# MASTERING

# PRINCIPLES OF ACCOUNTS

# MACMILLAN MASTER SERIES

Basic Management
Biology
Chemistry
Commerce
Computer Programming
Computers
Data Processing
Economics
Electronics
English Language
French
German
Italian
Marketing
Mathematics
Modern World History
Office Practice
Physics
Principles of Accounts
Sociology
Spanish
Statistics
Study Skills

Other books by J. Randall Stott
published by Macmillan

BASIC COMMERCE

# MASTERING
# PRINCIPLES OF
# ACCOUNTS

J. RANDALL STOTT, F.C.A.

*First published 1982 by*
THE MACMILLAN PRESS LTD
*London and Basingstoke*
*Companies and representatives throughout the world*

Filmset by
Reproduction Drawings Ltd
Sutton, Surrey

ISBN 0 333 31289 9  (hard cover)
      0 333 30446 2 (paper cover – home)
      0 333 31066 7 (paper cover – export)

This book is also available under the title
*Basic Principles of Accounts*
published by Macmillan Education.

# CONTENTS

# CONTENTS

# CONTENTS

# PREFACE

The subject of accounting in this new textbook is built up progressively, step by step, with the interest of the student maintained through the recognition that 'double entry' is a working tool of management and not simply an exercise in balancing up sets of figures.

The book is designed specifically to cover the latest syllabuses of all major examining bodies in Book-keeping and Accounts.

The questions at the end of each chapter are based upon recent examination papers, and brief answers to all the problems questions are listed at the back of the book.

J. Randall Stott.

# INTRODUCTION TO ACCOUNTING

## 1.1 HISTORICAL NOTE

Records of business transactions were kept before the days of the Pharaohs. Evidence of this has been found on crumbling clay tablets, buried deep in the sand of Ancient Babylonia.

Four thousand years ago a kind of paper was manufactured from reeds growing on the banks of the Nile. This was called papyrus, a Greek word from which our own word 'paper' is derived.

Centuries later, the Romans recorded their written word, command and deed on parchment vellum made from goatskin or calfskin. At that time, too, in south-east Asia, the Buddhist monks engraved an everyday 'account' of the revenue and expense of their monasteries upon *olas*, narrow strips cut from the young leaf to the talipot, a giant palm.

## 1.2 ORIGIN OF DOUBLE-ENTRY BOOK-KEEPING

Book-keeping, known in its correct form as 'double entry', has generally been attributed to Italy in the fifteenth century, when Venice was the centre of the maritime trade and merchant banking was being born. It is possible, however, that the Venetians adapted a system to suit their needs, copied perhaps from Moorish traders or some Semitic race who were extending their trade and commerce far from their native land.

For the past five hundred years huge leather-bound ledgers have recorded the rise and fall of financial empires, privately owned family businesses, monopolies of the State, and many firms of international repute.

Most of these cumbersome handwritten ledgers have been superseded by typewritten loose-leaf sectional ledgers, or by the even more up-to-date easy-for-reference individual files and folders housed in vertical or horizontal steel cabinets.

## 1.3 AGE OF BUSINESS EFFICIENCY

Specialisation and mass-production methods have led to mechanisation of office work, and machine accounting is now a characteristic of large and medium-sized firms.

Aids to speed and accuracy are to be seen in every modern office. The adding machine and calculator are within the reach, and purse, of every small trader.

Here again, we have an affinity with the past. The abacus of the Arab world was (and still is) similar in operation to the adding machine of today. The latter is simply the mechanical improvement and development of the other. The purpose of both is the same: to add up quickly and find an accurate total.

Despite modernistic trends in the method of recording transactions, accounting principles remain the same; there are still many handwritten ledgers, too, in various sections of the mercantile world of today.

Book-keeping is an essential part of the world of credit in which we live. Without credit in a limited form, everything would come to a stand-still. There would be a brake on forward planning and the many uncertainties and risk of the businessman would hold back production and large-scale enterprise.

Double entry is a complete system. It tells the true story about the financial affairs of a business: the capital it started with, what it has bought and sold; the profit made or the loss incurred; what it was worth yesterday and what it is worth today.

## 1.4 ACCOUNTING

The term 'accounting' in the sense it is used here, simply means *correct* book-keeping.

'Accounts' is rather a loose term, meaning either the written (or type-written) books of account, the recorded details made up from these books or ledgers, or the statements of account to be presented in summary form at the annual general meeting by the chairman of a company or by the treasurer of a cricket club.

## 1.5 LIABILITY TO KEEP ACCOUNTS

Limited companies are compelled by law to keep proper records of their financial transactions. The regulations of Companies Acts safeguard the interests of company members (shareholders) and also those of the creditors, to whom money is owing by the company for goods supplied and for services rendered.

Although sole traders and partnerships are not subject to a legal obligation, it is very much in their interests to keep proper records so that audited copies may be submitted to the Inland Revenue as proof of their business profits or losses. Failure to do so will render them liable to over-assessment of income tax, which means that they will pay more than what they need, simply because they cannot prove that they are liable for less. There are also severe obligations imposed upon most trading firms to keep records of Value Added Tax (V.A.T.), which, periodically, must be handed over to the Commissioners of Customs and Excise.

Clubs, societies and associations, generally, are non-trading organisations, but there is the responsibility towards members and supporters. The elected committee must produce a periodic statement giving information about subscriptions and donations received, and show how the money has been spent.

## 1.6 THE LANGUAGE OF THE BUSINESS WORLD

Some of the following words and terms may already be familiar to you, but from now on you must think of them in their accounting sense:

ASSETS  Property, machinery, equipment, stock and money belonging to a business, including money owing by customers. (*See* Debtor.)

LIABILITIES  Obligations and debts owing by the business for goods supplied or for services rendered, and, in some instances, for loans made. (*See* Creditor.)

CAPITAL OR NET WORTH  This is the proprietor's financial interest or holding in the business, represented by the value of net assets, i.e. total assets less liabilities.

BALANCE SHEET  A final statement of reckoning; the conventional style in the United Kingdom, until quite recently, has been to list the capital and liabilities on the left of the statement, and the assets on the right. It is not an account.

DEBIT  May mean the left-hand side, a posting to the left-hand side, or the actual invoice or charge to a customer's account.

DEBTOR  A person or firm owing money. Normally a customer who has not yet paid his account. The debt owing to the firm is a business asset.

CREDIT  May mean the right-hand side, a posting to the right-hand side, or may refer to goods bought to be paid at a later date.

CREDITOR  Is owed money by the business. Normally a supplier or wholesaler whose account has not yet been paid, but can refer to expense creditors whose services have been used, and to whom money is owing.

CASH TAKINGS OR CASH SALES   Money taken daily in exchange for goods sold across the counter. No record need be kept of the customer's name. The money paid into the till takes the place of the goods taken off the shelf.

TURNOVER   Trading revenue from cash sales, cash takings and credit sales.

CREDIT SALE   The goods are handed over against a written or implied promise to pay later. The name and address of the customer must be recorded, the amount being part of a debtor's list until paid.

PURCHASES   The total amount of goods bought for resale for cash or on credit during a trading period.

STOCK   Goods bought for resale but *not yet sold*.

## QUESTIONS

1. State briefly three reasons for the 'keeping of accounts'.
2. Distinguish between:
   (a) debit and credit
   (b) debtor and creditor
   (c) purchases and stock
   (d) an asset and a liability
   (e) a cash sale and a credit sale.

# CAPITAL AND THE

# BALANCE SHEET

Capital is something more than money in the bank. The capital of a business, shown on a statement called the 'balance sheet', comprises:

| | |
|---|---|
| ALL BUSINESS ASSETS | The property and possessions owned by the business, consisting of 'fixed assets' such as machinery, furniture and fittings, office equipment, and 'current assets' of money, stocks of goods and debts owing to the business by debtors. |

LESS

| | |
|---|---|
| BUSINESS LIABILITIES | Debts owing to suppliers of goods and services (called trade creditors and expense creditors) and obligations also to people who have loaned money to the business (called loan creditors). |

The difference, in the case of a sole trader, being his NET WORTH or CAPITAL.

## 2.1 THE BALANCE SHEET

A balance sheet is a statement of assets and liabilities showing their money values or estimated worth on a certain date. The date is important. The asset and liability values are *as shown on that date* – not the day before, nor the day after, when their values may be quite different.

It is customary for most trading firms to produce a summary record of their financial dealings at least once every twelve months. Many firms 'close their books' on December 31 each year and a large number adopt March 31 as their balancing-up date to coincide approximately with the Income Tax year.

Balance Sheet as at December 31

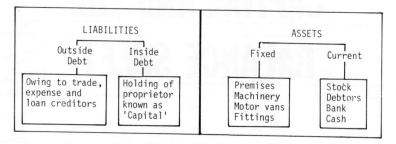

*Note* that the capital and financial holding of the proprietor is also a liability of the business, and that the two sides of the balance sheet should agree in their arithmetic totals in accordance with the simple equation:

CAPITAL + LIABILITIES = ASSETS

## 2.2 THE CHANGING FORM OF ASSETS AND LIABILITIES

Fixed assets are more permanent than current assets. Fixed assets are purchased for the long term by the business, whereas current assets change from day to day in the process of trading. Similarly with the liabilities, a mortgage or a long-term loan is regarded as a long-term or fixed liability, whereas amounts owing to trade and expense creditors fluctuate as debts are incurred and payments are made by the business, and consequently are referred to as 'current liabilities'.

Since statements of profit and loss are drawn up only at intervals of perhaps six or twelve months, you are not visibly aware of the effect of every small trading transaction.

BUT each change of an asset or of a liability affects the business (and the balance sheet if one was drawn up) in TWO WAYS.

Take, for example, three common instances, of goods bought on credit, the payment of the creditor's account, and the purchase of a fixed asset for cash.

(a) £100 of goods are bought on credit on January 5
A current asset comes into the business. At the same time a liability is created.

(b) The creditor's account is paid on January 15
An asset (cash) goes out and a liability is cancelled.

(c) £50 of fittings are bought for cash on January 20
A fixed asset comes into the business, and the current assets are reduced by the payment.

These are all characteristics of *double-entry book-keeping* where every transaction has a *twofold aspect*.

Assuming you start in business on January 1 with £500 cash and a van worth £1000, your balance sheet on this date will show total assets of £1500, and one liability (your commencing capital) of £1500, thus:

Balance Sheet as at January 1

| | £ | | £ |
|---|---|---|---|
| Capital Account | 1500 | Fixed assets | |
| | | Van | 1000 |
| Current liabilities | - | Current assets | |
| | | Cash | 500 |
| | 1500 | | 1500 |

Note the *two-way* changes after the transactions recorded above.

(a) After £100 value in goods has been bought *on credit* on January 5

Balance Sheet as at January 5

| | £ | | £ |
|---|---|---|---|
| Capital Account | 1500 | Fixed assets | |
| | | Van | 1000 |
| Current liabilities | 100 | Current assets | |
| | | Stock | 100 |
| | | Cash | 500 |
| | 1600 | | 1600 |

(b) After the creditor's account has been paid on January 15

Balance Sheet as at January 15

| | £ | | £ |
|---|---|---|---|
| Capital Account | 1500 | Fixed assets | |
| | | Van | 1000 |
| Current liabilities | - | Current assets | |
| | | Stock | 100 |
| | | Cash | 400 |
| | 1500 | | 1500 |

(c) After £50 of fittings have been bought on January 20

Balance Sheet as at January 20

|  | £ |  | £ |
|---|---|---|---|
| Capital Account | 1500 | Fixed assets | |
| | | Van | 1000 |
| | | Fittings | 50 |
| Current liabilities | – | Current assets | |
| | | Stock | 100 |
| | | Cash | 350 |
| | 1500 | | 1500 |

Note the order generally adopted for the marshalling and grouping of the assets, the fixed assets preceding the current assets; and, on the liabilities side, the proprietor's capital, in the nature of a fixed or long-term liability of the business, quite separate and always preceding the current liabilities.

Note also that the capital figure of £1500 has remained constant on these small balance sheets, simply because the proprietor's holding and interest in the business has not yet been affected by the transactions of *trading proper* (no sales have taken place and no business expenses incurred beyond the exchange of money for stock and fittings). In Chapter 4, capital too is shown as a varying factor, dependent upon the profit element and the withdrawals of money for the private use of the proprietor.

## QUESTIONS

1. Explain the term 'capital' as applied to the net worth of a business. Why is money only part of business capital?

2. Paula Jameson commences in business on January 31 with £500 cash. The following day she pays £150 for goods which she intends to sell. She also buys a showcase for £80. Show her balance sheet on February 1.

3. Pick out the assets and liabilities from the following and make up a balance sheet, using your own figures:

Cash : fittings : creditors : stock of goods

4. Robert Wells starts business on March 1 with £250 cash, £300 of stock and £200 of shop fittings and fixtures. He owes £100 to Village

Stores for goods already supplied. Show his opening balance sheet on March 1.

5. Assume you start in business on June 1 with £600 cash and an old van worth £400. Make up a balance sheet at *each* stage of the following transactions:

(a) the purchase of £50 of goods for cash on June 3
(b) the purchase of £180 of goods on credit on June 12
(c) the payment of £120 for some fittings on June 20
(d) the payment, on June 30, of £100 off the wholesaler's account who supplied goods on June 12, leaving a balance of £80 still owing.

*Note* The bank account and payment by cheque are not explained until Chapter 8, consequently the cash balances in some of these early exercises may appear rather more substantial than would be the case in practice; the large payments in cash will later be superseded by cheque payments.

# CHAPTER 3

# THE THEORY OF DOUBLE ENTRY

We now come to the 'book work', the recording of the routine daily transactions of a small trading business. The transactions are classified and grouped according to the principles laid down by a system known as 'double-entry book-keeping'.

In addition to assembling accurate information required by management, the double-entry system ensures that a full and complete record is kept of the receipt and payment of money, the purchase and sale of merchandise, the amounts owing to suppliers on credit (creditors), the amounts due from credit customers (debtors) and the details of the many and varied expenses incurred by the business.

Industrial and commercial undertakings, large and small, transfer their goods, commodities or services at a price measured in money's worth. An exchange or transfer of value is called a 'transaction', and *where value is given, it must also be received.*

This is the crux of double-entry book-keeping. There are *two parts or aspects to every transaction – one which gives or pays, the other which receives. Both must be recorded* in the same set of books.

## 3.1  LEDGER ACCOUNTS

The information with regard to transactions is recorded, in money value, on ledger accounts, which may relate to assets, liabilities, persons (firms and individuals), or to business gains and profits, or to losses and expenses.

Those ponderous leather-bound tomes housing the accounts at the beginning of this century have been superseded by the more manageable loose-leaf ledgers and steel filing-cabinets with visible indexes so that individual files can be located quickly.

Many of the ledger rulings have also changed to suit the needs of different businesses. The bank statement type of ruling, with its three columns, all on the right for debit, credit and a progressive balance, lends itself to the mechanised office, but for the purpose of explaining elementary book-keeping, we shall continue to use the older and original style of ledger ruling, shown below.

## 3.2  THE ACCOUNT

The individual record of a person, firm, asset, liability or expense is called an 'account'.

Two separate accounts are involved to record the dual parts or aspects of every transaction.

The account which *receives or benefits is debited.*

The account which *gives or pays is credited.*

This is the ruling of the orthodox style of Ledger Account:

| Debit (Dr.) | | | Name of Account | | (Cr.) Credit | |
|---|---|---|---|---|---|---|
| | | £ | | | | £ |
| Date | Value COMING IN | | Date | Value GOING OUT | | |

Note that this ledger account has two distinct sides, the debit on the left and the credit on the right.

The name of the account is shown clearly as a central heading.

There is a date column on both sides, followed by a fairly wide space for the description of the posting and guide to its related account.

A narrow 'folio' column in front of the figures column is used to record the page number and ledger abbreviation of the related opposite entry.

The amount or figures column on both sides shows the financial value of the transactions.

From this stage onwards every business transaction, whether buying or selling goods, giving a service, paying expenses or purchasing assets, will *involve two separate accounts* and you must begin to think in terms of double entry. Whether in the field of commerce, or scanning through an examination paper, you must now think and decide which account is to be debited and which account is to be credited.

Ignoring money values, consider the following list of transactions, and in each instance decide which ledger account should be debited and which account should be credited. If at first you find it difficult, glance down the answer columns, and then cover them up and try to reason out the double entry yourself. One or two terms may be confusing to begin with (such as purchases) but with practice you will soon get used to the new language of accounting.

| Transaction | Account to be debited | Account to be credited |
|---|---|---|
| Bought goods for cash | Purchases (NL) | Cash (CB) |
| Bought goods on credit from Brown | Purchases (NL) | Brown (BL) |
| Sold goods for cash | Cash (CB) | Sales (NL) |
| Sold goods on credit to Smith | Smith (SL) | Sales (NL) |
| Bought new van for cash | Van A/c (GL) | Cash (CB) |
| Bought desk on credit from Office Supplies Ltd | Office equipment (GL) | Office Supplies Ltd (BL) |
| Paid wages | Wages A/c (NL) | Cash (CB) |
| Bought stationery for cash | Stationery (NL) | Cash (CB) |
| Paid insurance premium | Insurance (NL) | Cash (CB) |
| Paid half-yearly rates | Rates A/c (NL) | Cash (CB) |
| Credit sale to Johnson | Johnson (SL) | Sales (NL) |
| Drew cash for 'self' | Drawings A/c (PL) | Cash (CB) |
| Paid Brown's account | Brown (BL) | Cash (CB) |
| Smith called and paid his account | Cash (CB) | Smith (SL) |

The various account books of the ledger system are divided up and section-ised for convenience; explained in greater detail in Chapter 13. The recog-nised abbreviations for the different ledgers, used in the folio columns of ledger accounts for cross-referencing purposes are:

CB   Cash Book            BL   Bought or Purchase Ledger
PL   Private Ledger       SL   Sales Ledger
GL   General Ledger       NL   Nominal Ledger

### 3.3  CASH SALE CONTRASTED WITH CREDIT SALE

Double-entry procedure can only be introduced gradually, building up from one simple illustration to the next.

First let us take a simple everyday transaction of a customer spending £10 in the supermarket. The housewife will collect her weekly needs from the shelves and deep-freezes and pay for them as she passes through the check-out point. Her name is not recorded when she hands over her money as this is a cash sale, and the supermarket stock has been reduced by £10 (selling price) and the cash balance of the store increased by £10.

In double-entry terms, cash is debited with £10 and Sales Account credited with £10. If this isolated sale was recorded (instead of by mechanised totals) the two accounts would appear thus:

| Dr. | | | Cash Account | | | | Cr. |
|---|---|---|---|---|---|---|---|
| Jan. 3 | Money COMING IN from Sales (the related account) | | £ 10 | | | | |

| Dr. | | | Sales Account | | | | Cr. |
|---|---|---|---|---|---|---|---|
| | | | Jan. 3 | Money value GOING OUT replaced by Cash (the re-lated account) | | £ 10 | |

By way of contrast let us now take a *sale on credit* of £20 worth of goods to John Green on January 3.

Sales account is affected as before since goods are sold or relinquished, but *no money is paid* at the time of the sale, so an account must be opened in the name of the debtor customer.

An account for John Green is opened in the Sales Ledger and debited with £20, the contra and opposite entry to the credit recorded on sales account, thus:

| Dr. | | | John Green (5) | | | | Cr. |
|---|---|---|---|---|---|---|---|
| Date | Debit money value of the goods COMING IN | | £ | | | | |
| Jan. 3 | Sales Account | NL8 | 20.00 | | | | |

| Dr. | | | | Sales Account (8) | | | Cr. |
|---|---|---|---|---|---|---|---|
| | | | | | | | £ |
| | | | Date | Credit money value of the goods GOING OUT | | | |
| | | | Jan. 3 | John Green | SL5. | 20.00 | |

From the two entries above, the book-keeper will understand that merchandise has been sold *on credit* by his firm to a customer, whose account has been opened on folio (page) 5 of the sales ledger. No money has passed, so the Cash Book is not involved, but the money value of these goods is recorded on the credit of sales account on folio 8 of the Nominal Ledger, and the first principles of accounting are maintained by a *debit* to the account which *receives*, and a *credit* to the account which *gives*.

To go a stage further on, Cash Account will be involved when John Green settles his account on January 24, the two accounts now affected being cash, always kept in the cash book, and of course, John Green's account again, in this way:

| Dr. | | | Cash Book (3) | | | | Cr. |
|---|---|---|---|---|---|---|---|
| | | | £ | | | | |
| Date | Debit money COMING IN | | | | | | |
| Jan. 24 | John Green | SL5 | 20.00 | | | | |

| Dr. | | | John Green (5) | | | | Cr. |
|---|---|---|---|---|---|---|---|
| | | | £ | | | | £ |
| Date | Debit money value of the goods COMING IN | | | Date | Credit money PAID, i.e. GOING OUT | | |
| Jan. 3 | Sales Account | NL8 | 20.00 | Jan. 24 | Cash | CB3 | 20.00 |

Note that the payment of £20.00 by John Green on January 24 in no way affects sales account. His debt is cancelled and he is no longer a debtor of the firm selling him the goods on credit. The retailing firm receives the money for the goods already handed over, and the position now is virtually that of a cash sale.

Neatness and clarity are the essence of ledger accounts. Emphasis has been placed on the headings of 'Debit value Coming In' and 'Credit value Going Out' for the sake of first principles, but these headings will be omitted after this chapter.

The folio column in front of the money columns on both sides of the account is used for cross-referencing to the opposite or dual aspect of each entry; it also makes the task and checking of the cashier or book-keeper easier. For example, John Green's account is kept on folio 5 of the sales (or debtors') ledger; sales account is on folio 8 of the Nominal Ledger, and the payment from John Green on January 24 is posted to folio 3 of the cash book, which is part of the ledger system, but has special rulings to suit the needs of the business.

Indexes are kept at the front of the various ledgers to allow quick and easy access to all the accounts within the ledgers.

## QUESTIONS

1. Explain, by illustration, what you understand by a 'ledger account'. Show descriptive headings and connect the account by a posting to another part of the ledger system such as the cash book.

2. Show the distinction between a cash sale and a credit sale by recording the following transactions on ledger accounts:

(a) £5 of goods sold for cash on November 4.
(b) £15 of goods sold on credit to Robert Hall on November 5.

3. Sarah Lawson started in business on March 1 with £2000 cash her only asset. Show her balance sheet on March 10, after the following transactions have taken place:

March
2   Paid £800 for machinery and equipment
4   Bought £500 of stock on credit from Leonard Pye
5   Cash sales £120 (cost price of goods sold £80)
8   Paid £300 'on account' to Leonard Pye
10   Personal drawings £100.

4. John Ford has the following assets and liabilities on July 1:

| | £ | | £ |
|---|---|---|---|
| Premises (at cost) | 8000 | Trade debtors | 1480 |
| Fixtures/equipment | 650 | Trade creditors | 820 |
| Second-hand van | 2200 | Cash | 490 |

His stock on July 1 was valued at £1500.

You are required to make up a balance sheet to show clearly:

(a) John Ford's capital account.
(b) His fixed and current assets.
(c) His current liabilities.

5. As a continuation of question 4, John Ford's business dealings during the first week of July are listed below:

(a) a safe was bought for £80 cash.
(b) one-third of the stock was sold for £750 cash, and another one-third to a credit customer for £800.
(c) a debtor paid his outstanding account of £130.
(d) a creditor's June account for £60 was paid.
(e) John Ford withdraw £100 cash for household use.

Redraft the balance sheet of John Ford as at July 8, giving full effect to these transactions.

*Note.* Accounting for profit is explained in the next chapter, though it will be seen that a profit or gain has been made in questions 3 and 5 above, with goods being sold at a higher price than their cost. Stocks are adjusted to their correct figures, and this profit, calculated arithmetically, is added to the proprietor's capital on the balance sheet.

# PRACTICAL
# BOOK-KEEPING (1)

## 4.1 BASIC PRINCIPLES

Let us suppose that you start in business, in a small way, as a retail grocer, working from your home address, on June 1 with £500 cash as your commencing capital.

Your transactions for the time being are for cash only. The bank account and cheques will be explained in Chapter 8. All business dealings for the first week in June are listed below:

|  |  | £ |
|---|---|---|
| June 2 | Bought various supplies and paid cash | 120.00 |
| 4 | Money received for goods sold | 85.50 |
|  | Made a number of small purchases and put to stock for resale | 22.20 |
| 5 | Cash takings (all stock being sold) | 94.80 |
| 6 | Withdrew cash for private use | 40.00 |

You can now 'post up' your cash account for the first week of June, although in practice this would be done day by day.

Dr.                              Cash Book (folio 1)                         Cr.

| June |  |  | £ | June |  |  | £ |
|---|---|---|---|---|---|---|---|
| 1 | Balance in hand (capital) | PL3 | 500.00 | 2 | Purchases | NL15 | 120.00 |
| 4 | Sales | NL8 | 85.50 | 4 | Purchases | NL15 | 22.20 |
| 5 | Sales | NL8 | 94.80 | 6 | Drawings | PL6 | 40.00 |
|  |  |  |  | 6 | Balance c/d |  | 498.10 |
|  |  |  | 680.30 |  |  |  | 680.30 |
| June 6 | Balance b/d |  | 498.10 |  |  |  |  |

The abbreviations NL8 and NL15 refer to the page numbers of the nominal ledger where the accounts recording the total sales and the total purchases for the month of June will be found.

## 4.2 POINTS TO NOTE ON CASH BOOK ILLUSTRATION

(a) All wording within the account, as far as possible, should be condensed to one word which *identifies the opposite or dual aspect of each entry*, and makes the work of the cashier and ledger clerk easier. Instead of 'money received for goods sold' and 'cash takings' we simply write 'sales'; instead of 'bought various supplies and paid cash' and 'made a number of small purchases, etc.' we write 'purchases'.

There is no need to repeat the word 'cash' within the cash book, as all entries refer to money received or money paid.

(b) Goods and supplies bought for stock and to be resold are always identified by the word 'purchases' to distinguish them from asset purchases and routine everyday business expenses.

(c) Money withdrawn for the private use of the proprietor is called 'drawings' to distinguish from employees' wages and salaries. Drawings is not a business expense, but a withdrawal of part of the proprietor's holding (capital) in the business, represented, generally, by available profits.

(d) There is no need to repeat the name of the month in the same date column, and the £ sign is only necessary at the top of each money column. The abbreviations Dr. and Cr. are used now in place of 'Debit' and 'Credit' at the top of the account, and often these are dispensed with altogether in practice.

(e) The cash account is balanced up simply by deducting the total of the credit side (the payments) from the total of the debit side receipts including the commencing balance. In this instance the cash balance of £498.10 is inserted as an *additional credit to balance the account*, and then *brought down as a debit balance below the total of the left-hand side*. The abbreviations c/d and b/d signify 'carried down' and 'brought down'.

## 4.3 POSTING UP THE LEDGER ACCOUNTS

Each item in the cash book (except the closing balance and the totals) is now posted up to its related account in the ledger.

First of all, your Capital Account will be *credited* with £500, the money you have given or loaned to the business. In effect, you have become a creditor of the business with a financial holding at June 1 of £500.

| Dr. | | | | | Capital Account (3) | | Cr. |
|---|---|---|---|---|---|---|---|
| | | | | June<br>1 | Cash | CB1 | £<br>500.00 |

Next the cash takings or sales are posted to the *credit* of sales account in the ledger. Ultimately these grouped sales will give you the total sales figure for the month of June.

| Dr. | | | | | Sales Account (8) | | Cr. |
|---|---|---|---|---|---|---|---|
| | | | | June<br>4<br>5 | Cash<br>Cash | CB1<br>CB1 | £<br>85.50<br>94.80 |

The credit side of the cash book is now posted to the *debit* of two separate ledger accounts, recording your goods bought and the money withdrawn for private use.

| Dr. | | | | Purchases Account (15) | | | Cr. |
|---|---|---|---|---|---|---|---|
| June<br>2<br>4 | Cash<br>Cash | CB1<br>CB1 | £<br>120.00<br>22.20 | | | | |

| Dr. | | | | Drawings Account (6) | | | Cr. |
|---|---|---|---|---|---|---|---|
| June<br>6 | Cash | CB1 | £<br>40.00 | | | | |

## 4.4 THE TRIAL BALANCE

The postings of the double entry are now complete for the first week of June. The next stage is to group and assemble the account balances in the books. This information is listed on a statement called the Trial Balance, normally drawn up prior to working out the trading results for the period.

The total debits equal the total credits. This acts as a check on the *arithmetical* accuracy of your postings.

There is no particular order for listing the balances. Often they are taken in the sequence the book-keeper selects as he checks through his books. Sometimes the fixed assets and the trading expenses are grouped.

Trial Balance June 6

|  | Debit balances £ | Credit balances £ |
|---|---|---|
| Cash balance June 6 | 498.10 | |
| Capital June 1 | | 500.00 |
| Purchases | 142.20 | |
| Sales | | 180.30 |
| Drawings | 40.00 | |
| | 680.30 | 680.30 |

Trade debtors and trade creditors are shown *not by name*, but in separate totals. It is suggested that beginners should head their trial balances with the closing cash (and bank) balances, as these are sometimes overlooked.

The trial balance is not part of the double entry, nor is it an account. It is simply a list of debit and credit balances, assembled together to check the arithmetical accuracy of the postings, and to provide information, in total form, to render the task of the book-keeper or accountant easier, when he starts to prepare the final accounts for the period under review.

## 4.5  THE TRADING ACCOUNT

From the information now shown on the trial balance at June 6, we can find out the profit made for the first week of trading. In this small illustration the varied and routine expenses of running a business have been ignored, to aid simplicity. In working out the trading profit, we are concerned only with items directly to do with trading (i.e. buying and selling), which in this instance simply means offsetting the total purchases against the total sales. There are no stocks of goods on hand to take into account in this example, and the fact that the cash balance is £1.90 lower on June 6 than it was on June 1 has no significance in so far as trading profit is concerned.

A simplified form of Trading Account is shown on p. 21.

The main object of the trading account is to ascertain the gross profit (or loss) on trading. The gross profit is the difference or balance between the cost of the goods sold and the total money value of the sales; in effect, it is the excess sales revenue, a credit balance on the trading account, and still part of the double-entry system.

Trading Account for the week ended June 6

| | £ | | | £ |
|---|---|---|---|---|
| Purchases | 142.20 | | Sales | 180.30 |
| Gross profit c/d | 38.10 | | | |
| | 180.30 | | | 180.30 |
| | | | Gross profit b/d | 38.10 |

## 4.6 THE BALANCE SHEET

We can now make up a statement showing the financial position of your business, and the net worth of your interest or holding as at June 6. This statement is called a balance sheet. It is not an account, but a statement of assets and liabilities, the final balances in the books, at a certain date.

It has been customary to show, in the older horizontal style of presen-

Balance Sheet as at June 6

| Capital and liabilities | £ | £ | Assets | £ |
|---|---|---|---|---|
| Capital June 1 | 500.00 | | Cash in hand | 498.10 |
| Add: profit for period | 38.10 | | | |
| | 538.10 | | | |
| Less: drawings | 40.00 | 498.10 | | |
| | | 498.10 | | 498.10 |

| Dr. | | | | Capital Account (3) | | Cr. | |
|---|---|---|---|---|---|---|---|
| | | | £ | | | | £ |
| June 6 | Transfer from Drawings A/c | PL6 | 40.00 | June 1 | Cash | CB1 | 500.00 |
| 6 | Balance c/d | | 498.10 | 6 | Transfer from Trading A/c | | 38.10 |
| | | | 538.10 | | | | 538.10 |
| | | | | June 6 | Balance b/d | | 498.10 |

tation, the capital and the liabilities of a business on the left-hand side of the balance sheet, and the business assets and property on the right-hand side, as already shown in the earlier chapters of this book.

Finally, your capital account is made up to correspond with the detail shown on the balance sheet. The trading profit (a credit) is transferred from the trading account to the *credit* of the capital account, and the balance on Drawings Account is transferred to the *debit* of capital account.

### Points to remember

(a) Neatness in handwriting and figuring are important. Untidiness will lose you marks.

(b) Align your figures correctly. Valuable time is lost checking for errors due to bad alignment.

(c) Use clear bold headings for ledger accounts and for the final accounts. Allow ample space under all headings and subheadings.

(d) Corresponding totals must be ruled on the same horizontal.

(e) Pencil in totals as a temporary measure before rechecking and then inking-in.

(f) Do not omit dates on your ledger accounts or in the headings of the final accounts.

(g) Remember that a trading account always *covers a specific period*, whereas a balance sheet is drawn up *as at a certain date*. Show clearly in each instance.

(h) Do not scratch out or obliterate wrong figures. Rule through the error neatly - one ruled line only. No marks will be lost if this advice is followed.

### QUESTIONS

1. Enter up the details of receipts and payments of money in your cash book from the information listed below. Carry down the balance in hand from January to February, and from February to March, to show the final balance on March 31.

(a) January
    1  Started in business with £600 cash
    4  Bought supplies of goods for £200
    15 Cash takings amounted to £120
    22 Received from cash customers £65
    30 Bought further goods for £150
    31 Balanced up at end of month.

(b) February
  1 Balance brought down from January
  5 Cash sales amounted to £135
 12 Withdrew cash for 'self' £100
 18 Further purchases £110
 26 Cash sales to date £95
 28 Cash sales £80
   Carried balance down to March.

(c) March
  1 Balance brought down from February
  6 Purchased goods for cash £115
  8 Cash takings to date £145
 15 Drawings for 'self' £100
 25 Cash sales £90
 31 Balanced up at end of month.

**2.** (a) Explain the meaning of these abbreviations:

CB  BL   SL  PL   GL   NL
c/d and b/d   c/f and b/f

Why does c/d precede b/d, and c/f precede b/f?
(b) Make up a balance sheet as at June 30, with your figures, embodying the following assets and liabilities under their proper groupings of 'fixed and currents assets' etc.

  Fittings and fixtures : stock of goods : cash : debtors
  creditors : drawings : profit for month.

**3.** You start in business on July 1 with £400 cash, your only asset. At present you are working from your home address to reduce your expenses to a minimum. The transactions during your first month's trading are listed below:

July
|  |  | £ |
|---|---|---|
| 2 | Bought various supplies for cash | 250 |
| 5 | Received from cash customers | 85 |
| 12 | Cash takings amounted to | 115 |
| 18 | Bought further goods | 120 |
| 22 | Cash sales | 135 |
| 25 | Cash sales | 170 |
| 31 | Drawings for private use | 100 |

All stock is completely sold out at the month end.
You are required to make up and balance your cash book, post the double entry to all ledger accounts, and take out a trial balance to prove the accuracy of your postings on July 31.
 **4.** From the trial balance in question 3 above, make up a trading account for the month of July and a balance sheet as at July 31.
 **5.** Continue with the posting of the cash book and ledger accounts

where applicable in question 3 for the month of August from the additional details now given below, and take out another trial balance on August 31:

August

|  |  | £ |
|---|---|---|
| 3 | Cash purchases | 240 |
| 8 | Bought further supplies | 160 |
| 10 | Cash sales to date | 185 |
| 15 | Cash sales | 155 |
| 19 | Bought a record-player for private use | 120 |
| 24 | Cash purchases | 50 |
| 28 | Received from cash customers | 145 |
| 31 | Cash sales | 85 |
|  | Withdrew cash for own use | 60 |

**6**. Rudolph Rudd's transactions for the month of March are given below. His capital, represented by one asset – cash – was £300 on March 1.

March

|  |  | £ |
|---|---|---|
| 2 | Bought goods for resale | 124 |
| 5 | Cash sales | 106 |
| 10 | Purchases | 80 |
| 13 | Cash sales | 84 |
| 18 | Bought further goods | 59 |
| 25 | Cash sales | 98 |
| 28 | Purchases | 17 |
| 30 | Withdrew for 'self' | 60 |
| 31 | Sold remainder of the stock | 125 |

Post up Mr Rudd's cash account, and the double entry to the ledger, take out a trial balance at March 31, and then make up his trading account for the month of March and a balance sheet at March 31.

7. Complete the following table.

|  | Capital June 1 | Capital June 30 | Profit for month | Drawings |
|---|---|---|---|---|
|  | £ | £ | £ | £ |
| A | 1500 | 2200 | 900 | – |
| B | 2000 | 1400 | 200 | – |
| C | 4500 | – | 1200 | 1500 |
| D | 3300 | 3800 | – | 600 |
| E | – | 4200 | 750 | 250 |

# PRACTICAL

# BOOK-KEEPING (2)

## 5.1 FULL-LENGTH ILLUSTRATION TO THE TRIAL BALANCE

Your friend Tom Brown has a small lock-up shop stocked with household supplies, catering for the village needs in hardware and ironmongery. He took over the shop, starting a new business on October 1, with a capital of £800 in cash and an initial stock, brought from his home and valued at £200.

Early in November, Tom Brown asks for your help; you manage to put him on a suitable double-entry basis, and, after writing up his books for the month of October, decide to produce a full set of final accounts as at October 31. Here is the full list of Tom Brown's trading transactions for the month:

| October | | £ |
|---|---|---|
| 1 | Bought further supplies for cash | 140.00 |
| 2 | Paid rent for the month | 30.00 |
| 3 | Cash takings | 76.60 |
| 5 | Sold goods on credit to A. Jones | 45.00 |
| | Paid general office expenses | 16.50 |
| 8 | Bought fittings and equipment for shop | 130.00 |
| | Paid for advertising | 17.40 |
| 9 | Bought supplies on credit from F. Smith & Co. | 160.00 |
| 10 | Paid carriage on goods bought | 10.80 |
| 12 | Cash takings | 88.80 |
| 14 | Credit sale to S. Simpson | 52.70 |
| | Bought stationery | 8.50 |
| 16 | Cash takings | 78.40 |
| 18 | Bought gardening supplies for cash | 108.50 |
| 19 | Cash takings | 55.60 |
| 20 | Paid £50 'on account' to F. Smith & Co. | 50.00 |

| 24 | Paid for advertising | 17.40 |
| 26 | Drew cash for 'self' | 80.00 |
| 28 | Cash sales | 115.00 |
| 30 | Paid wages to part-time assistant | 60.00 |
| 31 | Cash sales | 144.20 |

*Note.* In this exercise credit transactions are introduced, a fixed asset is bought for the permanent use of the business, and among the payments are a variety of routine nominal expenses.

As you have a complete list of Tom Brown's transactions in front of you, first of all make up his cash book for the month of October, taking care to *exclude all credit purchases and sales.*

| Dr. | | | | | Cash Book | | | | Cr. |
|---|---|---|---|---|---|---|---|---|---|
| | | £ | | | | | | £ | |
| Oct. | | | Oct. | | | | | | |
| 1 | Balance in hand | | 1 | | Purchases | | | 140.00 | |
| | (Capital Account) | 800.00 | 2 | | Rent | | | 30.00 | |
| 3 | Sales | 76.60 | 5 | | General expenses | | | 16.50 | |
| 12 | " | 88.80 | 8 | | Fittings/equipt | | | 130.00 | |
| 15 | " | 78.40 | | | Advertising | | | 17.40 | |
| 19 | " | 55.60 | 10 | | Carriage | | | 10.80 | |
| 28 | " | 115.00 | 14 | | Stationery | | | 8.50 | |
| 31 | " | 144.20 | 18 | | Purchases | | | 108.50 | |
| | | | 20 | | F. Smith & Co. | | | 50.00 | |
| | | | 24 | | Advertising | | | 17.40 | |
| | | | 26 | | Drawings | | | 80.00 | |
| | | | 30 | | Wages | | | 60.00 | |
| | | | 31 | | Balance c/d | | | 689.50 | |
| | | 1358.60 | | | | | | 1358.60 | |
| Oct. | | | | | | | | | |
| 31 | Balance b/d | 689.50 | | | | | | | |

Before starting to post up the dual aspect of each entry in the ledger, note that the credit purchases of October 9 and the credit sales of October 5 and 14 have not been entered in the cash book, because these are *credit items and no money passes* at the time the goods are handed over. *The cash book is simply a record of money receipts and money payments.*

Later in the month, however, on October 20, the business pays F. Smith & Co. £50 on account of the debt owing. This payment naturally appears as a credit in the cash book on that date, the dual aspect being explained a little further on.

Again, note the one-word abbreviation, as far as possible, of the cash book entries, and note the blank space left on the debit side of this cash account for October, to even up the record and ensure the totals are on the same horizontal. Total payments amount to £669.10, which are deducted from total receipts, including the commencing balance of £800, leaving a closing month-end balance of £689.50. This closing balance is inserted above the total on the credit, *to balance the account*, and *brought down as a debit balance* at October 31. It is thus the commencing balance for the new month of November.

Normally cash book balances are carried forward or brought down from one period to the next, and are not posted up to other parts of the ledger system. But in this particular instance, Tom Brown's opening cash balance is also *part of his commencing capital*, the other part being his stock of goods, valued on October 1 at £200.

| Dr. | | | | | Capital Account Tom Brown | | Cr. |
|---|---|---|---|---|---|---|---|
| | | | | | | | £ |
| | | | | Oct. 1 | Cash | | 800.00 |
| | | | | 1 | Stock Account | | 200.00 |

The first credit entry (£800) on the capital account is the double or opposite aspect of the opening cash balance, but a corresponding debit must now be made on Stock Account, now that a record of this *capital asset* has been shown on Tom Brown's capital account.

| Dr. | | | | Stock Account | | | Cr. |
|---|---|---|---|---|---|---|---|
| Oct. 1 | Capital Account | | £ 200.00 | | | | |

Pausing to think at this stage, you will realise that the double-entry principles are being maintained, as we have two separate debits on cash and stock accounts totalling £1000 and agreeing with the full credit of £1000 now on capital account.

The remainder of the items on the debit side of the cash book refer to cash sales, and are all posted to the credit of sales account, thus:

| Dr. | | | | | Sales Account | | Cr. |
|---|---|---|---|---|---|---|---|
| | | | | | | | £ |
| | | | | Oct. | | | |
| | | | | 3 | Cash | | 76.60 |
| | | | | 5 | A. Jones | | 45.00 |
| | | | | 12 | Cash | | 88.80 |
| | | | | 14 | S. Simpson | | 52.70 |
| | | | | 16 | Cash | | 78.40 |
| | | | | 19 | " | | 55.60 |
| | | | | 28 | " | | 115.00 |
| | | | | 31 | " | | 144.20 |
| | | | | | | | 656.30 |

Note that the *credit* sales to A. Jones and S. Simpson on October 5 and 14 have also joined the cash sales on the credit side of sales account, increasing the main turnover for the month, now totalling £656.30. The purpose of the sales account is to arrive at the total revenue from sales, both cash and credit.

The double entry for the credit sales is shown on the *debit* of the personal accounts of A. Jones and S. Simpson, who become debtors of Tom Brown.

| Dr. | | | | A. Jones | | | Cr. |
|---|---|---|---|---|---|---|---|
| | | | £ | | | | |
| Oct. | | | | | | | |
| 5 | Sales Account | | 45.00 | | | | |

| Dr. | | | | S. Simpson | | | Cr. |
|---|---|---|---|---|---|---|---|
| | | | £ | | | | |
| Oct. | | | | | | | |
| 14 | Sales Account | | 52.70 | | | | |

We now turn to the credit side of the cash book and post up the payments to related and opposite accounts in the ledger. Separate accounts will be opened for each kind of expense, and a clear distinction made between the goods bought for resale (purchases) and fixed assets bought for the permanent use of the business. There are three transactions for the purchase of goods, one of them a purchase of goods on credit, as shown now on the Purchases Account for October:

| Dr. | | | Purchases Account | | | Cr. | |
|---|---|---|---|---|---|---|---|
| Oct. | | | £ | | | | |
| 1 | Cash | | 140.00 | | | | |
| 9 | F. Smith & Co. | | 160.00 | | | | |
| 18 | Cash | | 108.50 | | | | |
| | | | 408.50 | | | | |

The item of £160 debited on October 9 joins the other cash purchases for the month to provide the aggregate total purchases of £408.50 for October. This credit purchase is not recorded in the cash book, as no money was handed over at the time the goods were bought. F. Smith & Co. become the creditor of Tom Brown. An account is opened for them in the Bought Ledger, and credited with the opposite entry to that shown on purchases account, thus:

| Dr. | | | F. Smith & Co. | | | Cr. | |
|---|---|---|---|---|---|---|---|
| | | | Oct. | | | £ | |
| | | | 9 | Purchases A/c | | 160.00 | |

Later in the month, when Tom Brown pays £50 on account to his creditor, cash account is credited and the above account of F. Smith & Co. is debited with this payment, leaving a balance of £110.00 still to be paid. The account is brought up to date:

| Dr. | | | F. Smith & Co. | | | Cr. | |
|---|---|---|---|---|---|---|---|
| Oct. | | | £ | Oct. | | | £ |
| 20 | Cash | | 50.00 | 9 | Purchases A/c | | 160.00 |
| 31 | Balance c/d | | 110.00 | | | | |
| | | | 160.00 | | | | 160.00 |
| | | | | Oct. | | | |
| | | | | 31 | Balance b/d | | 110.00 |

The creditor's account has been balanced up to show the debt owing by Tom Brown to his supplier at the end of the month.

Students are sometimes confused by the effect of payments in settlement of outstanding accounts in so far as the purchases (or sales) account is concerned. This payment in no way affects purchases account. The double entry is simply between cash account and the creditor's personal account. Similarly on the sales side, payments from debtors in no way affect sales account; the double entry simply being between cash book and the personal account of the debtor.

A new kind of business payment needs explanation. The payment of £130 on October 8 refers to the purchase of 'Fittings and equipment for the shop'. Obviously, these are not goods for resale, and it is not a routine trading expense like advertising. This is a 'fixed asset' purchase, the acquisition of something to be kept for the permanent use of the business. The procedure is to debit the asset account (under its own name) and bring the debit balance on to the balance sheet as part of the business property, at the end of the accounting period. Asset accounts, generally, are kept in the private ledger of the proprietor, and a clear distinction is made between capital and revenue expenditure, explained in the next chapter.

| Dr. | | | | Fittings and Equipment Account | | | | Cr. |
|---|---|---|---|---|---|---|---|---|
| Oct. 8 | Cash | | £ 130.00 | | | | | |

The remainder of the payments, with the exception of Drawings on October 26, relate to routine everyday expenses of a trading business. They are all debited direct from the credit of the cash book to the debit of their individual accounts in the nominal ledger, kept for the purpose of recording gains and losses, profits and expenses.

| Dr. | | | | Rent Account | | | | Cr. |
|---|---|---|---|---|---|---|---|---|
| Oct. 2 | Cash | | £ 30.00 | | | | | |

| Dr. | | | | General Expenses | | | | Cr. |
|---|---|---|---|---|---|---|---|---|
| Oct. 5 | Cash | | £ 16.50 | | | | | |

| Dr. | | | | Advertising | | | | Cr. |
|---|---|---|---|---|---|---|---|---|
| Oct. 8 24 | Cash " | | £ 17.40 17.40 | | | | | |
| | | | 34.80 | | | | | |

| Dr. | | | | Carriage | | | | Cr. |
|---|---|---|---|---|---|---|---|---|
| Oct. 10 | Cash | | | £ 10.80 | | | | |

| Dr. | | | | Stationery | | | | Cr. |
|---|---|---|---|---|---|---|---|---|
| Oct. 14 | Cash | | | £ 8.50 | | | | |

| Dr. | | | | Wages | | | | Cr. |
|---|---|---|---|---|---|---|---|---|
| Oct. 30 | Cash | | | £ 60.00 | | | | |

Finally, the money withdrawn by Tom Brown for his own use on October 26 is debited to his drawings account in the Private Ledger. The proprietor of a business has full conrol over his finances, and may withdraw any sums to suit his private needs at any time. Consequently, drawings are not admissible expenses allowed by the Inland Revenue to be charged against business profits. Amounts withdrawn by the proprietor are kept quite separate from wages and salaries of employees.

| Dr. | | | | Drawings | | | | Cr. |
|---|---|---|---|---|---|---|---|---|
| Oct. 26 | Cash | | | £ 80.00 | | | | |

**The trial balance**
The arithmetical accuracy of your postings may now be checked by taking out a trial balance, a list of all the account balances in the books:

Trial Balance October 31

|  |  | Debit £ | Credit £ |
|---|---|---|---|
| Cash balance   October 31 | CB | 689.50 |  |
| Capital   Tom Brown   Oct. 1 | PL |  | 1000.00 |
| Stock   Oct. 1 | NL | 200.00 |  |
| Sales | NL |  | 656.30 |
| Trade debtors (total) | SL | 97.70 |  |
| Purchases | NL | 408.50 |  |
| Creditors | BL |  | 110.00 |
| Fittings and equipment | PL | 130.00 |  |
| Rent | NL | 30.00 |  |
| General expenses | NL | 16.50 |  |
| Advertising | NL | 34.80 |  |
| Carriage | NL | 10.80 |  |
| Stationery | NL | 8.50 |  |
| Wages | NL | 60.00 |  |
| Drawings | PL | 80.00 |  |
|  |  | 1766.30 | 1766.30 |

## QUESTIONS

1. Explain each entry in the two ledger accounts below, and say which is the debtor's account and which is that of the creditor.

J. C. Box

| Feb. |  | £ | Feb. |  | £ |
|---|---|---|---|---|---|
| 8 | Cash | 48.80 | 1 | Balance b/f | 48.80 |
| 28 | Balance c/d | 25.00 | 15 | Purchases A/c | 25.00 |
|  |  | 73.80 |  |  | 73.80 |
|  |  |  | Mar. |  |  |
|  |  |  | 1 | Balance b/d | 25.00 |

J. B. Cox

| | | £ | | | | £ |
|---|---|---|---|---|---|---|
| Feb. | | | Feb. | | | |
| 1 | Balance b/f | 35.00 | 6 | Cash | | 35.00 |
| 18 | Sales A/c | 15.50 | 28 | Balance c/d | | 15.50 |
| | | 50.50 | | | | 50.50 |
| Mar. | | | | | | |
| 1 | Balance b/d | 15.50 | | | | |

**2.** Enter up the following transactions in Frank Dobson's cash book for the month of September, bringing down the closing balance for October 1.

September
- 1   Cash in hand £400
- 2   Bought £250 of goods on credit from S. Parker Ltd
- 3   Paid insurance £25.50
- 4   Cash sales £82.30
- 5   Paid wages to part-time assistant £35.50
      Paid £44 for some office fittings and shelving
- 10   Cash takings amounted to £176.70
- 14   Bought office furniture for £65
      Cash sales £93.10
- 18   Paid £88 for further supplies of goods
- 20   Paid £5 carriage on goods bought
      Sold £160 of goods on credit to P. Dawson
- 25   Paid advertising account £15.20
- 26   Paid £100 to S. Parker Ltd 'on account'
- 28   Paid wages £35.50
      Cash sales totalled £185.40
- 30   Frank Dobson withdraw £80 for private use

*N.B.* Do not enter purchases and sales *on credit* in your cash book.

**3.** From the cash account now made up for Frank Dobson, you are required to post the double entry to the related ledger accounts, and take out a trial balance on September 30. For the purpose of this exercise, the cash on hand on September 1 should be regarded as Dobson's commencing capital.

**4.** Percy Potter has the following assets and liabilities on June 1
     Cash in hand    £500      Stock on hand    £200
     Money owing by Matthew Reid    £100
     Money owing to William Carey £200 for goods bought on May 31.

Ascertain Mr Potter's capital from the above figures, and make up his cash book from the transactions following for the month of June.

*N.B.* Only the cash balance and the cash transactions will be posted to Potter's cash book; the original book debts (and credit purchases and sales) will be posted direct to ledger accounts.

June

2 Bought some office furniture for £85
3 Cash sales £56.20
4 Bought further supplies on credit from Carey for £150
Paid rent for month £20
8 Cash sales £82.70
10 Credit sale of £105 to F. H. Moon
12 Paid £60 wages
Cash purchases £72.10
15 Potter withdrew £50 cash for himself
16 Cash sales £45.40
18 Reid paid £100 balance owing on May account
Cash sales £118.60
20 Paid balance of Carey's old account £200
22 Paid £60 wages
23 Cash takings £128.80; paid advertising £28.50
25 Cash sales £76.50
Moon called and paid £55 'on account'
27 Bought office desk for £66
28 Cash sales £136.40; paid wages £60
30 Potter withdrew another £50 for 'self'

5. From the cash account of Percy Potter in the previous exercise, post up the double entry to the related ledger accounts, and take out a trial balance on June 30.

Note that the final balances of the assets and liabilities which formed part of Potter's original capital must also be shown on the trial balance, but with stock at its commencing figure of £200, distinct and separate from the purchases total for the period.

6. You are required to assemble the information given below in trial balance form, and ascertain the commencing capital of the proprietor, Horatio Hogg, by deducting the total credits from the total debits:

|  | £ |  | £ |
|---|---|---|---|
| Net sales | 1940 | Net purchases | 630 |
| Stationery | 52 | Insurance | 8 |
| Rent | 210 | Salaries | 750 |
| Drawings | 500 | Advertising | 60 |
| Cash | 400 | Sundry expenses | 40 |

7. Make up a trial balance from the following balances extracted from the books of Wilfred Wearwell on June 30:

|  |  | £ |
|---|---|---|
| June 1 | Opening capital | 1000 |
|  | Stock at start | 300 |
| June 30 | Net sales for month | 2400 |
|  | Net purchases for month | 1180 |
|  | Advertising | 150 |
|  | Wages/salaries | 440 |
|  | Drawings | 260 |
|  | Carriage on purchases | 30 |
|  | Insurance | 20 |
|  | Petrol and oil | 40 |
|  | Cash on hand     June 30 | 980 |

# PRACTICAL
# BOOK-KEEPING (3)

## 6.1  STOCK AND THE REVENUE ACCOUNTS

In both the wholesale and the retail trade, business profits are made through selling merchandise, in competitive markets, at higher prices than cost.

The true cost price of goods cannot be found unless stocks are taken into account. Stock refers to merchandise available for sale, but unsold, both at the beginning and at the end of a specific trading period. Its correct valuation is important. If stock is undervalued at the close of the accounting period, profits are understated. If it is over-valued, profits are inflated. But, although stock valuation is important, profits (or losses) are in fact levelled out and adjusted during the ensuing period, since the closing valuation at the end of one period (December 31) becomes the commencing figure for the beginning of the new period (January 1).

First let us deal with a simple stock problem by arithmetic. A trader has a stock, on January 1, of 200 articles, the balance remaining of purchases made during December at an average cost of £1 each. This stock has been valued at its cost price of £200 for the accounting period ended December 31.

The old stock at December 31 now becomes the new opening stock for January 1, the beginning of the new period.

The trader buys 1500 more articles of the same type during January at the average price of £1.20 per article, and sells 1200 articles during the month at £1.60 each.

By mental arithmetic he would appear to have made 40p on each of the 1200 articles sold (i.e. a total profit of £480), but is this his true profit? The opening and closing stocks have been ignored.

The true profit is worked out in this way.

It is reasonable to assume that the old stock will be sold first, and that the balance of purchases remaining (the stock) at the end of January was bought at the more recent price of £1.20.

|  |  | £ |
|---|---|---:|
| Net sales of 1200 articles at £1.60 each |  | 1920 |
| *Deduct* the cost of goods sold |  |  |

|  | £ |  |
|---|---:|---:|
| Opening stock 200 at £1 | 200 |  |
| Purchases 1500 at £1.20 | 1800 |  |
|  | 2000 |  |
| *Less*: closing stock |  |  |
| (500 at £1.20) | 600 | 1400 |
| Showing a gross profit of |  | £520 |

The combination statement shown below incorporates both the physical stock numbers and the financial values which would appear on a trading account for the month ended January 31:

Trading Account (and Stock Record) for January

| Jan. |  | Nos | £ | Jan. |  | Nos | £ |
|---|---|---:|---:|---|---|---:|---:|
| 1 | Stock on hand | 200 | 200 | 31 | Sales | 1200 | 1920 |
| 31 | Purchases during | | | 31 | Stock | 500 | 600 |
|  | month | 1500 | 1800 |  |  |  |  |
| 31 | Profit on | | | | | | |
|  | trading | – | 520 |  |  |  |  |
|  |  | 1700 | 2520 |  |  | 1700 | 2520 |

## 6.2  COST, EXPENSE AND REVENUE

The cost of living and the prices of foodstuffs, commodities, clothing and all manner of goods will continue to rise on account of world commodity prices and the ever-increasing wages demands.

The manufacturer must obtain his basic raw material and pay his heavy factory and labour costs before he can supply the needs of the wholesaler and retailer. In their turn, both wholesaler and retailer must be prepared to bear the expenses of warehousing, storage, advertising, packing and delivery costs.

At all stages of production and distribution there are all manner of routine and varied expenses such as the wear and tear of vehicles, insurance and paper work of all description.

The manufacturer's cost comprises the cost of the raw materials, wages of the factory workers and the maintenance expenses of the factory (rent, rates, insurance, lighting and heating, power and machinery repairs and replacement).

The financing of any form of production requires *capital investment,* which means that a fairly substantial percentage must be added to the total manufacturing cost to cover probably both heavy interest charges and an adequate profit element expected from the investing public.

The general expenses of the wholesaler and the retailer, after warehousing and preparing the goods for sale, relate either to selling or administration, the former including advertising, sales commission and delivery, whereas the latter is mainly executive and office work.

The *revenue* of a business refers to its turnover or sales, or the work done and charged to customers. *Revenue expenditure*, on the other hand, relates to the expenses incurred in connection with or on account of *creating that revenue.*

## 6.3 THE TRADING AND PROFIT AND LOSS ACCOUNT

When making up the periodical accounts of a small trading business it is customary to divide the revenue accounts into two main sections:

(a) the first section is called the trading account. It is concerned with the cost of the goods sold, all expenses directly attributable to production and preparing the merchandise for sale. The difference or balance between the total cost of the goods sold and the net turnover is the gross profit (or loss) on trading. This figure, normally a gross profit and credit balance, is carried down to:

(b) the second and lower section of the combined account. This serves to group and assemble the many routine office, selling and administration expenses of the business, all debited to this account. The difference or balance between the gross profit and the total profit and loss account expenses is the net trading profit (or loss) which, in the case of a sole trader, will be transferred to the credit or debit of his capital account.

It is now time to refer back to the trial balance of Tom Brown at the end of Chapter 5. From the details on this trial balance you can now make up the final accounts of Tom Brown's business for the month of October.

Only one additional figure is needed, and that is Tom Brown's valuation of his closing stock at October 31. Let us assume that he values it at £250. (In most examinations, students are given the stock figures; it is unusual for them to have to calculate the stock, unless it is a stock problem.)

Looking again at this trial balance, first of all you will need to extract, for the revenue accounts, only those items specifically concerned with trading and selling, and those expenses, mainly of a routine and recurring nature, necessary for the promotion of sales and the smooth running of the business. Note that this will include everything on the trial balance *except* for cash, debtors, creditors, fittings, capital and drawings. These exceptions are assets and liabilities of the business, to be shown on the balance sheet; they are certainly aids and ancillaries of a trading business, but do not directly influence profits and losses, and are not what are termed 'revenue' items.

All items on the trial balance are taken *once only*, either to the *Trading and Profit and Loss Account, or to the Balance Sheet.* Those taken to the revenue accounts lose their identity, being absorbed in the net profit or loss, whereas the assets and liabilities, with full details of capital and drawings, are displayed prominently on the balance sheet.

Note the long combined heading of the trading and profit and loss account, with almost all the items on the debit, the two sections being split at the gross profit stage:

Trading and Profit and Loss Account
for the month ended October 31..

| | £ | £ | | £ |
|---|---|---|---|---|
| Stock Oct. 1 | 200.00 | | Net sales | 656.30 |
| Purchases | 408.50 | | | |
| | 608.50 | | | |
| Less: Stock Oct. 31 | 250.00 | 358.50 | | |
| Carriage | | 10.80 | | |
| Wages | | 60.00 | | |
| COST OF SALES | | 429.30 | | |
| Gross profit c/d | | 227.00 | | |
| | | 656.30 | | 656.30 |
| Rent | | 30.00 | Gross profit b/d | 227.00 |
| General expenses | | 16.50 | | |
| Advertising | | 34.80 | | |
| Stationery | | 8.50 | | |
| Net trading profit to be taken to Capital Account | | 137.20 | | |
| | | 227.00 | | 227.00 |

## 6.4 COMMENTS ON THE REVENUE ACCOUNTS

(a) The period of trading is designated as part of the long heading of the trading and profit and loss account, in this case 'for the month ended October 31' in contrast to the balance sheet, which is a statement (not an account) drawn up *on a certain date.*

(b) The basic elements of trading, purchases, sales and stocks appear in the first section, together with other expenses directly affected by the turnover of the business, such as carriage inwards (i.e. on purchases) and wages, which, generally, relate to warehousing or preparing the goods for sale.

Carriage on purchases increases the cost of the goods bought, and is a trading account expense. On the other hand, carriage 'outwards' is a distribution expense, and is debited to the lower account. *Both* are expenses and debits.

A distinction is generally made between wages and salaries, the former being charged to trading account if to do with warehousing or putting the goods in a suitable condition for sale; but office and administrative salaries (and wages of cleaners) are not affected by the turnover to the same extent, and are debited to the profit and loss section as more in the nature of a fixed expense like rates and insurance.

(c) Remember that closing stock is a *credit* brought into the books for the first time at the end of the trading period. It may *either be added to sales or deducted from purchases.* In this instance the final stock has been deducted from purchases in order to arrive at the cost of sales (cost of the goods sold) to give management a figure for comparative purposes. The gross profit is the difference between the cost of sales and the net sales. It is carried down to the credit of the lower account. In this instance there are few entries on the right-hand side of the two sections, but in practice there are sometimes a few miscellaneous small profits and gains shown on the credit side of the profit and loss account, such as discounts received, rents or commissions received or bad debts recovered.

(d) Again it is emphasised that these revenue accounts are only to do with the profit and loss elements of trading, income and gains, losses and expenses, and in *no circumstances must fixed assets, cash and bank balances, capital or drawings be brought into these accounts.*

## 6.5 CLOSING OF THE REVENUE ACCOUNTS

All the nominal accounts, whose totals have already been transferred either to the trading or to the profit and loss accounts, should now be closed in this manner:

Dr.                          Purchases Account                          Cr.

| Oct. | | £ | Oct. | | | £ |
|---|---|---|---|---|---|---|
| 1 | Cash | 140.00 | 31 | Transfer to | | |
| 9 | F. Smith & Co. | 160.00 | | Trading A/c | | 408.50 |
| 18 | Cash | 108.50 | | | | |
| | | 408.50 | | | | 408.50 |

Dr.                            Rent Account                             Cr.

| Oct. | | £ | Oct. | | | £ |
|---|---|---|---|---|---|---|
| 2 | Cash | 30.00 | 31 | Transfer to | | |
| | | | | P & L A/c | | 30.00 |

Similarly with the debits of the old stock account, carriage, wages, general expenses, advertising, stationery, and also the sales account credit total.

The only accounts left open in the books are the asset and liability accounts, capital and drawings, all to appear on the balance sheet, together with the new stock figure of £250, still to be shown on a ledger account, and explained at the beginning of Chapter 7.

## 6.6  CAPITAL AND REVENUE EXPENDITURE

A business either starts from scratch with a sum of money in the bank, or is bought as a 'going concern'. In any event, fixed assets are bought, or acquired, out of the original capital of the business. This is known as capital expenditure.

Any further money spent on additional fixed assets is capital expenditure and any money spent on improving or extending existing fixed assets is also a capital expense.

Revenue expenditure is normal business expense, spent on routine trading requirements such as wages, rent, rates, insurance and advertising, all items which appear on the debit of trading and profit and loss account.

The distinction between capital and revenue is important from the points of view of both the trader and the Inland Revenue.

| Revenue expense | Capital expense |
|---|---|
| is debited to a nominal account and transferred to the trading or profit and loss account.<br><br>This decreases the net profit and often means a consequent reduction of income tax | is debited to an asset account and appears on the balance sheet under the heading of fixed assets.<br><br>Business profits are not affected. |

Some difficulty is generally experienced in the early stages of learning accounting, in distinguishing between the two types of expense.

Briefly, anything which is *used up* in the ordinary course of trading is revenue expense, whereas anything *kept* for the permanent use of the business for a number of years may be regarded as a fixed asset and capital expenditure.

**QUESTIONS**

1. What do you understand by:

   (a) manufacturer's cost
   (b) the revenue of a garage?

2. This is the trading account of Georgina West for the month of October:

| | £ | | £ |
|---|---|---|---|
| Stock Oct. 1 | 2000 | Net sales | 7200 |
| Purchases | 4200 | Stock Oct. 31 | 1400 |
| Gross profit | 2400 | | |
| | 8600 | | 8600 |

Give the figures for (a) the cost of goods sold (cost of her sales); (b) the gross profit percentage on turnover; and (c) the gross profit percentage on cost.

3. Business *A* has a stock of £2250 on April 1. During the month purchases bought amounted to £3600 and sales grossed £5640. If the profit margin is 25 per cent of turnover, what is the approximate value of the stock at April 30?

The estimated sales of Business *B* are £80,000. For the past three years selling prices have averaged 30 per cent of the turnover and selling and administrative expenses have averaged 8 per cent and 6 per cent respectively. What is your estimate of the net profit of the business for this year?

4. Why is it so important to distinguish between capital and revenue expenditure? How would you classify the following?

    (a)  erection of a new showroom
    (b)  fire insurance premium
    (c)  commission to travellers
    (d)  stationery supplies
    (e)  decoration of old offices
    (f)  rates and taxes
    (g)  purchase of second-hand duplicator
    (h)  advertising
    (i)  new tyres for van
    (j)  repairs to van
    (k)  new heating installation
    (l)  embezzlement loss

5. The specimen trial balances below relate to questions 3 and 5 at the end of Chapter 5. Note that the *closing stocks* of both Frank Dobson and Percy Potter are shown to the left of these trial balances. You are required to make up the trading and profit and loss account for each trader.

(a)          Frank Dobson Trial Balance September 30

|  |  | £ | £ |
|---|---|---:|---:|
|  | Capital Sep.1 |  | 400.00 |
|  | Drawings | 80.00 |  |
|  | Sales A/c |  | 697.50 |
|  | Purchases A/c | 338.00 |  |
|  | Insurance | 25.50 |  |
|  | Fittings | 109.00 |  |
|  | Carr. inwards | 5.00 |  |
|  | Advertising | 15.20 |  |
|  | Debtors | 160.00 |  |
| Closing | Creditors |  | 150.00 |
| stock | Wages | 71.00 |  |
| Sep. 30 | Cash balance | 443.80 |  |
| £75.00 |  |  |  |
|  |  | 1247.50 | 1247.50 |

(b)          Percy Potter Trial Balance June 30

|  |  | £ | £ |
|---|---|---:|---:|
|  | Capital June 1 |  | 600.00 |
|  | Drawings | 100.00 |  |
|  | Purchases/Sales | 222.10 | 749.60 |
|  | Debtors/Creditors | 50.00 | 150.00 |
|  | Fittings | 151.00 |  |
|  | Rent | 20.00 |  |
|  | Wages | 180.00 |  |
|  | Advertising | 28.50 |  |
|  | Stock  June 1 | 200.00 |  |
| Closing | Cash balance | 548.00 |  |
| stock |  |  |  |
| June 30 |  | 1499.60 | 1499.60 |
| £120.00 |  |  |  |

# PRACTICAL

# BOOK-KEEPING (4)

## 7.1 THE BALANCE SHEET

Before making up the final statement, the balance sheet, stock and capital accounts should be brought up to date.

The old debit of £200 on stock account has already been transferred to the trading account; that part of the account is now closed.

However, in making up the trading account, the new (closing) stock of £250 at October 31 has been brought into the books by a *credit* to trading account (shown as a deduction on the debit). Its corresponding *debit* must now be posted to stock account, thus:

| Dr. | | Stock Account | | | Cr. |
|---|---|---|---|---|---|
| | | £ | | | £ |
| Oct. 1 | Capital Account | 200.00 | Oct. 31 | Transfer of old stock to Trading Account | 200.00 |
| Oct. 31 | Trading Account (new stock figure) | 250.00 | | | |

The new stock has now been brought into the books. It is a current asset and will be taken to the right-hand side of the balance sheet at October 31.

The valuation of stock is not a theoretical figure to be worked out by the ledger clerk. Physical stocktaking is a continuous process in large trading organisations. In examinations, however, students are normally given the stock figures.

Tom Brown's capital account is made up by transferring to its credit the net profit from the Profit and Loss Account, and to its debit the total of drawings account for the month.

| Dr. | | | Capital Account | | Cr. |
|---|---|---|---|---|---|
| | | £ | Oct. | | £ |
| Oct. 31 | Transfer from Drawings A/c | 80.00 | 1 1 | Cash Stock | 800.00 200.00 |
| 31 | Balance c/d | 1057.20 | 31 | Transfer of net profit | 137.20 |
| | | 1137.20 | | | 1137.20 |
| | | | Oct. 31 | Balance b/d | 1057.20 |

The phrase 'final accounts' includes the balance sheet, but it should be realised that the double entry has already served its purpose and debit and credit no longer applies to the balance sheet. It is simply a statement of assets and liabilities, made up for interested parties in a manner approved by management, and, in the case of limited companies, in conformity with the requirements of the Companies Acts.

The final picture or presentation of the financial structure of the business *at a certain date*, discloses the business property and possessions on that date, and both its internal and external debts and obligations, in total form.

The two styles of balance-sheet presentation are now shown in connection with Tom Brown's balance sheet, first the modern 'vertical narrative' style, in general use by most of the larger organisations and which allows a break-down of information and ancillary notes in anticipation of questions by company members and shareholders. In this style of balance sheet there are usually wide margins and the comparative figures of the previous year, and one big advantage is that it helps to prevent students thinking of the balance sheet as an account with debit and credit sides.

There is, of course, much more detail on the balance sheets of public and private companies than that shown. It is customary, too, to deduct the current liabilities from the current assets, to give the working capital of the business.

To switch over to the older conventional style, in common use among the smaller firms, all that is necessary is to tilt the modern style (with the capital shown first) over to the left, and we get the horizontal style of balance sheet which lends itself to visual presentation on the fixed blackboards. This is the style we shall use up to company account stage, in the last chapter of this book.

Balance Sheet of Tom Brown
as at October 31..

| Capital and liabilities | £ | £ | Previous year |
|---|---|---|---|
| Capital Account   Oct. 1 | 1000.00 | | |
| Net trading profit | 137.20 | | |
| | 1137.20 | | |
| Less:  drawings | 80.00 | 1057.20 | |
| Current liabilities | | | |
| Trade creditors | | 110.00 | |
| | | 1167.20 | |
| Represented by the following assets: | | | |
| Fixed assets | | £ | |
| Fittings and equipment | | 130.00 | |
| Current assets | £ | | |
| Stock | 250.00 | | |
| Trade debtors | 97.70 | | |
| Cash | 689.50 | 1037.20 | |
| | | 1167.20 | |

Balance Sheet of Tom Brown
as at October 31..

| Capital Account | £ | | Fixed assets | | £ |
|---|---|---|---|---|---|
| Balance Oct. 1 | 1000.00 | | Fittings/equipment | | 130.00 |
| Net trading profit | 137.20 | | | | |
| | 1137.20 | | Current assets | | |
| Less: drawings | 80.00 | 1057.20 | Stock | 250.00 | |
| | | | Trade debtors | 97.70 | |
| Current liabilities | | | Cash | 689.50 | 1037.20 |
| Trade creditors | | 110.00 | | | |
| | | 1167.20 | | | 1167.20 |

Note the general evenness of the statement above. It is divided into four main sections, Capital and Liabilities on the left, and Fixed and Current Assets on the right. These sections should be kept separate and distinct. In no circumstances should current (or fixed) liabilities be thrust into the capital section. Capital is an internal debt of the business due to its owner, whereas trade creditors are external debts owing to suppliers of goods or services.

If, occasionally, a fixed (long-term) liability (such as a mortgage or large bank loan) is included, this should be placed under its own heading between the Capital Account and the Current Liabilities.

Fixed assets have been bought for the retention and permanent use of the business, and not for sale in the trading sense. Current assets, on the other hand, change their form from day to day, as goods are sold for cash or on credit, creating book debts, and further merchandise is bought for stock by cash or credit.

The two sides of Tom Brown's balance sheet are listed in order of permanency, the fixed assets (kept for the permanent use of the business) preceding the current assets, which fluctuate and change day by day. Similarly, on the liabilities side, the net worth or capital of Tom Brown, his interest and holding valued at £1057.20, a fixed or long-term liability of the business and internal debt due to the proprietor, is kept quite separate from the current liabilities, and normally heads the left-hand side of this style of balance sheet.

All Tom Brown's *trading* transactions for the month of October (gains, losses and expenses) have been absorbed into the ultimate *net profit* figure, now transferred to the proprietor's capital account, and the remainder of the items shown on his balance sheet still have 'open' balances in the books, to be carried forward for use in the next trading period.

Every balance sheet has a story to tell.

In this small illustration, Tom Brown has increased the net worth of his business by £57.20 during the month of October, reflected by the amount

|  |  |
|---|---|
| of his trading profit | £137.20 |
| *less* his withdrawals | £ 80.00 |
|  | £ 57.20 |

Tom Brown's cash balance has decreased by £110.50, but he has acquired fixed assets of £130, and his stock is worth £50 more than that which he had when he started business. Counteracting this benefit, to a small degree, he owes his trade creditors, at October 31, a little more than what is owing to him by his own trade debtors.

## 7.2 CAPITAL OWNED AND CAPITAL EMPLOYED

'Capital owned' is the credit balance of the capital account, the financial holding or equity in the case of a sole trader (£1057.20 in this instance). Tom Brown, however, cannot withdraw or realise this sum until he has sold or borrowed its corresponding value of business assets.

'Capital employed' may be interpreted in two ways:

(a) As the total amount of fixed and current assets at the disposal and for the full use and benefit of the business (£1167.20 in this instance).
(b) The total fixed and current assets *less trade debtors*, i.e. £1069.50. It may be argued that the business is being deprived of the use of available funds represented by these debts. On the other hand, it could also be argued that there is also a substantial amount owing to creditors assisting the financing of trading operations at *their* expense.

## 7.3 WORKING CAPITAL

Working capital is simply a sufficiency of stock and money available to meet routine trading operations, which would include paying off a proportion of the creditors and the settlement of normal business expenses such as wages, advertising, insurance and rates.

Working capital is the excess of current assets over current liabilities. It is not merely the cash available, although cash is part of the working capital. Again referring to the balance sheet of Tom Brown:

|  |  | £ | £ |
|---|---|---|---|
| The current assets are: | Stock | 250.00 | |
| | Debtors | 97.70 | |
| | Cash | 689.50 | 1037.20 |
| Deduct the current liabilities – creditors | | | 110.00 |
| | Working capital | | 927.20 |

## 7.4 SOLVENCY

When a person is able to pay his debts, he is said to be solvent. This does not always mean that he must have a large bank balance. He might have a bank overdraft, but own a good deal of stock and property, or substantial sums of money may be owing to him by his debtors. Generally speaking, if the total assets of a business exceed the total liabilities (excluding capital) that business is solvent.

## 7.5  PERSONAL DRAWINGS

When money is withdrawn by the proprietor for his own or family use, there is a corresponding reduction of his holding or net worth in the business, shown by the reduction of his capital account. The same principle applies when a grocer takes butter and bacon from the shop for his family consumption. His stock of goods available for sale is reduced by the cost price of the commodities withdrawn, and again there is the corresponding reduction of his capital account.

These withdrawals bear no relationship to the proper trading expenses of the business. The money and goods are withdrawn, for private and personal use, in anticipation of profits to be made.

### QUESTIONS

1. Anne Bartel's balance sheet is shown in brief detail at March 24:

| | £ | | | £ |
|---|---|---|---|---|
| Capital | 5000 | Fixed assets | | 3500 |
| Trade creditors | 2750 | Current assets | | |
| | | Stock | 1600 | |
| | | Debtors | 2420 | |
| | | Cash | 230 | 4250 |
| | 7750 | | | 7750 |

You are required to draft another balance sheet at March 31, giving effect to the following transactions which took place during the last week of March:

(a)  £520 was received from credit customers and £300 paid to trade creditors.
(b)  Sales to cash customers totalled £250 showing a profit margin of 20 per cent on selling price.
(c)  Another £400 of goods were bought on credit.
(d)  A steel filing-cabinet was bought for £80 cash.
(e)  Miss Bartel withdrew £75 for her own use.

Say to what extent the working capital of Miss Bartel's business has changed between March 24 and March 31.

2. Refer back now to question 5 of Chapter 6 and make up the balance sheets of Frank Dobson's business as at September 30, and Percy Potter's business as at June 30. Use the older style of horizontal presentation and in each case show clearly the separate sections for capital, current liabilities, fixed assets and current assets.

3. Make up the final accounts (trading and profit and loss account and a balance sheet) from the following trial balance of Walter Page, dated December 31:

| | | | Debit £ | Credit £ |
|---|---|---|---|---|
| CASH BOOK | Balance on hand | | 816 | |
| BOUGHT LEDGER | R. Morton & Co. | | | 250 |
| | H. Frost | | | 130 |
| SALES LEDGER | E. Roberts | | 164 | |
| | L. Price | | 308 | |
| NOMINAL LEDGER | Advertising | | 372 | |
| | Insurance | | 260 | |
| | Rent/rates | | 1,760 | |
| | Wages | | 4,880 | |
| | Purchases | | 9,360 | |
| | Sales | | | 21,640 |
| GENERAL AND PRIVATE LEDGERS | Fixed assets at cost | | 9,600 | |
| | Stock Jan. 1 | | 2,500 | |
| | Capital | | | 11,000 |
| | Drawings | | 3,000 | |
| The closing stock at Dec. 31 was £2880 | | | 33,020 | 33,020 |

4. (a) Assuming that you have made up a horizontal-style balance sheet for question 3 above, now redraft to show its full detail on a vertical narrative style as shown in the text.

(b) Make up the capital account of Walter Page to show his commencing balance for the new trading year starting January 1.

(c) Show the complete sales ledger account of Edwina Roberts, who owed £122.80 at the beginning of September, bought supplies on credit amounting to £179.50 during October, returned some damaged goods and received a credit note for £15.50, and finally paid the balance outstanding at November 30 on December 5; the present outstanding balance of £164 refers to goods purchased during December.

5. Gentian Dale lists her transactions for the month of August and asks you to make up her cash book and ledger accounts, extract a trial balance

and draft a balance sheet as at August 31. Her final stock valuation was £100, and these are her figures for the month:

|  |  |  | £ |
|---|---|---|---|
| August | 1 | Cash (her only asset when she started business this date) | 500 |
|  | 3 | Cash paid for goods | 150 |
|  | 4 | Cash takings | 66 |
|  |  | Paid for shelving | 50 |
|  | 6 | Paid wages to part-time assistant | 48 |
|  |  | Cash sales | 154 |
|  | 10 | Bought stationery | 16 |
|  |  | Paid insurance | 15 |
|  | 15 | Bought further goods for sale | 72 |
|  |  | Paid wages | 48 |
|  | 18 | Cash sales | 113 |
|  |  | Paid travelling expenses | 4 |
|  | 20 | Drawings | 50 |
|  | 22 | Cash sales | 176 |
|  | 25 | Commissions received | 80 |
|  |  | Bought stamps | 5 |
|  | 28 | Paid wages | 48 |
|  |  | Bought filing-cabinet | 28 |
|  | 30 | Paid office salaries for month | 178 |
|  |  | Withdrew for own use | 50 |

# CASH AND BANK:
# CASH DISCOUNT

Up to this stage the principles of double entry with illustrative exercises have been based on physical cash, i.e. currency notes and pence.

This might apply to the very small types of retail business such as a shop, but even the local grocer and butcher are now very much cheque and bank conscious and like to keep abreast of the times. They also realise that it is not wise to keep large sums of money on the shop premises on account of the possibility of theft and fire, so a current account is opened at the nearest bank.

Cash and cheques from customers and trade debtors are paid into the current account, and cheques drawn on the bank in settlement of suppliers' account. The purpose of a current account is to have money ready and available for use as required.

The bank is a safe place for surplus funds, and banks rarely make charges or commission for their services providing a regular small balance (say an average of £100) is maintained on the current account. Excess accumulations of funds may be placed on a special deposit account to earn interest, varying according to the prevailing rates of the Bank of England and the Money Market.

## 8.1 THE TWO-COLUMN CASH BOOK

Cash payments are reduced to a minimum in the larger firms, and cheques are drawn to cover almost every kind of business expense. The bank may be instructed to make certain payments on behalf of a customer by standing order or credit transfer, explained at the end of this chapter.

As a rule the book-keeping beginner is introduced to the two-column type of cash book (shown overleaf) with separate debit and credit columns for the receipt and payment of both cash and cheques.

Dr.                          Two-column Cash Book                    Cr.

| Date | | Fol. | Cash | Bank | Date | | Fol. | Cash | Bank |
|------|--|------|------|------|------|--|------|------|------|
| | | | £ | £ | | | | £ | £ |
| Jan. | | | | | Jan. | | | | |
| 1 | Balance | | 10 | 500 | 2 | J. Brown | BL6 | | 20 |
| 2 | Cash sales | NL8 | 15 | | 3 | Rent | NL5 | | 8 |
| 5 | S. Smith | SL9 | | 60 | 4 | Stamps | NL3 | 2 | |

Cash and Bank columns in a cash book are *separate accounts* and are balanced up quite independently. They are merely kept alongside each other for convenience. If this small cash book illustration were balanced up, there would be a cash balance of £23 and a bank balance of £532 to enter in the two separate columns on the credit side of the cash book, and to bring down below the totals of £25 and £560 on the debit side.

Since these original entries in the cash book have yet to complete their double entry, the cash sales will be posted to the credit of the nominal ledger, and the payments for rent and stamps to the debit, of their respective accounts, also in the nominal ledger. Smith, who was presumably a trade debtor, will have his account in the sales ledger credited with his payment of £60, and Brown, a supplier, will have his account in the bought ledger debited with the £20 paid to him.

It is often usual, though not recommended, for the local retailer to pay many of his day-to-day expenses out of his daily takings, and also to withdraw money for his household needs and private use from the cash till. Unless an accurate record is kept by the shopkeeper, his accountant will not relish his task in preparing final accounts at the year end.

Wholesalers' accounts are settled monthly by cheque as a rule, and the money surplus to immediate requirements (including customers' cheques) is paid into the current account at the local bank once or twice a week, dependent upon the volume of business.

## 8.2 PROCEDURE WITH REGARD TO TEXTBOOK EXERCISES

It is customary for the student to assume that cheques are to be paid into the bank the same day they are received, unless there are instructions that cash and cheques are to be *banked in total* towards the end of the exercise. The correct procedure, in the latter instance, is to enter cheques *in the cash column as they are received*, and then make a contra posting when banked, *crediting cash and debiting the bank.*

The same rules apply to cheques as for cash, with regard to the posting of the opposite aspect of the original debit or credit.

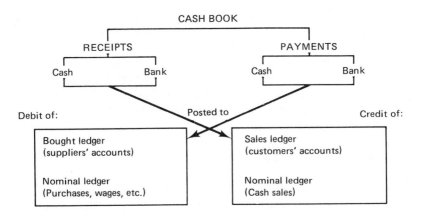

## 8.3 CHEQUES

A cheque is a direction given to a banker to pay or transfer a sum of money to a named payee.

The instructions are written or typed on an official printed form supplied by the bank, the main essentials shown in this specimen outline:

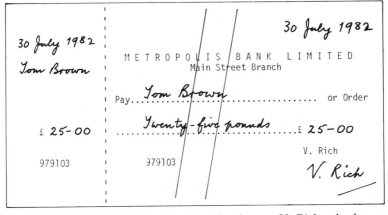

This cheque is dated and signed by the drawer, V. Rich, who has an account with Metropolis Bank Limited. His signature will be easily recognisable by the bank's counter clerks. The cheque is drawn in favour of Tom Brown, who in normal circumstances would pay this cheque into his own bank account. Tom Brown's bankers would then arrange to 'collect' this sum of money from Metropolis Bank. The amount, by mutual arrangement known as a 'clearing', would be transferred from one bank to the other, thereby reducing V. Rich's current account by £25 and increasing Tom Brown's current account by the same amount.

Two parallel transverse lines are drawn across this cheque as a safety precaution. The cheque must be paid into a bank account *before* the money can be collected from Rich's bank. It cannot be cashed across the bank's counter, as in the case of a cheque not crossed, and is a precaution against the cheque falling into the wrong hands; if stolen, it can be more easily traced. However, in the event of Tom Brown not having a bank account, he could endorse or sign it over to a friend or local tradesman, by adding his signature on the back of the cheque, the recipient then paying it into his own bank for collection.

## 8.4   CHEQUE COUNTERFOILS

The counterfoil on the left of the cheque is filled in at the time the cheque is made out. The perforation between the cheque and its counterfoil allows the cheque to be detached easily from its book when required by the drawer to make a payment.

The cashier of a firm posts up the credit side of his cash book *bank column* from these counterfoil stubs.

Bank regulations state that the bank is not in duty bound to honour cheques of customers drawn against uncleared cheques paid into their account for collection. Uncleared cheques (cheques not yet cleared) are those cheques handed in to the bank for collection, but not yet collected or transferred over to the customer's account.

## 8.5   PAYING-IN SLIP

When surplus cash and cheques are paid into the bank, details are entered into an official paying-in book issued by the bank for the use of customers. The counter clerk (teller) detaches the main part of the slip from its counterfoil, stamping and initialling the latter, which serves the same purpose as the stubs of the cheque book, although for the reverse side of of the cash book. The cashier enters up his debit bank column from these paying-in slips, and then files them safely away, as sometimes the auditor requires to see them.

## 8.6   DISHONOURED CHEQUES

Occasionally a cheque may be returned by your bank with the initials R/D or N/S noted on it. These are abbreviations for 'Refer to drawer' and 'Not sufficient funds, implying that the person who has given you the cheque has no available funds in his bank account to meet the cheque. Your bank returns it to you so that you may take any action you think fit. It is important to remember that the bank cannot give you credit for a returned cheque, and if you have already shown it as a receipt in your cash book, you must *now reverse it*, and debit it back to the customer's account.

**Example**

George Smith owes you £10, and sends you a cheque in settlement. You debit your bank column and credit his personal account in your sales ledger. Two days later your bank informs you that the cheque has been refused by Smith's bank.

The entries in both the cash book and the ledger must be reversed. The bank column of the cash book will be credited and the debit posted back to the debtor's account in the sales ledger, as he still owes you this money.

| Dr. | | | | Cash Book | | | | Cr. |
|---|---|---|---|---|---|---|---|---|
| | | | £ | | | | | £ |
| | George Smith | SL | 10 | | George Smith (Returned cheque) | SL | | 10 |

| Dr. | | | | George Smith | | | | Cr. |
|---|---|---|---|---|---|---|---|---|
| | | | £ | | | | | £ |
| | Balance b/f | | 10 | | Cheque | CB | | 10 |
| | Returned cheque | CB | 10 | | | | | |

## 8.7 CASH DISCOUNT AND THE THREE-COLUMN CASH BOOK

Trade discount, the fairly large rebate given by the wholesaler to the retailer, is explained in Chapter 11.

For the present we are concerned only with *cash discount*, a much smaller allowance than trade discount, and offered by the creditor (wholesaler or retailer) as an inducement for customers to pay their accounts (in particular monthly statements) more quickly.

From the point of view of the creditor firm this fractional reduction of the profit is more than compensated for by the regular settlement of customers' accounts, and often avoids the worry of large outstanding balances and possible bad debts. Probably, too, there is not the same concern for the negotiation of bank loans as the working capital is built up again at the beginning of every month.

The three-column cash book is now brought into use to provide that extra column, on both sides, to record cash discount.

Cash discount is entered into its appropriate column alongside the payment to which it relates, *but for convenience only*. The double entry is:

(a) the posting of both *discount and cash (or cheque)* to the personal account of either payee or payer, and

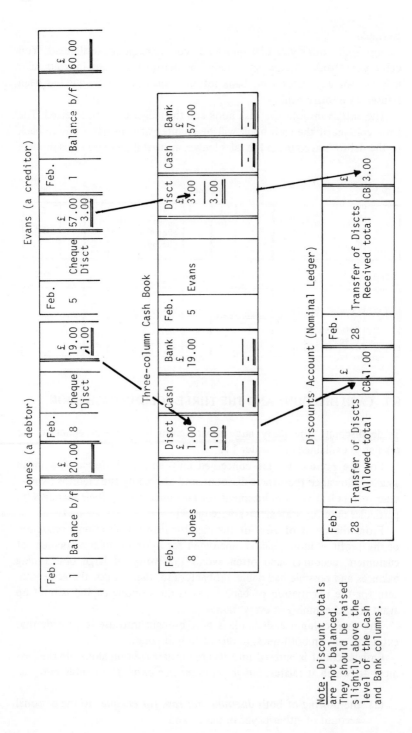

(b) the posting of the *discount* to a Discounts Account in the nominal ledger.

It is better explained by illustration, as shown on page 56.

## 8.8 POSTING THE DISCOUNT TOTALS

The personal accounts of Jones and Evans have been settled and balanced off. At this stage the double entry might appear complete, but, because the discount columns are only *memoranda* columns it is still necessary to deal with the debits or credits within those columns. This is dealt with, in total form, in a way similar to the day books.

Discounts allowed (debit) total is *transferred to the debit* of Discounts Allowed Account as a loss and expense to the business. Discounts received (credit) total is *transferred to the credit* of the Discounts Received Account as a profit or gain of the business. Alternatively, these totals are transferred to the same account, Discounts Account, in the nominal ledger, though, generally, the totals are shown separately on the profit and loss account.

Remember that the discount totals are merely *transferred*, as the entries within their columns have already completed their double entry.

The final destination of the discount totals is the profit and loss account, and if a trading and profit and loss account were made up, in the last illustration, for the end of February, the totals would appear thus:

Profit and Loss section of the Trading
and Profit and Loss Account
for the period ended February 28

| | £ | | £ |
|---|---|---|---|
| Discounts allowed | 1.00 | Gross profit b/d | – – |
| | | Discounts received | 3.00 |

## 8.9 BANKING TERMS

CURRENT ACCOUNT
: The ordinary business account. Money may be withdrawn on demand.

DEPOSIT ACCOUNT
: Earns interest on excess funds. Interest varies according to Bank of England and Money Market rates; used to be 2 per cent below the Bank Rate.

BANK CHARGES
: No charges for cheque books now, and no poundage on cheques. Fairly high interest rates on overdrafts and sometimes notional interest on current accounts maintained at low and marginal levels.

OVERDRAFT — Where the bank permits a customer to overdraw his account balance. Usually of a temporary nature, for a few weeks or a few months, at fairly high interest. Do not confuse with Bank Loans, fixed sums, to be repaid at interest, over agreed periods.

STANDING ORDER — The bank undertakes to pay recurring expense on behalf of the customer. In particular applicable for annual subscriptions to clubs and associations, insurance premiums, television rentals, and mortgage repayments. The bank makes the payment and debits the customer's current account, indicated on his statement by the abbreviation SO.

CREDIT TRANSFER — The paying customer authorises his bank to make certain payments by direct transfer from his account to the credit of accounts of named persons. In this way it is only necessary to draw one cheque in payment, and it also saves time and trouble in making out slips for the various payees. Quarterly electricity and gas bills can be settled direct through the bank, and monthly paid employees are now, in the main, paid by credit transfer, direct from their employer's bank account to the credit of their own.

## QUESTIONS

1. Write up the cash book of Anita Trent from the following information and bring down the balances on March 31:

March
- 25 Cash balance brought forward £25.20
  Bank balance brought forward £374.80
- 26 Cash takings £66.30
  Received cheque from James Denton for £35.50
  Charles Garratt called and paid his old account £8.80 in cash
- 27 Cash takings £80.70
  Paid £100 cash into bank
- 28 Received cheque for £60.10 from Henry Masters
  Paid £4 cash for stationery and stamps
  Paid Central Stores their February account £120.00 by cheque
- 30 Counter sales totalled £90.30
  Miss Trent paid £50 cash into bank and withdrew £25 cash for herself
- 31 Balanced up cash and bank columns.

2. Post the cash and bank transactions to your cash book for the next three months, balancing up at the end of each month, and bringing down the final balance on December 31:

*N.B.* All payments over £2 should be made by cheque, unless otherwise stated. The only exceptions to this rule are payments for wages and stamps, normally paid in cash.

October
1   Cash balance brought forward £42.40
      Bank balance brought forward £483.50
2   Cash takings £55.60
4   Paid sundry expenses in cash £3
8   Cash sales £42.20
12   Received cheque for £60 from Herbert Lovell
15   Paid Roberts & Evans Ltd £80.00 by cheque
20   Cash sales £77.40
24   Paid £100 cash into bank
27   Paid wages £60 for part-time assistance
31   Cashed £50 cheque for 'self'.

November
1   Cash sales £67.20
3   Paid fire insurance premium £15
      and Electricity Board account for £30.30
8   Alan Mansel paid his account £70 by cheque
10   Paid window cleaner £2
14   Received £15 cash from Derek Main
18   Cash sales £84.30
22   Paid £100 cash into bank
28   Paid wages £60
30   Withdrew £50 cash for 'self'.

December
1   Cash sales £90.40
4   James Dean paid his November account for £54.60
9   Bought some stationery for £2
12   Received £24 cash from Hilary Farrar
16   Paid window cleaner £2
18   Paid half-year's rates £130
22   Cash sales £92.50; paid £100 into bank
28   Paid wages £60
31   Cashed £50 cheque made out for 'self'.

3. Explain these terms and abbreviations:

| Contra | paying-in slip | credit transfer |
|---|---|---|
| current account | deposit account | cheque stubs |
| R/D | N/S    O/D | SO |

4. Assume your first job, on July 8, is with the local grocer, who has

a good little business with up-to-date equipment. Occasionally, though, he gets a little behind with his figure work.

He asks you to make up his cash book, for the week previous to your arrival, from the following information:

The balances brought forward from June 30 were:

Cash balance £22.50    :    Bank balance £385.70

The cash register details extracted gave the till roll details as follows:

|  |  | £ |  |  | £ |
|---|---|---|---|---|---|
| July 1 | total for day | 44.80 | July 2 | total for day | 68.10 |
| 3 | ,, | 58.20 | 4 | ,, | 76.80 |
| 5 | ,, | 87.30 | 6 | ,, | 134.70 |

During the week three credit customers had paid their accounts:

July 2   Cheques were received from Arthur Gosling £16.60 and George Fisher £24.00

5   Herbert Kemp called and paid £12.20 in cash.

The two cheques were banked on July 6 with some cash.

There were three entries in the bank paying-in slip (as shown on the counterfoils):

July 4   Cash banked  £150.00
5   Cash banked  £200.00
6   Cash and cheques banked £140.60

Cheque book counterfoil stubs showed the following payments to suppliers and creditors during the first week of July:

July 2   Marston & Sons Ltd   £115.00
3   Ronald Ward   36.80
5   Grange Products   42.30

Another cheque was drawn on July 6 for £120.00 specifically for the payment of wages. Routine cash payments made from the till during the week were extracted as follows:

July 2   Postages £3;   July 4 Cleaning £6;   July 5 Packing material £8.

You are required to bring down the cash and bank balances on July 6, and indicate, in the folio columns of the cash book, the abbreviation of the particular ledger for the related or opposite entry for each item.

5. Make up a three-column cash book from the details given below:

November
1   Bank balance £450   :   cash balance £50
4   Cash takings £35.80

5   Paid Edwina Smith's October account for £60 less 5 per cent cash discount

6   Bought supplies for resale £22.20

9   Henrietta James called and paid her October account for £40; allowed her 5 per cent off

13   Received settlement of Hazel Hughes's account, outstanding since May. This was for £19.50 but Miss Hughes only forwarded £18.80, so put the difference down to discounts allowed

18   Allowed Jennifer Johnson 5 per cent discount when she paid her account invoiced at £25

24   Paid £30 into bank

30   Sent Katrina Brown a cheque for £63.27 in settlement of account due for £66.60. This was according to past dealings with this supplier.

**6.** At the close of business on April 27 the totals of Richard Henry's cash book were:

| | Discount £ | Cash £ | Bank £ | | Discount £ | Cash £ | Bank £ |
|---|---|---|---|---|---|---|---|
| | 28 | 428 | 1876 | | 16 | 375 | 1420 |

The following transactions took place during the last three days of April:

April

28   Cash takings £42, paid £40 into bank. Cheque for £9 received from Horace Walker. Richard Henry cashed a cheque for £25 for his private use.

29   Cash sales £39, paid £30 into bank. Paid £80 rates for half-year. Cheque received from Alan Peel for £24 which was accepted in settlement of his account for £25. Horace Walker's cheque for £9 was returned by the bank with remarks thereon 'refer to drawer'.

30   Bought a filing-cabinet for the office for £50. Paid £4 to office cleaner, and drew wages cheque for £190. Cash sales amounted to £66, of which £50 was paid into bank. Received a cheque for £76 from Bryan Gale. His sales ledger debit was for £80 but had previously agreed to this allowance.

You are required to write up Richard Henry's cash book and bring down his cash and bank balances at April 30.

# BANK RECONCILIATION

When the cashier of a firm makes out a cheque to send off to one of the firm's creditors he enters the amount of the payment in the credit column of his cash book, thereby reducing the bank balance *according to the cash book*. Actually, the firm's balance at the bank will not be affected by this particular cheque sent to the creditor for several days, which time must elapse before that cheque is presented for collection. The time lag is due to postal delay, in particular the second-class post, further delay in making out the paying-in book and handing over its contents for collection, and again, at least another day's delay for the creditor's bank to 'clear' the cheque and obtain payment from the debtor's bank.

Similarly, when a cheque is received in settlement of a customer's account, the cashier records the receipt when the paying-in book is made out, as a debit to his bank column and a posting (by the ledger clerk) to the credit of the customer's account. The cheque, however, has yet to be 'cleared' and collected from the debtor's bank. If the 'clearing' is local, i.e. within the same town area, settlement may be a little quicker, but provincial cheques cleared by London will take four to five days.

Normally, twice a year, the bank debits the customer's current account with any commission and charges for services or temporary overdrafts, and until the firm's cashier receives the bank statement, he is unaware of the extent of these charges. Again, dividends from the firm's investments may have been paid direct to the firm's bank account, and have yet to be debited to the bank column of the cash book.

The firm's cashier or accountant must agree and reconcile the figures shown by the cash book bank columns with the entries shown on the bank statement, before the true bank balance is established for the balance sheet at the end of the trading period.

A reconciliation statement is made out, sometimes by the cashier on the last page of the period in his cash book. Cheques in transit are listed and added or subtracted and the existing bank balance amended to its true figure.

## 9.1  PROCEDURE IN PRACTICE

Normally, reconciliation takes place at least once a month. The cashier checks his cash book against the bank statement, ticking off all postings in the bank columns of his cash book which correspond to those shown on the bank statement.

Any items not ticked in the firm's cash book will either be cheques not yet presented for payment, or cheques not yet cleared and credited to the firm's current account.

On the other hand, items not ticked or unaccounted for on the bank statement will refer to standing orders, certain bank charges or commission, and dividends paid direct to the bank. All these items will be posted by the cashier to the receipt or payment bank columns of his cash book. He will then have brought his own bank balance up to date, as far as possible.

## 9.2  GENERAL RULES FOR RECONCILIATION

(a)  Where there is a debit bank balance in the cash book
   (i) Bring the cash book up to date by adding any interest and dividends paid direct to bank, and deducting any bank charges.
   (ii) Now turn to the bank statement and add to the statement any cheques not yet cleared by the bank.
   (iii) Deduct from the bank statement any cheques not yet presented for payment.

The balance of the bank statement should now agree with the amended cash book balance.

(b)  Where there is a credit balance in the bank columns of the cash book, and a bank overdraft shown on the bank statement.

   (i) Again adjust the cash book bank balance, but remember that interest and dividends paid direct to the bank will *decrease* the overdraft shown by the cash book, and bank charges will *increase* it.
   (ii) Turn now to the bank statement and deduct cheques not yet cleared by the bank.
   (iii) Add cheques not yet presented for payment.

The balance should agree with that in the cash book.

## 9.3  PRACTICAL EXAMPLES

(a)  The cash book for the month of June is first checked over, item for item, with the bank statement underneath it.

Cash Book
(Bank columns only)

| June | | | | £ | June | | | £ |
|---|---|---|---|---|---|---|---|---|
| 1 | Balance b/f | ✔ | | 250 | 2 | Roberts | ✔ | 18 |
| 2 | Cash sales | ✔ | 24 | | 8 | Wages | ✔ | 48 |
| 3 | " | ✔ | 36 | 60 | 12 | Rates | ✔ | 120 |
| | | | — | | 18 | Shaw | ✔ | 30 |
| 10 | Jones | ✔ | 12 | | 24 | Wages | ✔ | 52 |
| 12 | Brown | ✔ | 54 | 66 | 28 | Johnson | | 78 |
| | | | — | | 30 | Stevens | | 40 |
| 18 | Evans | ✔ | | 58 | 30 | Balance c/d | | 157 |
| 24 | Cash sales | ✔ | | 44 | | | | |
| 28 | Somers | | 38 | | | | | |
| 30 | Hancox | | 27 | 65 | | | | |
| | | | — | | | | | |
| | | | | 543 | | | | 543 |
| July | | | | | | | | |
| 1 | Balance b/d | | | 157 | | | | |

Bank Statement

| Date | Details | | Debit | Credit | Balance |
|---|---|---|---|---|---|
| June | | | £ | £ | £ |
| 1 | Balance b/f | | | | ✔ 250 |
| 3 | Cash and cheques | | | ✔ 60 | 310 |
| 4 | Roberts | | ✔ 18 | | 292 |
| 8 | Self | | ✔ 48 | | 244 |
| 12 | Cheques | | | ✔ 66 | 310 |
| 15 | Corpn rates | | ✔120 | | 190 |
| 18 | Cheque | | | ✔ 58 | 248 |
| 22 | Shaw | | ✔ 30 | | 218 |
| 24 | Cash | | | ✔ 44 | 262 |
| 24 | Self | | ✔ 52 | | 210 |
| 28 | Bank charges | | 1 | | 209 |
| 30 | Treasury Stock | | | 40 | 249 |
| 30 | SO | | 6 | | 243 |

When the firm's cashier receives the bank statement on July 1 he will bring his cash book up to date as at the end of June by posting the £40 Treasury Stock divident (paid direct to bank) as a receipt in his cash book. He will also post the bank charges of £1 and annual trade subscription of £6 to the credit column of his cash book.

The amended cash book bank balance (acceptable for audit purposes) is now shown as £190:

| June | | £ | June | | £ |
|---|---|---|---|---|---|
| 30 | Balance b/f | 157 | 30 | Bank charges | 1 |
| 30 | Treasury | | 30 | Trade sub. | 6 |
| | Stock | | | Balance c/d | 190 |
| | dividend | 40 | | | |
| | | 197 | | | 197 |
| July | | | | | |
| 1 | Balance b/d | 190 | | | |

We can now reconcile the amended cash book bank balance of £190 with the balance according to the bank statement of £243 by ticking the various items in the cash book against those shown on the bank statement. The items left unticked on the credit of the cash book are the unpresented cheques of Johnson and Stevens, totalling £118; the items left unticked on the debit of the cash book are the two cheques received from Somers and Hancox, totalling £65, and not yet cleared by the bank.

Reconciliation Statement June 30

| | £ | | £ |
|---|---|---|---|
| Amended balance as per CB | 190 | Reverse (i.e. deduct) from CB balance cheques not yet cleared by bank (£38+27) | 65 |
| Reverse (or add back) cheques not yet presented for payment (£78+40) | 118 | Balance as per bank statement | 243 |
| | 308 | | 308 |

## (b) Bank reconcilation: illustration working from a bank overdraft

You are asked to find the bank balance, at December 31, according to the firm's cash book, from the information given below:

Bank Statement

| December | | Debit £ | Credit £ | Balance £ |
|---|---|---|---|---|
| 23 | Brought forward | | | 72.18 |
| 27 | Cash and cheques | | 222.44 | 294.62 |
| 28 | Thomas | 185.49 | | 109.13 |
| 30 | Salaries | 166.00 | | 56.87 OD |
| 31 | Petty cash paid in | | 36.61 | 20.26 OD |
| 31 | Bank charges | 6.30 | | 26.56 OD |

In addition to the petty cash paid into bank at the year-end, the paying-in book on December 31 also showed customers' cheques totalling £144.22, but these were not cleared by the bank until early in the New Year.

A cheque of £56.52 had been sent to Stationery Supplies Ltd on December 28, but this was not presented until January 2. The bank charges of £6.30 were not picked up by the firm's cashier and posted to his cash book until the office reopened on January 2. He then made out the following reconciliation statement, later to be checked and agreed by the chief accountant.

Bank Reconciliation Statement

| Dec. 31 | | £ | Dec. 31 | | £ |
|---|---|---|---|---|---|
| | Cheques not yet credited by bank | 144.22 | | Overdraft according to bank statement | 26.56 |
| | Bank charges to be posted in CB | 6.30 | | Cheques not yet presented | 56.52 |
| | | | | Balance as per Cash Book | 67.44 |
| | | 150.52 | | | 150.52 |

## QUESTIONS

1. (a) What do the terms 'cheques not yet presented' and 'cheques not cleared' mean on a bank reconciliation statement?

(b) Make up Tarquina Lane's reconciliation statement at February 28 from the following information, and show the bank balance according to her cash book:

Balance of the bank statement dated February 28 was £273.45. The cashier had sent two cheques to creditors by post on February 26 (to Fred Daneway and R. P. Disney for £67.20 and £24.80 respectively). These had not yet been presented for payment.

Bank charges of £2.50 shown on the bank statement had not yet been entered in the cash book, and a trade subscription paid annually direct by the bank for £10.50 had not yet been posted in the cash book.

2. George Percival's cash book shows a bank balance of £410.68 on September 30. On checking with his bank statement at the beginning of October he finds that all entries in the bank columns of his cash book agree with those on the bank statement except for the following:

(a) Cash takings (including cheques cashed for customers) amounting to £126.60 paid into the bank late on Friday afternoon of September 30 had not yet been credited by the bank to the business account.

(b) Cheques drawn in settlement of two creditors' accounts (G. Shaw £15 and V. Thornton £42.20) had not yet been presented for payment.

(c) A dividend on Treasury Stock £80 net had been paid direct to the bank and not yet been entered in the cash book.

You are required to draw up a reconciliation statement to confirm the balance according to the bank statement.

**3.** Reconcile the overdraft shown on this bank statement with the bank balance according to the cash book £63.10.

Bank Statement

| Sep. | | | Debit £ | Credit £ | Balance £ |
|---|---|---|---|---|---|
| 20 | Brought forward | | | | 109.30 |
| 25 | Cash and cheques | | | 118.20 | 227.50 |
| | J. Bradford | | 132.50 | | 95.00 |
| 26 | R. A. Gorton | | 46.40 | | 48.60 |
| 28 | Salaries | | 240.00 | | 191.40 O/D |
| | Cash and cheques | | | 84.70 | 106.70 O/D |
| 30 | Bank charges | | 8.50 | | 115.20 O/D |

Cheques paid into the current account on September 30 amounted to £218.40. These were not credited until the following day. A cheque sent by the firm's cashier to Eurodox Ltd for £48.60 was not presented for payment until October 5.

**4.** Reconcile the bank balance of Kenneth Dent's cash book below with the bank statement shown overleaf:

Cash Book (bank columns only)

| Sep. | | | £ | Sep. | | | £ |
|---|---|---|---|---|---|---|---|
| 1 | Balance b/f | | 286.00 | 3 | D. Law | | 52.50 |
| 2 | D. Lyon | 22.50 | | 6 | T. France | | 12.20 |
| | Cash takings | 32.20 | 54.70 | 10 | Self | | 50.00 |
| | | | | 12 | G. Lewis | | 18.30 |
| 10 | S. Worth | | 72.50 | 18 | J. Eaton | | 26.40 |
| 15 | P. Barker | | 56.80 | 25 | R. Alderton | | 68.00 |
| 22 | Cash takings | 44.40 | | | Wages | | 150.00 |
| | S. Thomson | 15.90 | 60.30 | 30 | P. Harris | | 35.50 |
| | | | | 30 | Balance c/d | | 218.70 |
| 26 | H. Norris | 22.70 | | | | | |
| 30 | M. Draper | 78.60 | 101.30 | | | | |
| | | | 631.60 | | | | 631.60 |
| Oct. 1 | Balance b/d | | 218.70 | | | | |

Bank Statement

| Sep. | | Debit £ | Credit £ | Balance £ |
|------|--------------------|---------|----------|-----------|
| 1 | Brought forward | | | 286.00 |
| 3 | Cash/cheques | | 54.70 | 340.70 |
| 5 | D. Law | 52.50 | | 288.20 |
| 9 | T. France | 12.20 | | 276.00 |
| 10 | Self | 50.00 | | 226.00 |
| | S. Worth | | 72.50 | 298.50 |
| 15 | G. Lewis | 18.30 | | 280.20 |
| | P. Barker | | 56.80 | 337.00 |
| 21 | J. Eaton | 26.40 | | 310.60 |
| 24 | Cash/cheques | | 60.30 | 370.90 |
| 25 | Wages | 150.00 | | 220.90 |
| 30 | SO (trade sub.) | 2.50 | | 218.40 |
| | Building Soc. interest | | 45.00 | 263.40 |

# PETTY CASH

## 10.1    IMPREST SYSTEM OF PETTY CASH

The petty cashier relieves the main cashier of a good deal of routine work. It is also useful experience for the office junior to take on a job which is easily understood and yet which carries a minor degree of responsibility.

**Imprest means 'loan'**
A small sum of money is loaned or advanced for the special purpose of paying routine small expenses as they crop up day by day. The petty cash book is regularly balanced up and the main cashier hands over to the petty cashier the exact amount of money spent in the previous week (or month). This refund or reimbursement brings the commencing balance for the start of the new period up to the amount of the original imprest.

An important thing to remember is that the totals of all the analysis columns of the petty cash book must be posted to the debit of nominal ledger accounts to complete their double entry. In the illustration shown, the petty cash balance of £8 would be included as an asset on any balance sheet made up on January 6; the totals of the four expense columns would be debited to accounts in the nominal ledger and charged against profits for the period. If a trial balance was made up at this stage it would also include the *petty cash balance and all these expenses - as debits*, as the credit for £20 has already appeared in the main cash book.

Vouchers (i.e. receipts for money paid) should be insisted upon by the petty cashier, and each week the petty cash book should be scrutinised and initialled by the main cashier or the chief clerk of the department.

Make a mental note not to omit the petty cash balance when extracting balances for the trial balance.

Petty Cash Book

| Received from cashier | Date | Details of payment | Total | Voucher number | Stamps Stationery | Cleaning | Travelling expenses | Sundries |
|---|---|---|---|---|---|---|---|---|
| £ | | | £ | | £ | £ | £ | £ |
| 20.00 | Jan. 2 | Imprest balance | | | | | | |
| | 3 | Bus fares | 0.25 | | | | 0.25 | |
| | 3 | Cleaning | 2.00 | | | 2.00 | | |
| | 4 | Bus fares | 0.56 | | | | 0.56 | |
| | 5 | Stationery | 2.15 | | 2.15 | | | |
| | 6 | Milk and tea | 1.04 | | | | | 1.04 |
| | 6 | Postages | 6.00 | | 6.00 | | | |
| | | | 12.00 | | 8.15 | 2.00 | 0.81 | 1.04 |
| | | Balance c/d | 8.00 | | | | | |
| 20.00 | | | 20.00 | | | | | |
| 8.00 | Jan. 6 | Balance b/d | | | | | | |
| 12.00 | 8 | Cashier | | | | | | |

The totals of all these expense columns will be posted to the debit of Nominal Ledger Accounts. Sometimes an additional column is included for small payments to Bought Ledger Accounts, the individual amount being posted direct to the account of the creditor.

# QUESTIONS

**1.** Richard Walker is a petty cashier with a monthly float of £40. His petty cash payments for the month of February are listed below:

| February | Expense | Voucher No. | Amount £ |
|---|---|---|---|
| 1 | Postages | 1 | 2.30 |
| 2 | String/ball pens | 2 | 0.86 |
| 4 | Cleaning | - | 3.50 |
| 5 | Milk | - | 0.60 |
| - | Bus fares | 3 | 0.66 |
| 8 | Donation to Oxfam | 4 | 2.00 |
| 10 | Bus fares | 5 | 0.45 |
| 12 | Postages | 6 | 2.52 |
| 14 | Milk | - | 0.60 |
| 15 | Cleaning | - | 3.50 |
| 18 | Advertising | 7 | 4.75 |
| 20 | Milk | - | 0.60 |
| 21 | Postages | 8 | 1.82 |
| 24 | Parcel post | - | 1.24 |
| 26 | Bus fares | 9 | 0.76 |
| - | Cleaning | - | 3.50 |
| 28 | Tea | 10 | 0.46 |

Rule up a petty cash book with four columns, enter up the above expenses, balance the book for February and show the amount of money to be refunded to Richard Walker on account of his imprest.

**2.** From the information below, rule up a petty cash book to show five analysis columns for postages, stationery, cleaning, travelling and sundries. Bring down the balance on December 31 to show the amount to be reimbursed by the main cashier to cover the original imprest amount of £50.

December

| | | £ |
|---|---|---|
| 1 | Balance of petty cash on hand | 21.50 |
| | Received from main cashier on account of November disbursements | 28.50 |

| December | Voucher No. | Expense | Amount £ |
|---|---|---|---|
| 2 | 1 | Stationery | 2.20 |
| 4 | 2 | Bus fares | 0.45 |
| 5 | 3 | Postages | 3.68 |
| 8 | – | Cleaner | 4.00 |
| 10 | 4 | Chair repairs | 2.50 |
| | 5 | Postages | 3.26 |
| 14 | – | Milk | 0.60 |
| 18 | 6 | Parcel post | 1.35 |
| 21 | – | Cleaner | 4.00 |
| | 7 | Postages | 2.80 |
| 24 | 8 | Bus fares | 0.64 |
| 26 | – | Milk | 0.60 |
| 28 | 9 | Donation Red Cross | 2.00 |
| | – | Cleaner | 4.00 |
| 30 | 10 | Postages | 3.20 |
| 31 | – | Tea and milk | 1.15 |

**3.** Daniel Dare commenced business on May 1, his financial position listed as follows: bank account £1200 credit; petty cash £50; stock £150; motor van £600; fittings £200; debtors, Grey £80, Green £120; creditors, Black £160, Brown £180.

Open all ledger accounts, and also a separate petty cash book (using only the bank columns in the main cash book), and post up the following transactions for the month of May, and then take out a trial balance for the month.

May

2  Paid from petty cash, stationery £4, office cleaning £3
3  Cash sales paid direct to bank £44
   Bought further supplies from Black £60, and paid his outstanding debts for April, less 5 per cent cash discount
5  Drew cheque for private use £25
8  Cash sales £66 paid into bank
   Paid repairs to typewriter £10 from petty cash
12  Cashed £50 cheque for petty cash
16  Grey called and paid his April account less 5 per cent
20  Bought stamps £3 and paid sundry small expenses from petty cash £12
21  Paid bus fares £2 out of petty cash
   Sold £40 goods to Green. He paid £50 'on account' of his April purchases.
23  Paid Brown's account for April less 5 per cent cash discount
   Bought further goods £48 from him
25  Cash sales £88 paid direct to bank
28  Bought a new typewriter for £140
30  Paid wages to part-time assistant £40 out of petty cash
   Drew cheque for self £100

# THE DAY BOOKS,

# ORIGINAL RECORDS

# AND V.A.T.

Credit transactions have already been explained.

When goods are bought or sold on credit the possession of the merchandise passes at the time of the transaction, but payment is not made until a later date.

Transactions become four-sided, viz.

(a) Between a personal account and either purchases or sales account when the goods are handed over, and
(b) between the same personal account and the cash book when payment is made, often concluding the transaction.

## 11.1 PURCHASES DAY BOOK

In most trading businesses credit purchases are so numerous that it is found convenient to record the original entry for each purchase in a special book called the Purchase Day Book or Bought Journal.

The primary accounting document for merchandise bought on credit is the invoice, sent to the purchaser by the supplier of the goods. The invoice is date-stamped and given a number when received and checked against the goods-received book of the receipt storeman to ensure that the goods charged have actually been received.

Brief details of each invoice are entered, in date order, in the purchase day book, and the total of each separate invoice is posted to the credit of the supplier's account in the bought ledger. This procedure is exactly the same as before, in so far as the recording the amount owing on each creditor's account.

However, to avoid duplication of work, we do not immediately post each individual purchase to the debit of Purchases Account. Instead we total each day's purchases in the day book and carry forward the totals day by day until the *end of the month.* Then the total credit purchases for the month are posted to the debit of purchases account.

This completes the double entry. The single figure for the month's purchases absorbs all the separate debits from individual suppliers.

## 11.2 THE INVOICE

| Customer's name and address | | | No. 2206 Date | |
|---|---|---|---|---|
| B O U G H T   O F | | | | |
| WILLIAM MORRIS & SONS Manchester | | | | |
| Stock Ref. No. | Details | Quan-tity | £ | £ |
| | Brief description of the number of articles, quality, size, etc., of the goods | | 60.00 | |
| | Less:   trade discount 20% | | 12.00 | 48.00 |
| | | | | 48.00 |
| | E. & O.E. Terms 3% monthly | | | |

Note that it is only the *net amount* (after deduction of trade discount) which is taken to the creditor's account and also shown in the total column of the day book. The invoice is filed away in a box or a folder after the extraction of essential details are taken to the day book. See the illustration on p. 75.

## 11.3 TRADE DISCOUNT

Trade discount has been deducted from the gross amount of the last entry in the day book illustration. The amount due to the supplier is posted *net,* and the double entry is not affected as only the net amount of the invoice is shown in the total column.

Trade discount must not be confused with cash discount. The former is an allowance or rebate from the catalogue or list price of the manufacturer or wholesaler, generally a substantial amount (or percentage) which forms the basis of the retailer's gross profit. Cash discount, a much smaller percentage, is offered as an inducement for prompt payment by the supplier, wholesaler or retailer.

Purchases Day Book

| Jan. | Invoices from | | £ | £ |
|------|---------------|------|-----|----|
| 5 | Hugh Smith | BL | | 10 |
| 18 | Stanley Jones | BL | | 32 |
| 28 | Wm. Morris & Sons | BL | 60 | |
| | Less: trade disct of 20% | | 12 | 48 |
| | | | | 90 |
| | Posted to Purchases Account Jan. 31 | | | |

Bought Ledger

**Hugh Smith**

| Dr. | | | | Cr. |
|-----|--|--|--|-----|
| | | | | £ |
| | | Jan. 5 | PDB | 10 |

**Stanley Jones**

| | | | | £ |
|--|--|--------|-----|----|
| | | Jan. 18 | PDB | 32 |

**Wm. Morris & Sons**

| | | | | £ |
|--|--|--------|-----|----|
| | | Jan. 28 | PDB | 48 |

Nominal Ledger

Purchases Account

| Dr. | | | | Cr. |
|-----|--|--|--|-----|
| £ | | | | |
| Jan. 31 | Total purchases for month | PDB | 90 | |

Note. Many traders have additional columns for Value Added Tax in their day books, but at this stage it is thought advisable not to make the explanation too complicated. V.A.T. is explained separately at the end of the chapter.

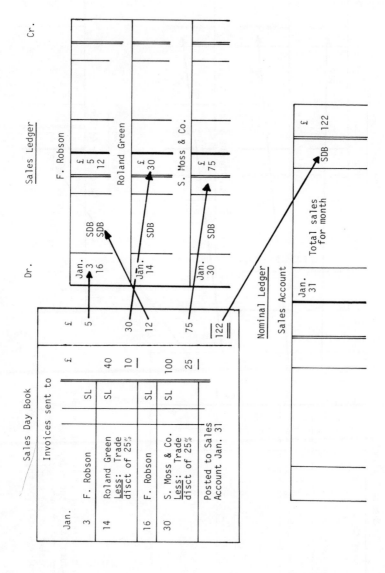

## 11.4  SALES DAY BOOK

Exactly the same principles are followed on the sales side.

An invoice is sent to each credit customer and from the carbon copy of the invoice the sales day book is made up.

Customers' accounts are debited immediately as the goods are handed over, but the sales total is carried forward day by day, and the total sales for the month posted to the credit of Sales Account at the end of the month, as shown in the illustration on p. 76.

In practice the work of the ledger clerks is made easier through these day book procedures, as a good deal of routine listing and totalling is done by the clerk typists in the mechanised office. The grouping and assembling of monthly totals provides useful information for management and for control purposes.

Day books are like diaries or journals in that they furnish a brief day-to-day record of the origination of each credit purchase or sale. Although memoranda and not an integral part of the ledger system itself, they serve as an aid, assembling information in date order and providing useful and necessary totals required by the accountant and management.

Purchases and sales of *fixed assets* must not be posted in the day books. The asset account should be debited or credited by direct posting from the cash book or personal account. Cash purchases and cash sales should also be excluded from the day books, being posted direct from the cash book to the Cash Purchases and Cash Sales Accounts in the nominal ledger.

Day books can be adapted to suit the needs and purposes of each business. Where there are several departments, analytical records may be designed to show the turnover and cost of each department, so that small trading accounts may be prepared to determine the profit or loss of the various sections or departments.

An analysis or columnar ruling of the purchase day book, to break down the material or merchanting costs of a business with three separate departments, might take the following form:

| Date | Supplier | Invoice no. | Ledger fol. | Total | Dept A | Dept B | Dept C |
|------|----------|-------------|-------------|-------|--------|--------|--------|
| May  |          |             | BL          | £     | £      | £      | £      |
| 2    | R. Mason | 156         | 23          | 86    | 50     | 22     | 14     |
| 4    | C. Lawson| 157         | 36          | 24    |        | 9      | 15     |
| 5    | J. Timmins| 158        | 44          | 38    | 25     | 13     |        |

## 11.5  RETURNS AND ALLOWANCES

(a) Goods are returned to the supplier for a variety of reasons. Mistakes may have been made in the sales or despatch department; they may have been packed badly and damaged; they may not be exactly what was ordered; the sizes, texture or the colour may be wrong.

In these instances a reduction or rebate may be expected from the original charge for the merchandise.

Allowances, too, are sometimes made for packages and containers returned to the supplier.

They are dealt with in a similar way.

The original invoice is allowed to stand and is posted up in the books in the ordinary way. A *credit note* is then forwarded by the supplier, both in acknowledgement of goods returned and in reduction or cancellation of the overcharge. These credit notes are also issued for returned 'empties'. In appearance the credit note resembles an invoice, with the words BOUGHT OF being substituted by CREDITED BY. Quite often the credit note is printed in red type.

The accounting procedure is not complicated. It is simply a matter of *reversing the original entry, or part of it*, the value of the goods returned back to the supplier. The creditor is debited back with the value of the returns (if a purchase); and the debtor is credited with the value of what he returns (if it refers to an original sale); the monthly totals on purchases or sales accounts also being reduced by the value of the goods returned.

In practice, where returns are fairly frequent, they are entered in special Returns Books, and the procedure followed is similar to that of the Day Books of the last chapter, with one important point to be borne in mind – the same percentage of trade discount already taken off the original purchase or sale must also be taken off the amount of any *gross* returns. Otherwise a debtor retailer could make a very handsome profit out of his wholesaler by returning all the goods he has bought.

### (b) Sales returns

In the example now shown, M. Shaw bought goods value £40 (less trade discount of 20 per cent) on May 8. He telephoned on examining them, and said one-quarter of the consignment was faulty. He returned the faulty goods and a credit note was sent to him on May 12. This was the only return during the month of May. At the end of the month the sales total posted from the Sales Day Book (SDB) was £654. Assume V.A.T. does not apply to these particular goods.

| Dr. | | | | M. Shaw | | Cr. |
|-----|-----|-----|-----|-----|-----|-----|
| May 8 | SDB | | £ 32.00 | May 12 31 | SRB Balance c/d | £ 8.00 24.00 |
| | | | 32.00 | | | 32.00 |
| May 31 | Balance b/d | | 24.00 | | | |

Sales Returns Book

| May 12 | M. Shaw (goods damaged in transit) | £ 8.00 |
|--------|-----|-----|
| | | 8.00 |

Sales Account (Nominal Ledger)

| May 31 | Total returns from Sales Returns Book | £ 8.00 | May 31 | Total sales for May from Sales Day Book | £ 654.00 |
|--------|-----|-----|--------|-----|-----|

Purchase returns will be dealt with in a similar manner, bringing the Purchase Returns Book (PRB) into operation.

Sometimes, in practice, separate accounts are kept in the nominal ledger for Returns Inwards and Returns Outwards, to give them their alternative names. At the end of the trading period the totals of these two accounts will either be transferred to sales and purchases accounts as indicated, or be taken direct to trading account and deducted from gross sales and gross purchases respectively. The misplacement of the returns on the trial balance is a common error of students. Returns OUT are purchase returns going back to the supplier and are *credited* to the trial balance. Returns IN are sales returns coming back from the customer, and are *debited* to the trial balance.

## 11.6 SUMMARY OF DAY BOOK PROCEDURE

| Day Book | Document | Debit | Credit |
|---|---|---|---|
| Purchases or Bought | Supplier's invoice Details posted to PDB | Monthly total of purchases debited to Purchases Account | Individual purchases posted to creditors' accounts in the Bought Ledger |
| Returns Outwards | Credit note posted to PRB | Individual returns debited to creditors' accounts | Monthly total credited to Purchases Account or Returns Outward |
| Sales | Firm's copy invoice. Details posted to SDB | Individual sales debited to customers' accounts in Sales Ledger | Monthly total of sales credited to Sales Account |
| Returns Inwards | Copy credit note. Details posted to SRB | Monthly total of sales returns debited to Sales Account or Returns Inwards Account | Individual sales returns credited to customers' accounts |

## 11.7 VALUE ADDED TAX

Value added tax, commonly known as V.A.T., is a tax on the consumer levied at all stages of distribution and applicable to most trades and professions. The tax is on the selling price of the merchandise or the charge made for services.

Some kinds of services are exempt from V.A.T., such as insurance, the postal service and education, while firms selling food, fuel and newspapers are 'zero-rated'. No V.A.T. tax is charged on the production and sale of these goods, and suppliers can reclaim all tax which may have been paid on zero-rated purchases.

Accounting records disclosing V.A.T. charged or paid must be kept by those traders, manufacturers and professional firms liable for registration. Credit sales invoices passing between taxable firms must show the full tax due to H.M. Customs and Excise.

On the sales side the full amount of the invoice, plus the tax, is charged to the credit customer, but the sales day book has a separate column to record the tax part of every gross sale, and the cumulative total of this column will be *credited to a Customs and Excise Account* at the end of every month when the normal monthly sales are posted to the credit of sales account.

The reverse procedure is adopted on the purchase side. Suppliers' invoices are split between the net charge for the goods and the tax, and shown in separate columns of the bought day book. The total (of both the net price plus the V.A.T.) is posted to the credit of the supplier's account in the bought ledger, and at the end of the month the separate totals for purchases and for V.A.T. are *debited* respectively to Purchases Account and Customs and Excise Account.

The settlement period for V.A.T. is one month or three months, at the option of the trader. The sum due to or owing by Customs is worked out on an 'Input and Output' basis.

Assuming V.A.T. at 10 per cent, the final details would be shown on a statement in this manner:

Period ended June 30

| Total purchases | £44,000 | | Total sales | £72,000 | |
|---|---|---|---|---|---|
| June | | £ | June | | £ |
| 30 VAT Input total 10% on purchases | | 4400 | 30 VAT Output total 10% on sales | | 7200 |
| Due to Customs c/d | | 2800 | | | — |
| | | 7200 | | | 7200 |
| July | | | July | | |
| 1 Cheque in settlement | | 2800 | 1 Balance b/d | | 2800 |

There is a further description of V.A.T. in Appendix (A.2).

## QUESTIONS

**1.** Write up your sales and purchases day books from the following details of goods bought and sold on credit:

November
1   Bought goods from Albert King invoiced at £90 less $33\frac{1}{3}$ per cent trade discount
5   Sold Norman Peach goods priced at £44 net

12  Received invoice from George Crocker for £56 net for goods delivered the previous day. He had made an allowance of £4 as agreed

17  Invoiced Harold Mason for £80 less 25 per cent trade discount

24  Bought £60 further goods from Albert King on same terms as before

26  Sold £48 goods to Sam Hilton less 25 per cent

30  Sent Mason a similar consignment as two weeks before, and on same terms.

2. (a) From the information below write up the ledger account of John Fryer in the books of Cobbett & Co., and bring down the balance at March 31:

Fryer owes Cobbett & Co. £88.80 on February 28.

The sales day book of Cobbett & Co. showed the following debits against Fryer for the month of March:

```
March  8   Invoice No. 51   for £36.00
       12      ,,   No. 83    ,,  £44.40
       18      ,,   No. 114   ,,  £64.80
```

Each invoice was subject to 25 per cent trade discount and 10 per cent value added tax.

Fryer settles his February account on March 15.

(b) Illustrate the main details of invoice No. 114 dated March 18 and show all three invoices on the detailed statement sent by Cobbett & Co. to John Fryer on March 31.

3. Douglas Hume's assets and liabilities on May 1 were:

|          | £    |          |       | £   |
|----------|------|----------|-------|-----|
| Van      | 1500 | Debtors: | Mills | 150 |
| Fittings | 350  |          | Bone  | 80  |
| Stock    | 820  | Creditors: | Bull | 60  |
| Bank     | 340  |          | Grove | 180 |

Cash Book details for May

| May |            | £   | £   | May |             | £   | £   |
|-----|------------|-----|-----|-----|-------------|-----|-----|
| 1   | Balance    |     | 340 | 3   | Contra      | 100 |     |
| 2   | Cash sales | 105 |     | 5   | Grove       |     | 180 |
| 3   | Contra     |     | 100 | 8   | Sundry exps | 15  |     |
| 8   | Cash sales | 75  |     | 14  | Drawings    | 25  |     |
| 12  | Mills      |     | 150 | 20  | Electricity |     | 35  |
| 18  | Bone       |     | 40  | 25  | Wages       | 80  |     |
| 24  | Cash sales | 84  |     | 30  | Bull        |     | 87  |
| 31  | Harris     |     | 54  | 31  | Balance c/d | 44  | 382 |
|     |            | 264 | 684 |     |             | 264 | 684 |
| June |           |     |     |     |             |     |     |
| 1   | Balance b/d | 44 | 382 |     |             |     |     |

The purchases and sales day books for May showed these details:

|  |  | Net | V.A.T. | Total |
|---|---|---|---|---|
| | Purchases Day Book | | | |
| May | | Net | V.A.T. | Total |
| 5 | Grove | £75 | £6 | £81 |
| 8 | Bull | 25 | 2 | 27 |
| 18 | Grove | 150 | 12 | 162 |

|  |  | Net | V.A.T. | Total |
|---|---|---|---|---|
| | Sales Day Book | | | |
| May | | Net | V.A.T. | Total |
| 4 | Mills | £125 | £10 | £135 |
| 7 | Fell | 75 | 6 | 81 |
| 12 | Mills | 125 | 10 | 135 |
| 28 | Harris | 50 | 4 | 54 |

You are required to post the above information to the individual and appropriate ledger accounts of Douglas Hume, and extract a trial balance on May 31.

4. The balance sheet of Susan Bardale as at July 1 is shown in brief:

| | £ | | | £ |
|---|---|---|---|---|
| Capital Account | 1840 | Fixed assets | | 1300 |
| Loan Account | 1000 | Stock | 1280 | |
| | | Debtors | 630 | |
| Trade creditors | 840 | Bank | 470 | 2380 |
| | 3680 | | | 3680 |

Open ledger accounts for the balances on Miss Bardale's balance sheet, using 'total' debtors' and creditors' accounts. Post the transactions shown underneath for the first week of July and extract a trial balance on July 8.

*N.B.* Cash and cheques are paid into the bank at the end of the week.

July
2 Miss Bardale drew £50 cash from the bank for private use.
Cash sales amounted to £84
Received cheque for £136 in settlement of a debtor's account
Paid one creditor's account £64 by cheque
3 Bought further goods on credit for the total cost of £192
4 Cash sales £114 (including cheque for £24)
Received £20 cash from a debtor
5 Paid the following out of office cash:

Wages £70 : Stamps £4 : Stationery £10

6 Paid a supplier's account £104 and bought another £150 of goods on credit
7 Credit sales totalled £252
Cash sales amounted to £118

84

8 Cheques from credit customers £108
Paid cash and cheques totalling £200 into bank, leaving a small balance of cash on hand.

5. Your financial year ends on June 30, and on June 1 your Purchases and Sales Accounts are shown posted up to date:

Purchases Account

| May 31 | PDB total to date<br>Cash purchases total | £<br>5886<br>363 | May 31 | PRB total to date | £<br>180 |
|---|---|---|---|---|---|

Sales Account

| May 31 | SRB total to date | 482 | May 31 | SDB total to date<br>Cash sales total | 9468<br>1286 |
|---|---|---|---|---|---|

Transactions during the month of June affecting the bought and sales ledgers are shown below. Make up your books of original entry for the month of June, and complete the purchases and sales accounts for the year ended June 30.

June
3   £320 of goods bought from D. Richardson & Co. Ltd less 25 per cent trade discount
5   Returned £40 (gross) damaged goods to Richardson's
9   Credit sales £180 to Frank Manning less 10 per cent trade discount
15  £160 of goods sold to Arnold Clutten less special allowance of £15
26  Sent £35 of goods to Ron Ecclestone, who telephoned the order
30  Cash purchases for the month of June £36
30  Cash sales for the month £164.

6. Enter up your three-column cash book and make up all *personal* ledger accounts from the following information:

April
1   Cash balance £15.30   :   bank balance £422.70
2   Cashed cheque for office use £25
3   Paid sundry office expenses in cash £22.50
    Cash sales £75.10
    Paid A. J. Russell's March account £120 less 5 per cent cash discount
5   Cash sales £84.40
    Paid £100 cash into bank
8   Received cheque from Dan Winter for £57. Discount of £3 had been deducted as agreed
12  Credit sale to Samuel Moss of £40 less 20 per cent trade discount

14   Moss returned £10 (gross) goods bought two days before
16   Cash sales £112.30
      Banked £50 and withdrew £25 cash for 'self'
18   Sold £25 of goods to Adam Dell less 20 per cent trade discount
      Paid advertising account £28.80
      Bought stationery for £5.20 cash
22   Sold £35 of goods to Winter less 20 per cent trade discount
      Received cheque in settlement of Dell's account less 5 per cent cash discount
24   Paid the outstanding account of Gillian Tempest £148 less 5 per cent discount, and bought another batch of goods from her for £120 less 25 per cent trade discount
26   Cash sales amounted to £88.50
30   Paid all cash into bank except for £20 retained for general office use. Balanced up cash book.

After balancing up the cash book, make up all personal ledger accounts in your bought and sales ledgers, bringing down all balances at April 30.

7. Jack Daw's listed assets and liabilities on March 1 were:

|  | £ |  |  | £ |
|---|---|---|---|---|
| Fittings | 560 | Debtors | Fox | 160 |
| Motor van | 800 |  | Lamb | 280 |
| Stock | 1240 |  |  |  |
| Bank | 600 | Creditors | Wren | 100 |
| Cash | 50 |  | Sparrow | 130 |

The following transactions took place during the month of March:

Purchase Day Book

| Mar. |  | £ |
|---|---|---|
| 3 | Wren | 92 |
| 10 | Sparrow | 136 |
| 18 | Wren | 168 |
| 26 | Kite | 50 |

Sales Day Book

| Mar. |  | £ |
|---|---|---|
| 2 | Fox | 176 |
| 8 | Lamb | 240 |
| 16 | Hare | 192 |
| 25 | Lamb | 70 |

Returns Outward Book

| Mar. |  | £ |
|---|---|---|
| 20 | Wren | 28 |

Returns Inwards Book

| Mar. |  | £ |
|---|---|---|
| 10 | Lamb | 32 |

Cash Book details

| Mar. |  | £ | £ | Mar. |  | £ | £ |
|---|---|---|---|---|---|---|---|
| 1 | Balance b/f | 50 | 600 | 1 | Sundry exps | 8 |  |
| 3 | Cash sales | 110 |  | 6 | Sparrow |  | 130 |
| 15 | Fox |  | 160 | 14 | Wren |  | 100 |
|  | Cash sales | 146 |  | 22 | Drawings | 50 |  |
| 20 | Lamb |  | 200 | 30 | Wages | 120 |  |
| 31 | Contra |  | 100 | 31 | Contra |  | 100 |

You are required to post the above information to the appropriate ledger accounts, balance all accounts and extract a trial balance on March 31.

# THE GENERAL JOURNAL:

# CORRECTION OF

# ERRORS

All book-keeping transactions must originate from a book of prime entry.

The ordinary journals or day books have been described, showing the initiation of the credit purchase or credit sale and the posting to the ledger accounts. The cash book, too, is both a book of original entry and also an integral part of the ledger system.

During the year transactions sometimes occur which cannot be conveniently posted direct to a book of original entry already introduced. Examples of these transactions would be the sales of fixed assets, the correction of errors and transfers between accounts. In addition, at the end of each trading period, certain adjustments have to be made such as the writing off of bad debts and the bringing into the books the closing stock valuation.

We use a book called the General Journal for the recording of entries of this special nature.

## 12.1 THE GENERAL JOURNAL

The general journal is sometimes described as the main journal or the journal proper. It is not part of the ledger but merely a memorandum record showing the accounts to be debited and credited of transactions which cannot be conveniently entered in any other book of original entry.

Briefly, the main uses of the general journal are for the recording of:

(a) Opening and closing entries.
(b) Year-end adjustments.
(c) Transfers and correction of errors.
(d) Anything of a special nature such as the purchase of a new electric typewriter or the sale of the old machine.

Generally speaking, students do not like journalising. They imagine that it is unnecessary and can be circumvented, and often make the corrections or adjustments direct to the accounts affected. But if the examiner asks for journal entries, he will expect to see them.

In any event, the correction of errors, by scratching or rubbing out, whether during one's daily duties or in the examination hall, is a bad habit. It will lose you marks in an examination and, in practice, the alteration of figures will attract the notice of the auditor, who will probably ask for an explanation.

## 12.2 SPECIAL ENTRIES AND YEAR-END TRANSFERS

In addition to opening entries, where assets and liabilities are assembled in trial balance form to find the commencing capital of the business before opening the various accounts in a new set of books, the following entries are self-explanatory. They refer to the purchase of a fixed asset, the sale of a fixed asset, the writing off of a small debt regarded as irrecoverable and the transfer to trading account of year-end balances. Note that in most journal entries there is the dual aspect, the debit entry being shown first and slightly to the left of the credit entry, and there is a brief *narration* giving the reason for the entries.

Journal

| December | | | £ | £ |
|---|---|---|---|---|
| 5 | Furniture and fittings | Dr. | 75 | |
| | Office Supply Co. Ltd | | | 75 |
| | Being purchase of filing-cabinet for office | | | |
| 8 | Cash | Dr. | 12 | |
| | Furniture/fittings A/c | | | 12 |
| | Sale of old desk for cash | | | |
| 14 | Bad Debts Account | Dr. | 6 | |
| | H. Jones | | | 6 |
| | Old debt of customer considered irrecoverable | | | |
| 31 | Sales Account | Dr. | 8500 | |
| | Trading Account | | | 8500 |
| | Transfer of year-end total | | | |
| 31 | Trading Account | Dr. | 5400 | |
| | Stock at January 1 | | | 850 |
| | Purchases for year | | | 4300 |
| | Carriage inwards | | | 250 |
| | Transfer of year-end totals | | | |

Note that journal entries are not totalled. One reason for recording these special entries, apart from having a permanent record initiated from a book of prime entry, is to give the ledger clerk authority for his postings, should queries arise from the auditor.

## 12.3 THE CORRECTION OF ERRORS

All corrections and adjustments in the books should, in theory, be made through the general journal.

**Examples**

(a) M. Hale sends you a cheque for £8 in settlement of his account. Your cashier enters the receipt correctly in the bank column of his cash book, but the ledger clerk posts it in error to the credit of M. Hill's account in the sales ledger.

The correction is made through the journal in this manner, with the brief narration underneath explaining the entry.

Journal

| Date | M. Hill<br>    M. Hale<br>Being correction of error in<br>    posting of payment | Dr. | £8 | £8 |
|------|------|------|------|------|

The book-keeper or ledger clerk responsible for posting the sales or debtors' ledger will pick up this item from the journal and make the necessary adjustment on the two accounts, debiting Hill and crediting Hale.

(b) David Roberts owes you £45. After repeated reminders he calls and pays you £30 cash, at the same time offering you some old bookshelves in settlement of the balance. In view of his circumstances you accept the proposition, but value the bookshelves at only £10 and write off the difference of £5 on his account to Bad Debts as a business loss and expense.

This requires a composite journal entry as shown below. The debtor's account is credited with the full amount. Furniture and Fittings is debited with £10, Bank with £30 and the balance of £5 is transferred to Bad Debts, again to be transferred to profit and loss account as a loss at the end of the trading year.

Journal

| Date | Furniture/fittings<br>Bank<br>Bad Debts<br>David Roberts<br>Being cash £30 and bookshelves<br>valued at £10 accepted in<br>settlement, leaving £5 to be<br>written off to bad debts | Dr. | £<br>10<br>30<br>5 | £<br><br><br>45 |
|------|---|---|---|---|

(c) Four errors have been disclosed in checking the books. They are shown below, followed by the journal entries correcting the errors in the general journal:

(i) A £60 filing-cabinet has been charged to General Expenses.

(ii) A cash sale of £15 to Arthur Jones has been posted to the credit of his account in the sales ledger.

(iii) When paying the account of R. Hickson, a supplier to whom £20 was due, £1 discount was deducted. Hickson would not allow this.

(iv) An amount of £35 for machinery repairs has been debited to Machinery (asset) Account.

Note that in all 'Correction of Error' type questions, you are *told what error has been made*. All you have to do is to *correct the mistake by reversing the entry* on the account wrongly posted, and bring the item in to the right account.

Journal

| 1 | Office Furniture Account<br>General expenses<br>Capital item had been debited<br>to revenue account | Dr. | £<br>60 | £<br>60 |
|---|---|---|---|---|
| 2 | Arthur Jones<br>Cash Sales Account<br>Cash sale credited wrongly to<br>customer's ledger account | Dr. | 15 | 15 |
| 3 | Discounts Received Account<br>R. Hickson<br>Cash discount disallowed | Dr. | 1 | 1 |
| 4 | Machinery Repairs Account<br>Machinery Account<br>Revenue item wrongly posted to<br>asset account, now corrected | Dr. | 35 | 35 |

Note in all instances of journal entries, the debit is posted first, and the credit is shown underneath and a *few spaces to the right.*

## 12.4  THE TRIAL BALANCE AND LOCATION OF ERRORS

(a) The trial balance is not an account, and neither is it part of the ledger system. It is simply a list of debit and credit balances extracted from the books, normally with the twofold purpose of:

(i) proving the arithmetical accuracy of the postings, and
(ii) assembling and grouping balances to simplify the making up of the final accounts.

The trial balance rarely balances the first time. A good deal of checking is often necessary, in particular with the accounts of small traders.

Mistakes may be arithmetical, the result of incorrect addition and subtraction, wrong carry-forwards and extensions. These mistakes frequently occur through lack of concentration when postings are being made.

Even if the trial balance totals do agree, this is only proof of the *arithmetical accuracy* of the postings. There may be other errors not disclosed by the trial balance, generally found by the auditor and his staff during the annual audit.

The common form of errors not disclosed by the trial balance are errors of:

(i) *Omission.* The goods are handed over to the customer, but she receives no invoice for them. No record is made of the sale. (Mrs Brown has a small credit account with the local grocer, takes a bottle of sherry off his shelf, and asks him to 'charge it'. He forgets to do so, until she reminds him about it.)
(ii) *Commission.* Posting to the wrong person's account, as described in the previous section. (Hill being credited with the payment instead of Hale.)
(iii) *Original entry.* If there was a mistake on the original invoice the double entry would not be affected. (Say Mrs Brown had been charged £1 instead of £2 for her sherry, the books would still have balanced, despite the undercharge.)
(iv) *Principle.* This refers to a posting to the wrong class of account (as in the case of the machinery repairs being debited to machinery account, an asset account, instead of to machinery repairs, the revenue account.)
(v) *Compensating Errors.* The purchase day book may have been under-cast by £100 and at the same time there may be an overcast of

£100 on one of the big debtors' accounts. Purchases should be £100 more and debtors £100 less.
(iv) *Duplication.* Where the same transaction has been recorded twice, leading to the duplication of the original invoice.

## (b) Locating the errors

(i) Find the actual difference between the trial balance totals, halve the difference, and then look for an entry of this amount on the greater side of the trial balance.
(ii) Check all debtors' and creditors' balances to find out if any have been omitted, or if any should not be included.
(iii) Check all additions in the cash book, the day books, and returns books. Check the carry-forwards in all these books to the end of each month, and on to the sales and purchases accounts, in so far as the day books are concerned. Ascertain that the discount totals have been correctly *transferred* to the nominal ledger. Check the analysis columns of the petty cash book to see that they are posted to the expense accounts, and that the actual petty cash balance has been brought to the debit of the trial balance.
(iv) If the error is a round figure (£1, £10 or £100) it is likely to be a mistake in an addition.
   If the difference is £110 it could be two errors of £100 and £10.
   If the difference is £90 it could also be two errors, £100 and £10.
(v) Transposition (out of position) occurs a good deal.

## Examples

£383 instead of £833
£377 instead of £337
£140.00 instead of £1.40

Mistakes in transposition often take place through haphazard methods of 'calling over' on the part of the junior clerks and typists.

## (c) Rule of nine

If the error is a round figure in pounds and *divisible by nine* the cause of the trouble may be transposed figures. For example, any two number figure with a difference of 5 will cause an error of 45 (16, 27, 38, 49, 61, 72, 83, and 94 when transposed will *all* show a difference of 45).
   This is only included by way of general interest as differences on most trial balances tend to be an accumulation of errors rather than just one error.

# QUESTIONS

1. Journalise the following transactions of Davinia Wade:

January
   1 Started in business with £25 cash, £375 in the bank, fittings worth £250 and stock recently bought for £150. An invoice from the wholesaler showed his last account for £80 was still unpaid
   2 Bought a counter for £50 and a typewriter for £65 from The Office Supply Co., both on credit and second-hand
   3 Paid Percy Jennings (the wholesaler) the £80 outstanding and bought another £120 of goods on credit from him
   8 Cash takings amounted to £85.50
   12 Sold £40 of goods to Charles Baker, allowing him 10 per cent trade discount
   18 £5 (gross) goods were returned by Baker
   25 Paid rent £20 for month and drew £25 cheque for cash to pay some small private expenses
   31 Transferred private car, valued at £800, to be used by the business.

*Note.* Some of the transactions above would not normally be recorded in the general journal; they would be taken direct to ordinary day books or posted direct from the cash book to ledger accounts. Nevertheless, examiners expect students to be able to journalise any kind of transaction.

2. You are required to make the necessary corrections of the following errors through the general journal:

March
   2 A cash sale of £12 has been credited to the account of H. Burton
   5 A payment of £35 for machinery repairs has been debited to the machinery (asset) account
   8 The account of H. K. Smith has been debited with £10 goods sold to M. K. Smith
   12 An invoice of £70.60 has been posted from the sales day book as £76.00 to the debit of A. Walton's account
   20 A purchase of £15.50 from H. G. Bell Ltd has been credited in error to the account of G. H. Wells Ltd
   28 The proprietor's drawings of £50 have been debited to salaries account.

3. State how the following errors would affect your trial balance and your balance sheet. Tabulate your corrections.
   (a) The sales day book has been undercast by £200.
   (b) A cash sale of £6 has been posted from the cash book to the credit of a customer's account.
   (c) A petty cash column (£16 for travelling) has been overlooked in extracting the trial balance.
   (d) Some office furniture has been bought for £170 and debited to Purchases Account.

(e) £20 of goods sold to John Grant has been debited to the account of James Gaunt.

(f) The purchase of office stationery £4 has been debited to the nominal account as 40p.

(g) Some old fittings have been sold for £32 and credited to cash sales account.

4. These balances were extracted from the books of Francina Ellis on December 31:

|  | £ |  | £ |
|---|---|---|---|
| Cash in hand | 15 | Stock Dec 31 | 1480 |
| Cash at bank | 485 | Fixtures | 630 |
| Loan from P. Wynn | 2060 | Premises (cost) | 6000 |
| Trade debtors | 870 | Trade creditors | 820 |

The books were arithmetically correct, but certain errors of principle and incorrect postings were discovered by the auditor at the beginning of the New Year.

You are required to make the necessary adjustments for those errors (listed below) through the general journal and draft an up-to-date balance sheet after the amendments.

(a) A cash sale of £6 had been posted to one of the creditors' accounts

(b) Interest of £60 had been charged to the loan account

(c) Goods to the value of £45 had been delivered on December 31 and taken into stock, but were not invoiced until January 5

(d) Drawings of the owner £40 had been charged to salaries

(e) Old fixtures, shown in the books at £56, had been sold for £30 cash and credited to cash sales account.

5. From the trial balance of Jacquetta Wood on p. 94, make up separate (columnar) trading accounts for the month of December, a general profit and loss account, and a balance sheet as at December 31.

| | £ | £ |
|---|---|---|
| Stock of sweets   Dec. 1 | 115 | |
| Stock of cigarettes & tobacco   Dec. 1 | 341 | |
| Purchases & returns - sweets | 550 | 38 |
| Purchases/returns - cigarettes & tobacco | 1275 | 30 |
| Sales and returns - sweets | 27 | 1405 |
| Sales/returns - cigarettes & tobacco | 46 | 2015 |
| Wages and salaries | 732 | |
| Rent and rates | 240 | |
| Advertising | 65 | |
| Bank charges | 20 | |
| Discounts received | | 80 |
| Commission paid | 135 | |
| Fittings and equipment | 2165 | |
| Motor van (bought four years ago) | 900 | |
| Trade debtors | 390 | |
| Trade creditors | | 313 |
| Repairs to van | 16 | |
| Petrol, oil and new tyres | 84 | |
| Carriage on sales | 22 | |
| Cash on hand | 13 | |
| Bank overdraft | | 235 |
| Drawings during month | 480 | |
| Capital of Miss Wood   Dec. 1 | | 3500 |
| | 7616 | 7616 |

The item for wages and salaries £732 should be divided equally between the departments, taking one-third to each trading account, and one-third to the general profit and loss account.

Miss Wood checked and valued her closing stocks as follows:

Sweets £160   :   Cigarettes and tobacco £375

# CLASSIFICATION OF LEDGER ACCOUNTS

The size and nature of the accounting department grows with the expansion of the business, but whether a large firm, fully mechanised with all manner of modern equipment and filing systems, or a small one-man concern or a partnership, the basic principles of accounting remain the same.

The ledger accounts may be housed in various ways, in loose-leaf weighty binders, in vertical or horizontal filing-cabinets, in smaller metal index cabinets for quick reference, but their function and purpose remains the same – to record briefly and accurately detailed information of all business transactions, affecting people, firms and all manner of trading expenses in the world of commerce and industry.

For ease and convenience ledger accounts are divided into three main groups:

  (i) Personal accounts of persons, firms and companies.

 (ii) Real and property accounts such as cash, fittings and stock.

(iii) Nominal accounts, comprising profits and gains, losses and expenses.

In addition to these three main divisions, the capital and drawings accounts of the sole trader may also be regarded as the proprietor's *personal accounts*, as they disclose his holding and relationship with his own business; these two accounts are kept in his *private ledger*, whereas the business property is sometimes recorded in a separate *general ledger*, distinguishing the asset and capital expenditure from the trading expense and revenue posted to the nominal ledger.

## 13.1 SUBDIVISIONS OF LEDGERS

Large accounts departments are sectionised.

There will be the chief accountant's office, a separate section under the main cashier and separate sections for bought and sales ledger clerks, and

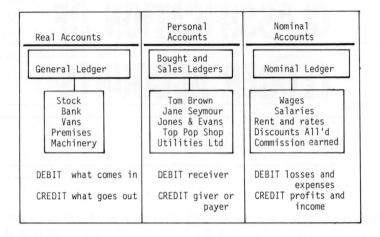

| Real Accounts | Personal Accounts | Nominal Accounts |
|---|---|---|
| General Ledger | Bought and Sales Ledgers | Nominal Ledger |
| Stock<br>Bank<br>Vans<br>Premises<br>Machinery | Tom Brown<br>Jane Seymour<br>Jones & Evans<br>Top Pop Shop<br>Utilities Ltd | Wages<br>Salaries<br>Rent and rates<br>Discounts All'd<br>Commission earned |
| DEBIT what comes in<br><br>CREDIT what goes out | DEBIT receiver<br><br>CREDIT giver or<br>payer | DEBIT losses and<br>expenses<br>CREDIT profits and<br>income |

for the nominal and general ledger clerks. Often, too, there is a separate wages department. Decentralisation and independent work reduces the risk of collusion and fraud.

In large selling organisations involving hundreds of credit customers all over the country, the sales ledgers are often subdivided, for example:

| *Alphabetically* | Sales Ledger 1 | Surnames A to D |
|---|---|---|
| | " 2 | " E to K |
| | " 3 | " L to R |
| | " 4 | " S to Z |

*or*

| *Geographically* | North-East | –North-West |
|---|---|---|
| | N. Midlands | –S. Midlands |
| | Wales | –West Country |
| | London | –Home Counties |

## 13.2 DESTINATION OF ACCOUNT BALANCES

First, a few samples of different classes of account are shown, and then, underneath, the ultimate destination of their balances.

### R. Raven (a creditor's personal account)

| | | | £ | | | | £ |
|---|---|---|---|---|---|---|---|
| May | | | | May | | | |
| 6 | Cheque | CB | 22.50 | 1 | Balance b/f | | 22.50 |
| 10 | Returns | PRB | 5.00 | 8 | Purchases | PDB | 40.00 |
| 31 | Balance c/d | | 35.00 | | | | |
| | | | 62.50 | | | | 62.50 |
| | | | | June | | | |
| | | | | 1 | Balance b/d | | 35.00 |

### P. Plover (a debtor's personal account)

| | | | £ | | | | £ |
|---|---|---|---|---|---|---|---|
| May | | | | May | | | |
| 1 | Balance b/f | | 36.20 | 18 | Returns | SRB | 4.00 |
| 15 | Sales | SDB | 24.00 | 20 | Cheque | CB | 36.20 |
| | | | | 31 | Balance c/d | | 20.00 |
| | | | 60.20 | | | | 60.20 |
| June | | | | | | | |
| 1 | Balance b/d | | 20.00 | | | | |

### Fixtures and Fittings (a real account)

| | | | £ | | | | |
|---|---|---|---|---|---|---|---|
| May | | | | | | | |
| 1 | Balance b/f | | 300 | | | | |
| 5 | Cheque for new desk | CB | 80 | | | | |

### Rates (nominal expense account)

| | | | £ | | | | |
|---|---|---|---|---|---|---|---|
| May | | | | | | | |
| 5 | Cheque (half-year's rates) | CB | 75 | | | | |

### Commission Received (nominal gains account)

| | | | | | | | £ |
|---|---|---|---|---|---|---|---|
| | | | | May | | | |
| | | | | 25 | Agency cheque | CB | 50.00 |

| | Trial balance | | Trading and P & L Account | | Balance sheet | |
|---|---|---|---|---|---|---|
| | Debit | Credit | Debit | Credit | Liabs | Assets |
| | £ | £ | £ | £ | £ | £ |
| R. Raven (creditor) | | 35 | | | 35 | |
| P. Plover (debtor) | 20 | | | | | 20 |
| Fixtures/fittings | 380 | | | | | 380 |
| Rates | 75 | | 75 | | | |
| Commissions Recd | | 50 | | 50 | | |

## QUESTIONS

**1.** A large firm of wholesalers has built up its connection by concentrating its advertising and sales activities almost entirely in the Midlands, approximately fifty miles on all sides of Birmingham, specialising in packaged and tinned groceries. What kind of ledger accounts might be found in this organisation?

**2.** Enter up the personal ledger account of Georgina Raft from the following information:

February

|   |   | £ |
|---|---|---|
| 1 | Miss Raft owed you | 17.60 |
| 2 | She bought more goods | 49.00 |
| 6 | Called and paid January account | 17.60 |
| 10 | Further sales to Miss Raft | 64.00 |
| 15 | She returned goods | 9.00 |
| 22 | Payment on account | 40.00 |
|   | Made an allowance for some faulty workmanship | 5.00 |
| 28 | Balanced up account | |

**3.** Matthew Hale is a wholesaler. His transactions with Roland Gale & Sons, small manufacturers, are shown below for the month of October:

October
- 1 Balance owing by Hale £150.00
- 5 £60 of goods bought by Hale less 20 per cent trade discount
- 6 Carriage of £4.75 charged on goods delivered the previous day
- 12 Hale paid balance owing for September less 5 per cent cash discount
- 20 Gale & Sons delivered another £80 of goods to their customer on the usual trade terms
- 22 Hale returned £10 (gross) goods of the recent consignment as 'not up to standard'
- 30 Packages and cartons returned to Gale & Sons, who issued a credit note for £6.50.

You are required to write up the account of Roland Gale & Sons as it would appear in the ledger of Matthew Hale.

**4.** A. Find the 'odd one out' in each of the following groups:

(a) Fittings, vans, premises and wages
(b) Sales day book, cash sales, bought ledger, returns inward
(c) Rates, stationery, commissions received, advertising
(d) Machinery account, repairs to machinery, plant extension.

B. How would you classify the following transactions? Indicate the accounts and the ledger group (or section) affected in each case.

(a) A cash sale of £10.
(b) A credit sale of £25 to Alfred Brett.
(c) Half-yearly rates of £80 paid by cheque.

(d) Repairs to van £72.
(e) Private drawings £50 cash.
(f) New typewriter bought on credit for £150 from Office Supplies Ltd.
(g) Credit purchase of £60 of goods from Darton Bros. less 20 per cent trade discount.
(h) Sale of old typewriter for £40 cash.
(i) Loan of £500 (paid into bank) from Sidney Smith.
(j) Return of £8 goods (gross) damaged in transit, to Darton Bros.

5. John Gilbert is your supplier and George Garrett is one of your main customers. Enter up the following transactions affecting their accounts in your bought and sales ledgers and bring down the account balances on January 31:

January
1 Balance owing to Gilbert £142.50: balance owing by Garrett £84.30
2 Bought £60 of goods from Gilbert less 20 per cent trade discount
5 Returned £15 (gross) goods bought on January 2
8 Garrett called and paid his outstanding account at December 31
10 Invoiced Garrett £56 of goods as ordered. Allowed him £2 for the return of the crate
15 Bought further goods from Gilbert £80 less usual discount and paid balance due to him at the year end
19 Cash sales totalled £96.60 to date
25 Sold Garrett £14 of goods for cash and £85 goods on credit
28 Sent Gilbert a cheque in settlement of his early January invoice, after adjusting for the returns of January 5; bought another £100 of goods from him less the usual trade discount.

# CHAPTER 14

# RECAPITULATION BY ILLUSTRATIVE EXERCISE

G. Finch is a retail trader. His commencing capital, shown by the opening entries in his journal on January 1, was £1500. Details of these entries were as follows:

Journal (folio 1)

| | | | Debit £ | Credit £ |
|---|---|---|---|---|
| Jan. 1 | Cash | CB1 | 10 | |
| | Bank | CB1 | 350 | |
| | Debtors: M. Thrush | SL8 | 45 | |
| | C. Gull | SL9 | 80 | |
| | Creditors: S. Lark | BL2 | | 35 |
| | H. Martin | BL5 | | 40 |
| | Stock | PL4 | 470 | |
| | Motor van | PL6 | 500 | |
| | Fittings | PL7 | 120 | |
| | Capital | PL2 | | 1500 |
| | | | 1575 | 1575 |

Mr Finch had already checked with Customs and Excise and been told that he was not liable for V.A.T. on account of a very moderate turnover, but was warned that he might have to register later, should his turnover exceed £15,000 a year.

Open a full set of books for Finch and post the transactions which follow for the month of January. Take out a trial balance and make up his trading and profit and loss account for the month, and a balance sheet as at January 31.

January

2    Received payment of Gull's account less 5 per cent cash discount
3    Sold £6 of goods to L. Heron
4    Bought £2 of postage stamps
5    Bought £35 of goods from S. Lark
8    Cashed £25 cheque for office use
     Paid £28 for part-time assistance
10   Cash sales £76
     Cash purchases £15
11   Paid £35 cash into bank
12   Sold £30 goods to S. Hawk less 20 per cent trade discount
     Cashed £15 cheque for 'self' and bought new pair of shoes for wife
14   Paid rent for month by cheque £30
     Bought £60 of goods less 25 per cent trade discount from H. Martin
15   S. Hawk returned goods £5 (gross) bought on January 12
     Paid Martin's December account less 5 per cent cash discount
16   Cash sales £96
     Paid £50 into bank
     Paid wages £28
20   Paid advertising account by cheque £12
24   Bought £40 showcase from Shop Fittings Ltd
26   Heron paid his account by cheque
     Cash sales £68
     Paid wages £28
30   Heron's cheque returned by bank 'refer to drawer'
31   Paid £6 sundry expenses and drew £60 for household use.

G. Finch valued his stock at January 31 at £515.

At this stage students sometimes have difficulty in deciding whether a payment should be paid by cheque or in cash.

First of all, when in doubt pay by cheque as this will avoid the complication of cash becoming overdrawn. Accept that it is usual to pay wages and stamps in cash, and also small expenses for cleaning, office sundries and cat's milk (which are generally petty cash expenses), but make it a rule to pay most creditors' accounts by cheque, certainly all accounts above £3, unless stated otherwise.

Credit transactions are also perplexing in these early stages. From now onwards, assume that all transactions to do with purchases and sales are on credit *where a personal name is mentioned*. There would be no point in mentioning a personal (or firm's) name unless the transaction is to be on credit.

With regard to the full-length illustration, we shall first of all extract the credit transactions, enter them in the day books, and then make up the cash book:

Purchase Day Book (folio 2)

| Jan. | | | £ | £ |
|---|---|---|---|---|
| 5 | S. Lark | BL2 | | 35 |
| 14 | H. Martin | BL5 | 60 | 45 |
| | Less: 25% TD | | 15 | |
| | | | — | |
| | Posted to NL24 | | | 80 |

Sales Day Book (folio 3)

| Jan. | | | £ | £ |
|---|---|---|---|---|
| 3 | L. Heron | SL10 | | 6 |
| 12 | S. Hawk | SL11 | 30 | 24 |
| | Less: 20% TD | | 6 | |
| | | | — | |
| | Posted to NL22 | | | 30 |

Sales Returns Book (folio 1)

| Jan. | | | £ | £ |
|---|---|---|---|---|
| 15 | S. Hawk | SL11 | 5 | 4 |
| | Less: 20% TD | | 1 | |
| | | | — | |
| | Posted to | NL22 | | 4 |

## Cash Book (folio 1)

**Receipts (Dr)**

| Jan. | | | £ | £ | £ |
|---|---|---|---|---|---|
| 1 | Balances b/f | | | 10 | 350 |
| 2 | Gull | SL9 | 4 | | 76 |
| 8 | Contra | c | | 25 | |
| 10 | Cash sales | N122 | | 76 | |
| 11 | Contra | c | | | 35 |
| 16 | Cash sales | NL22 | | 96 | |
| 16 | Contra | c | | | 50 |
| 26 | Heron | SL10 | | | 6 |
| 26 | Cash sales | NL22 | | 68 | |
| | | N129 | 4 | 275 | 517 |
| Feb. 1 | Balances b/d | | | 23 | 391 |

**Payments (Cr)**

| Jan. | | | £ | £ | £ |
|---|---|---|---|---|---|
| 4 | Stamps | NL25 | | 2 | |
| 8 | Contra | c | | | 25 |
| 10 | Wages | NL26 | | 28 | |
| 11 | Cash purchases | NL24 | | 15 | |
| 12 | Contra | c | | 35 | |
| 12 | Drawings | PL3 | | | 15 |
| 14 | Rent | NL18 | | | 30 |
| 15 | Martin | BL5 | 2 | | 38 |
| 16 | Contra | c | | 50 | |
| 16 | Wages | NL24 | | 28 | |
| 20 | Advertising | NL27 | | | 12 |
| 26 | Wages | NL24 | | 28 | |
| 30 | Retd cheque (Heron) | SL10 | | | 6 |
| 30 | Sundry expenses | NL28 | | 6 | |
| 31 | Drawings | PL3 | | 60 | |
| 31 | Balances c/d | NL30 | | 23 | 391 |
| | | | 2 | 275 | 517 |

## Private (or General) Ledger

### Stock Account (folio 4)

| | | | £ | | | | £ |
|---|---|---|---|---|---|---|---|
| Jan. 1 | Balance b/f | J1 | 470 | Jan. 31 | Transfer to Trading Account | | 470 |
| 31 | New stock credited to Trading Account | | 515 | | | | |

### Fittings (folio 7)

| | | | £ | | | | |
|---|---|---|---|---|---|---|---|
| Jan. 1 | Balance b/f | J1 | 120 | | | | |
| 24 | Shop Fittings Ltd | BL6 | 40 | | | | |

### Van Account (folio 6)

| | | | £ | | | | |
|---|---|---|---|---|---|---|---|
| Jan. 1 | Balance b/f | J1 | 500 | | | | |

## Bought Ledger

### S. Lark (folio 2)

| | | | | | | | £ |
|---|---|---|---|---|---|---|---|
| | | | | Jan. 1 | Balance b/f | J1 | 35 |
| | | | | 5 | PDB | 2 | 35 |

### H. Martin (folio 5)

| | | | £ | | | | £ |
|---|---|---|---|---|---|---|---|
| Jan. 15 | Cheque and disct | CB1 | 38 2 | Jan. 1 | Balance b/f | J1 | 40 |
| | | | | 14 | PDB | 2 | 45 |
| 31 | Balance c/d | | 45 | | | | |
| | | | 85 | | | | 85 |
| | | | | Feb. 1 | Balance b/d | | 45 |

### Shop Fittings (folio 6)

| | | | | | | | £ |
|---|---|---|---|---|---|---|---|
| | | | | Jan. 24 | Fittings Account | PL7 | 40 |

## Sales Ledger

### M. Thrush (folio 8)

| Jan. 1 | Balance b/f | J1 | £ 45 | | | | |
|---|---|---|---|---|---|---|---|

### G. Gull (folio 9)

| Jan. 1 | Balance b/f | J1 | £ 80 ═ | Jan. 2 | Cheque and disct | CB1 | £ 76 4 ═ |
|---|---|---|---|---|---|---|---|

### L. Heron (folio 10)

| Jan. 3 | SDB | 3 | £ 6 ═ | Jan. 26 | Cheque | CB1 | £ 6 ═ |
|---|---|---|---|---|---|---|---|
| 30 | Returned cheque | CB1 | 6 | | | | |

### S. Hawk (folio 11)

| Jan. 12 | SDB | 3 | £ 24 ⎯ 24 ═ | Jan. 15 31 | Returns Balance c/d | SRB1 | £ 4 20 ⎯ 24 ═ |
|---|---|---|---|---|---|---|---|
| Feb. 1 | Balance b/d | | 20 | | | | |

## Nominal Ledger

### Sales Account (22)

| Jan. 31 | Total sales returns | SRB1 | £ 4 | Jan. 10 16 26 | Cash book " " | CB1 CB1 CB1 | £ 76 96 68 |
|---|---|---|---|---|---|---|---|
| 31 | Trading Account | | 266 ⎯ 270 ═ | 31 | Total credit sales for month | SDB3 | 30 ⎯ 270 ═ |

### Purchases Account (24)

| Jan. 10 | Cash book | CB1 | £ 15 | Jan. 31 | Trading Account | | £ 95 |
|---|---|---|---|---|---|---|---|
| 31 | Total credit purchases | PDB2 | 80 ⎯ 95 ═ | | | | 95 ═ |

106

## Nominal Ledger

### Postages (folio 25)

| Jan. 4 | Cash book | CB1 | £ 2 | Jan. 31 | P & L Account | | £ 2 |
|---|---|---|---|---|---|---|---|

### Wages (folio 26)

| Jan. 8 | Cash book | CB1 | £ 28 | Jan. 31 | Trading Account | | £ 84 |
|---|---|---|---|---|---|---|---|
| 16 | " | CB1 | 28 | | | | |
| 26 | " | CB1 | 28 | | | | |
| | | | 84 | | | | 84 |

### Advertising (folio 27)

| Jan. 20 | Cash book | CB1 | £ 12 | Jan. 31 | P & L Account | | £ 12 |
|---|---|---|---|---|---|---|---|

### Rent Account (folio 18)

| Jan. 14 | Cash book | CB1 | £ 30 | Jan. 31 | P & L Account | | £ 30 |
|---|---|---|---|---|---|---|---|

### Sundry Expenses (folio 28)

| Jan. 31 | Cash book | CB1 | £ 6 | Jan. 31 | P & L Account | | £ 6 |
|---|---|---|---|---|---|---|---|

### Discounts Allowed (folio 29)

| Jan. 31 | Debit total for January | CB1 | £ 4 | Jan. 31 | P & L Account | | £ 4 |
|---|---|---|---|---|---|---|---|

### Discounts Received (folio 30)

| Jan. 31 | P & L Account | | £ 2 | Jan. 31 | Credit total for January | CB1 | £ 2 |
|---|---|---|---|---|---|---|---|

The Capital and Drawings Accounts of the proprietor are shown at the stage *before* the net trading profit is worked out, i.e. at the trial balance stage:

Private Ledger

Capital Account (folio 2)

| | | | | Jan.<br>1 | Balance b/f | J1 | £<br>1500 |
|---|---|---|---|---|---|---|---|

Drawings Account (folio 3)

| Jan.<br>12<br>31 | Cash book<br>" | CB1<br>CB1 | £<br>15<br>60 | | | | |
|---|---|---|---|---|---|---|---|

Although the nominal accounts have been shown balanced off, and the stock account has been brought up to date with the inclusion of the new stock at January 31, note that the trial balance below is made up *before the closure of these accounts.*

Trial Balance   January 31

| | Debit<br>£ | Credit<br>£ |
|---|---|---|
| Cash | 23 | |
| Bank | 391 | |
| Stock   Jan. 1 | 470 | |
| Fittings | 160 | |
| Van | 500 | |
| Capital   Jan. 1 | | 1500 |
| Drawings for month | 75 | |
| Trade debtors | 71 | |
| Trade creditors | | 155 |
| Sales for month | | 270 |
| Returns inwards | 4 | |
| Purchases for month | 95 | |
| Postages | 2 | |
| Wages | 84 | |
| Advertising | 12 | |
| Rent | 30 | |
| Sundry expenses | 6 | |
| Discounts allowed | 4 | |
| Discounts received | | 2 |
| | 1927 | 1927 |

Trading and Profit and Loss Account
for the month ended January 31

| | £ | £ | | £ | £ |
|---|---|---|---|---|---|
| Stock   Jan. 1 | 470 | | Sales for month | 270 | |
| Purchases | 95 | | Less:   returns | 4 | 266 |
| | 565 | | | | |
| Less:   Stock Jan. 31 | 515 | 50 | | | |
| Wages | | 84 | | | |
| Gross profit c/d | | 132 | | | |
| | | 266 | | | 266 |
| Discounts allowed | | 4 | Gross profit b/d | | 132 |
| Postages | | 2 | Discounts received | | 2 |
| Rent | | 30 | | | |
| Advertising | | 12 | | | |
| Sundry expenses | | 6 | | | |
| Net trading profit | | 80 | | | |
| | | 134 | | | 134 |

Balance Sheet of G. Finch
as at January 31..

| | £ | £ | | £ | £ |
|---|---|---|---|---|---|
| Capital Account | | | Fixed assets | | |
| Balance Jan. 1 | 1500 | | Fittings | 160 | |
| Add:   Net profit | | | Van | 500 | 660 |
|         for month | 80 | | | | |
| | 1580 | | Current assets | | |
| Less:   drawings | 75 | 1505 | Stock Jan. 31 | 515 | |
| | | | Trade debtors | 71 | |
| Current liabilities | | | Bank | 391 | |
| Trade creditors | | 155 | Cash | 23 | 1000 |
| | | 1660 | | | 1660 |

Finally, G. Finch's drawings account may be closed by transfer to the debit of his capital account, and the net trading profit will be credited to his capital account to agree with the detail shown on the balance sheet. It will be seen that he has increased his commencing capital by £5, the difference between his net profit and the money he has withdrawn on account of his expectation of profit.

Capital Account (folio 2)

| Jan. | | | £ | Jan. | | | £ |
|------|---|---|---|------|---|---|---|
| 31 | Transfer from Drawings A/c | PL3 | 75 | 1 | Balance b/f | J1 | 1500 |
| 31 | Balance c/d. | | 1505 | 31 | Net trading profit for January | | 80 |
| | | | 1580 | | | | 1580 |
| | | | | Feb. | | | |
| | | | | 1 | Balance b/d | | 1505 |

## QUESTIONS

1. As the sales ledger clerk of Lambert & Sons Ltd, make up the account of Roger Langton, one of your customers, from the information given below:

August
1 Debit balance brought forward £62.50
2 Further sales to Langton invoiced at £80 less 15 per cent trade discount
5 Langton paid his July account less cash discount on 4 per cent
6 One-quarter of goods consigned on August 2 were returned. Credit note issued
15 Another £60 of goods invoiced less usual 15 per cent
20 Langton paid £50 'on account' by cheque
24 The bank returned his cheque marked N/S
Langton was contacted and he made arrangements for the cheque to be met on August 28
28 Cheque met by the bank
31 Balanced his account.

2. What effect would the transactions below have upon the balance sheet of Simon Shaw, who started in business on July 1 with £1000 in the bank, a van valued at £1200 and £800 of goods for sale?
(a) A new van was bought for £2500 against a deposit of £500, the balance to be spread over two years. The old van was sold to a friend for £1180, the money being paid into the business account.
(b) A credit purchase of £200 more stock.
(c) The credit sale of £400 of goods at a profit of 20 per cent on sales.
(d) A filing-cabinet was bought for £120 cash less a discount of 10 per cent.
(e) Drawings of £50 by Mr Shaw.

Redraft his balance sheet giving full effect to these transactions.

3. Edward Leroy has the following assets and liabilities on June 1:

|  | £ |  | £ |
|---|---|---|---|
| Cash in hand | 15 | Cash at bank | 680 |
| Stock | 1225 | Fittings/fixtures | 230 |

Trade debtors: Cole £120 and Crawford £150
Trade creditors: Nutter £240 and Napier £180

The following transactions took place during the month of June:

June

|  |  | £ |
|---|---|---|
| 1 | Drew cheque for office to supplement cash in hand | 50.00 |
|  | Paid sundry expenses in cash | 20.20 |
| 2 | Cash sales | 75.50 |
|  | Crawford paid his May account less 4 per cent cash discount | 144.00 |
|  | Paid rent for month | 30.00 |
| 5 | Bought £180 goods from Nutter less 25 per cent trade discount. | |
| 6 | Returned £20 (gross) goods bought yesterday. | |
| 10 | Cash sales (banked £80) | 86.20 |
|  | Paid advertising account | 15.50 |
| 12 | Bought filing-cabinet invoiced at £60 from Office Supply Co. Ltd | |
| 14 | Cash purchases | 12.90 |
|  | Paid for stationery and stamps in cash | 8.20 |
|  | Cash sales | 92.40 |
| 15 | Sold Crawford £96 goods less 10 per cent TD. | |
| 16 | Crawford returned £30 (gross) goods bought on June 15. | |
|  | Cash sales | 132.70 |
|  | Paid cash into bank | 200.00 |
| 18 | Received cheque for commissions earned | 125.00 |
| 20 | Paid Nutter's May account less discount | 230.40 |
|  | Bought £160 more goods from Nutter less 25% trade discount. | |
| 24 | Returned containers to Nutter. He sent credit note for £4.50 | |
| 25 | Bought £80 of goods from Napier less 25 per cent trade discount | |
|  | Cash sales | 156.60 |
| 28 | Paid wages out of surplus cash | 120.00 |
| 30 | Leroy drew a cheque to cover £100 office salaries and £80 for himself | 180.00 |
|  | He then paid the remaining cash surplus into the bank. | |

You are required to ascertain Edward Leroy's commencing capital by listing his opening assets and liabilities, post all transactions to the original books of entry and to the personal and nominal ledger accounts. Balance all ledger accounts and take out a trial balance on June 30.

4. From the trial balance of Edward Leroy in the previous exercise, you are required to prepare a trading and profit and loss account for the month of June, and a balance sheet as at June 30.

Edward Leroy valued his closing stock at June 30 at £1450.

5. You decide to open a gown shop on May 1. Previously you have been working from your home address. Your assets and liabilities at this date are listed thus:

| | £ | | £ |
|---|---|---|---|
| Bank balance | 825 | Cash in hand | 75 |
| Stock of goods | 500 | 5-year lease | 1000 |
| | | Shop fittings | 100 |

Samuel Johnson owes you £150.

You owe your supplier Leslie Harris £400 for gowns recently delivered, and £50 is also owing to Shop Fittings Ltd for work done on your new premises.

The following transactions take place during May:

May
1  Sold two gowns to Consuela Hyde for £80. She promised to pay later in the month
2  Forwarded cheque to Shop Fittings in settlement of their account
4  Paid various office expenses in cash £15, and drew cheque for £20 to replenish cash in hand
8  Cash takings £75. Banked £50
10 Bought another £125 of gowns from Leslie Harris
   Paid his April account less 5 per cent cash discount
14 Samuel Johnson paid £100 off his April account and promised the other £50 early next month
   Returned £25 of goods bought on May 10
18 Bought a new office desk for £90. Paid by cheque
   Paid private car account £8 in cash
21 Consuela Hyde called and paid half the amount due
   Allowed her 5 per cent cash discount on her payment
   Cash sales £200. Paid £100 into bank
23 Made various purchases for cash £20
25 Paid travelling expenses of new sales assistant £2
30 Drew cheque for private expenses £85
31 Paid wages £66
   Paid all cash into bank leaving £5 in cash till.

Post all transactions from the cash book to the various accounts, open up all other necessary accounts, and extract a trial balance at May 31. After a final stock valuation of £350 you are required to prepare the final accounts of the business as at May 31.

# THE BANK CASH BOOK:
# CONTROL ACCOUNTS

## 15.1 THE BANK CASH BOOK

One main form of cash book has already been described. This is the three-column cash book, the kind generally required for elementary examinations.

A more modern form of cash book is now introduced. This is known as the Bank Cash Book. An essential feature is its simplicity. All money received (cash and cheques) is paid into the bank intact day by day, and all small cash disbursements are made from an entirely separate source, the Petty Cash Book.

Bank Cash Book (in brief detail)

| Date | | Fol. | Disct | Details | Bank | Date | | Fol. | Disct | Bank |
|------|--|------|-------|---------|------|------|--|------|-------|------|
| Jan. | | | | £ | £ | Jan. | | | £ | £ |
| 1 | Balance | | | | | 2 | Jones | BL8 | | 6 |
| | b/f | | | | 250 | 3 | Hudson | BL5 | 1 | 19 |
| 3 | Cash | | | | | 5 | Wages | NL4 | | 120 |
| | sales | NL3 | | 27 | | | | | | |
| | Evans chq | SL4 | | 10 | | | | | | |
| | Brown chq | SL3 | | 18 | 55 | | | | | |

The ruling of this type of cash book is slightly different from the older style. Cash columns are not required, but on the debit there is a column for the detailed grouping of cash and cheques received each day. The *total receipts* are banked each day (or at least the day following receipt, allowing for afternoon payments).

Each day the total receipts will be entered in the paying-in book and paid into the bank. The firm's cashier must accept the responsibility for this. The total of the paying-in slip each day will agree with the amount posted to the debit of the bank column for that day.

Cheque payments on the credit side of the cash book are dealt with as before. *All payments* are made by cheque from this type of cash book.

Where money is required for wages and petty cash, a cheque is drawn on the bank and cash obtained for the purpose.

Contra entries (cash from bank and vice versa) are no longer necessary, and many firms using the bank cash book analyse their debit and credit columns, providing information for management, and the relevant totals for the control system in force.

Specimen copies are now shown of the two separate sides of this type of bank cash book:

Debit side

| Date | | Fol. | Disct | Sales Ledger | Cash Sales | Sundries | Bank |
|---|---|---|---|---|---|---|---|
| | | | £ | £ | £ | £ | £ |
| Mar. 1 | Balance b/f | | | | | 500 | 500 |
| 2 | Cash sales | NL | | | 20 | | 20 |
| 4 | Thomas | SL | | 15 | | | |
| | Harris | SL | 2 | 48 | | | 63 |
| 5 | Cash sales | NL | | | 32 | | |
| | Sims (loan) | PL | | | | 200 | 232 |
| 6 | Office equipt (sale of old typewriter) | GL | | | | 25 | 25 |
| | | | 2 | 63 | 52 | 725 | 840 |

Credit side

| Date | | Fol. | Disct | Bought Ledger | Cash Purchases | Sundries | Bank |
|---|---|---|---|---|---|---|---|
| | | | £ | £ | £ | £ | £ |
| Mar. 2 | Morris | BL | 1 | 19 | | | 19 |
| | Kerr | BL | | 8 | | | 8 |
| 4 | Cash purchases | NL | | | 4 | | 4 |
| 5 | Wages | NL | | | | 150 | 150 |
| | Roland | BL | 4 | 76 | | | 76 |
| 6 | Petty cash | PCB | | | | 10 | 10 |
| | Drawings | PL | | | | 50 | 50 |
| | | | 5 | 103 | 4 | 210 | 317 |

The two sections of the bank cash book have not been balanced in this illustration, but balancing each month is a common feature and there is a control check on totals, with errors being located easily.

The sundries columns will include the opening balance, any sales of fixed assets, normal trade expenses such as wages and rent, the proprietor's drawings and cheques drawn for petty cash. For further detailed comparison, an additional analysis of the sundries columns would be required.

The big advantage of the bank cash book is that a daily check is maintained upon the money paid into bank. It is quickly verified by checking the bank statement against the cash book bank columns. Risk of mis-appropriation is much reduced.

Separate cash books are used on alternate days in the counting houses of many large firms. This allows the ledger clerks to post up the personal accounts of debtors and creditors without interrupting the duties of the cashier. Again, in other offices there may be separate cash books for receipts and payments, allowing for the economic division of time and labour.

## 15.2  TOTAL ACCOUNTS

An understanding of total accounts gives the student confidence to tackle the 'incomplete record' type of question, particularly where no figures are given for either credit purchases or credit sales.

**Illustration**
From the following information you are required to find the total credit purchases and credit sales for the year ended December 31.

|  | January 1 | December 31 |
|---|---|---|
| Debtors' balances | £440 | £455 |
| Creditors' balances | £330 | £285 |

During the year the payments from credit customers totalled £1225; the payments made to credit suppliers amounted to £920. Cash sales for the year amounted to £410.

**Answer in account form**

Total Debtors

| Jan. | | £ | Dec. | | £ |
|---|---|---|---|---|---|
| 1 | Balance b/f | 440 | 31 | Cash from credit customers (CB totals) | 1225 |
| 31 | CREDIT SALES for year | 1240 | | | |
| | | | 31 | Balance c/d | 455 |
| | | 1680 | | | 1680 |
| Jan. | | | | | |
| 1 | Balance b/d | 455 | | | |

Total Creditors

| Jan. 31 | Payments to suppliers (CB totals) | | £ 920 | Jan. 1 | Balance b/f | | £ 330 |
|------|------|------|------|------|------|------|------|
| 31 | Balance c/d | | 285 | 31 | CREDIT PURCHASES for year | | 875 |
| | | | 1205 | | | | 1205 |
| | | | | Jan. 1 | Balance b/d | | 285 |

*Note.* The cash sales of £410 must be added to the credit sales to bring the total net sales up to the figure of £1650 for the year.

## 15.3 CONTROL ACCOUNTS

Control or adjustment accounts are useful devices providing checks on the postings to the different ledgers. If there are errors on the trial balance, searches for discrepancies may be limited to certain sections of the accounting system.

The work of the personal (and nominal) ledger clerks is made easier, in particular when interim trading and profit and loss accounts are required by management. The task of the internal auditor is lightened considerably too, in so far as a good deal of routine checking is concerned.

### Control accounts are summaries of totals

The special adjustment or control accounts kept at the end of each ledger provide a check on the postings within the particular ledger.

Only totals appear in control accounts. For instance, the control account at the back of the bought ledger will be *debited with the total purchases* to that particular ledger, and *credited with payments made to suppliers*, discounts received and returns outwards.

The balances of control accounts at the back of the personal ledgers should agree with the total extracted lists of debtors and creditors in the particular ledgers which are being 'self-balanced'.

Books of prime entry must be adapted to suit the self-balancing system in operation. The bank cash book, for example, lends itself to mechanisation and the control system.

## 15.4 ILLUSTRATION OF BOUGHT LEDGER CONTROL

For this brief example a summary of totals is shown; these totals have been extracted from the purchases day book, the purchases returns book, the credit side of the bank cash book (explained earlier in the chapter) and the listed total of the creditors' balances taken from the bought ledger.

| Creditors | Purchases | Returns | Payments | Discount | Closing balances |
|---|---|---|---|---|---|
| | £ | £ | £ | £ | £ |
| Morris | 85 | 15 | 19 | 1 | 50 |
| Kerr | 20 | | 8 | | 12 |
| Roland | 120 | 10 | 76 | 4 | 30 |
| | 225 | 25 | 103 | 5 | 92 |
| Totals obtained from | PDB | PRB | CB | CB | BL |

Bought Ledger

General Ledger Control Account
(kept at the back of the Bought Ledger)

| Mar. 6 | Purchase Day Book on March 6 | | £ 225 | Mar. 6 | Cash/cheques | CB | £ 103 |
|---|---|---|---|---|---|---|---|
| | | | | | Discounts | CB | 5 |
| | | | | | Returns outwards | PRB | 25 |
| | | | | | Balance c/d | | 92 |
| | | | 225 | | | | 225 |
| Mar. 6 | Balance b/d | | 92 | | | | |

The figures recorded in the control accounts at the back of the *personal* ledgers are shown on the reverse side to the items appearing in the particular ledgers.

On the other hand, the general and nominal ledger clerks keep replica accounts (but with sides in reverse) corresponding to the bought and sales ledger control accounts at the back of their ledgers, providing a double check on the personal accounts. In large organisations, care is taken to ensure that the general ledger clerks work quite independently of the personal ledger clerks. This tightens up the internal check and is a safeguard against fraud.

## 15.5 TYPICAL EXAMINATION QUESTION

The following balances have been extracted from the books of a firm at December 31:

|  | £ |
|---|---|
| January 1 Debit balances in sales ledger | 6222 |
| Credit balances in sales ledger | 88 |
| Debit balances in bought ledger | 56 |
| Credit balances in bought ledger | 3650 |

Supplementary information at December 31:

| | £ | | £ |
|---|---|---|---|
| Sales for year | 45,560 | Purchases for year | 31,320 |
| Discounts allowed | 285 | Discounts recd | 316 |
| Purchase returns | 172 | Sales returns | 260 |
| Payments to suppliers | 30,824 | Bad debts written off | 118 |
| Payments from customers | 43,793 | | |

Other balances:

|  | £ |
|---|---|
| Debit balances in the bought ledger at the year end | 51 |
| Credit balances in the sales ledger at the year end | 344 |
| Credits transferred from the bought ledger to the sales ledger during the year | 147 |

From the information given above make up both the Sales and Bought Ledger Control Accounts as they would appear in the General Ledger of the firm, bringing down the balances to be carried forward to the following year.

## ANSWER

Bought Ledger Control Account

| Jan. | | £ | Jan. | | £ |
|---|---|---|---|---|---|
| 1 | Debit balance b/f | 56 | 1 | Credit balance b/f | 3,650 |
| Dec. | | | Dec. | | |
| 31 | Payments to suppliers | 30,824 | 31 | Purchases for year | 31,320 |
| | Purchase returns | 172 | | Debit balances c/d | 51 |
| | Discount recd | 316 | | | |
| | Transfers to SL | 147 | | | |
| | Credit balances c/d | 3,506 | | | |
| | | 35,021 | | | 35,021 |
| Jan. | | | Jan. | | |
| 1 | Balance b/d | 51 | 1 | Balance b/d | 3,506 |

Sales Ledger Control Account

| Jan. 1 | Debit balance b/f | £ 6,222 | Dec. 1 | Credit balance b/f | £ 88 |
|---|---|---|---|---|---|
| Dec. 31 | Sales for year | 45,560 | Dec. 31 | Payments from credit customers | 43,793 |
| | Credit balance c/d | 344 | | Sales returns | 260 |
| | | | | Discount allowed | 285 |
| | | | | Bad debts | 118 |
| | | | | Transfers from BL | 147 |
| | | | | Debit balance c/d | 7,435 |
| | | 52,126 | | | 52,126 |
| Jan. 1 | Balance b/d | 7,435 | Jan. 1 | Balance b/d | 344 |

*Note.* (a) Transfers from one ledger to another appear in both control accounts.

(b) Closing balances must be inserted above the totals before being carried down.

## QUESTIONS

1. Post up the entries in your *bank cash book* for the month of November from the information given below, bringing down the balance on November 30. Use additional columns for the receipts and payments with regard to cash sales and cash purchases, and the amounts to be posted to the sales and bought ledgers.

November
1   Bank balance £520.00
2   Cash takings £72.30. Paid into bank
    Drew cheque for petty cash reimbursement £15.80
5   Paid X (wholesaler's) account for October £120 less 4 per cent cash discount
8   Received payment of A's October account for £40 less 4 per cent cash discount
    Cash takings £88.60. Banked cash and cheque £127.00

12  Paid into bank cash sales receipts £66.20, together with cheques from *B* and *C* for £15.40 and £18.10 respectively

16  Paid into bank cash sales receipts £76.70, together with cheque from *D* for £57.60 (discount of £2.40 already deducted) and cheque from *E* for £65.00 (discount of £3.00 deducted)

20  Paid rates for half-year £180.00
Paid for office stationery £7.50

22  Cash takings £94.80. Paid into bank

24  Cash purchases £18.60, paid by cheque
Received cheque from *F* for £14.40 and paid into bank

28  Drew cheque for wages £240.00

30  Drew cheque for private expenses £50.00
Paid *Y*'s account for £80 less 4 per cent discount.

2. Make up the purchases and sales control accounts at the end of November from information extracted from the bank cash book in question 1, and the figures given below:

|  | Sales Ledger | Bought Ledger |
|---|---|---|
|  | £ | £ |
| Control balances Nov. 1 | 1180.50 | 824.20 |
| Day book totals for month | 524.20 | 275.60 |
| Returns book totals for month | 28.40 | 22.50 |

Bring down the control balances as at December 1.

3. From the following information you are required to find the total credit purchases and credit sales:

|  | Jan. 1 | Dec. 31 |
|---|---|---|
|  | £ | £ |
| Debtors' balances | 1260 | 1320 |
| Creditors' balances | 810 | 940 |

During the year receipts from credit customers totalled £5880, and payments to suppliers amounted to £3240. The cash sales figure for the year was £1350.

4. Make up the trading account of Roberta Rowan from the details given below:

|  | Stock | Debtors | Creditors |
|---|---|---|---|
|  | £ | £ | £ |
| January 1 | 2500 | 1650 | 1480 |
| December 31 | 3000 | 1825 | 1360 |

During the year Miss Rowan received £9820 from credit customers and £1930 from cash sales. Her payments to suppliers amounted to £3440 and she paid £122 for carriage inwards. Warehousing wages and storage expenses amounted to £6860.

**5.** Your assignment is to extract all the necessary detail from the figures listed below, and make up the sales ledger control account as it would appear in the general ledger, for the month ended April 30:

|  |  | £ |
|---|---|---|
| April 1 | Debit balances in sales ledger | 5866 |
| | ,, ,, ,, bought ledger | 54 |
| | Credit balances in sales ledger | 136 |
| | ,, ,, ,, bought ledger | 2868 |
| April 30 | Credit balances in sales ledger | 96 |
| | Debit balances in bought ledger | 72 |

|  | £ |
|---|---|
| Purchases for year | 19,820 |
| Sales for year | 35,620 |
| Purchase returns | 315 |
| Sales returns | 424 |
| Discounts allowed | 522 |
| Discounts received | 454 |
| Payments to suppliers | 18,246 |
| Payments from customers | 33,898 |

Bad debts written off during the year amounted to £124.

Credits transferred from the sales ledger to the bought ledger during the year totalled £88.

# DEPRECIATION OF FIXED ASSETS: PROVISION FOR BAD DEBTS

If you buy a car for £3000 on January 1 would you expect to receive £3000 for it on December 31, twelve months later?

Would it not be more reasonable to expect to receive about £2300, allowing, of course, for prevailing inflationary conditions?

In business, we have to take into account the reduction in value of fixed assets, and show their approximately true values on balance sheets. After all, certain assets lose value through continual use and wear and tear, and need to be replaced after a few years; they are no longer worth their original price.

The reduction or fall in value is called 'depreciation'. It is treated as a loss or expense to the business and charged (debited) to trading or profit and loss account, and at the same time, the asset account is correspondingly reduced in value. Depreciation in particular applies to machinery and automobiles, all manner of electrical equipment and leases, and to a reduced degree on fittings and fixtures. Not long ago it was also applicable to freehold buildings and premises, but these now often maintain or increase in value on account of industrial demand, rising prices and the high cost of ground sites.

## 16.1 DEPRECIATION METHODS

Three of the older methods, now only seen in the accounts of the sole trader, and occasionally a partnership, are explained at this elementary stage.

(a) *Fixed instalment or straight line.* The sum to be written off the asset account is a *fixed amount* each year. Its main advantage is the even cost, which is easy to work out (for example, a £5000 ten-year lease would be charged against profits at £500 a year).

(b) *Fixed percentage on reducing balance* is in general use for machinery,

122

motor vehicles, etc., where there are additions and replacements, and repairs become heavier as the depreciation debit to profit and loss account becomes lighter.

(c) *Revaluation method* is adopted sometimes in the case of loose tools and precision equipment. Additional tools and accessories are debited to the asset account, which is revalued annually, the loss in value (difference) being written off against profits.

Three ledger accounts are now shown of a lease, a motor van and loose tools, with depreciation reducing the asset account over the first two years:

£5000 Lease Account

| (The lease is for ten years, so equal instalments of £500 will be deducted and charged against profits each year) | | | | | | |
|---|---|---|---|---|---|---|
| Jan. 1 First year | Original cost | CB | £ 5000 | Dec. 31 | Depreciation A/c Balance c/d | £ 500 4500 |
| | | | 5000 | | | 5000 |
| Jan. 1 Second year | Balance b/d | | 4500 | Dec. 31 | Depreciation A/c Balance c/d | 500 4000 |
| | | | 4500 | | | 4500 |
| Jan. 1 | Balance b/d | | 4000 | | | |

Van Account

| (The van was purchased as a new vehicle for £4000 on January 1 and is to be depreciated at 25 percent on the asset's reducing balance) | | | | | | |
|---|---|---|---|---|---|---|
| Jan. 1 First year | Cheque | CB | £ 4000 | Dec. 31 | Depreciation 25% on £4000 Balance c/d | £ 1000 3000 |
| | | | 4000 | | | 4000 |
| Jan. 1 Second year | Balance b/d | | 3000 | Dec. 31 | Depreciation 25% on £3000 Balance c/d | 750 2250 |
| | | | 3000 | | | 3000 |
| Jan. 1 | Balance b/d | | 2250 | | | |

## Loose Tools Account

(The firm makes their own working tools. There was a balance brought forward valued at £400 on January 1; revalued at £250 at end of first year, and at £350 at end of second year, after allowing for £280 of additional tools made by own workmen)

| | | £ | | | £ |
|---|---|---|---|---|---|
| Jan. 31 | Balance b/f | 400 | Dec. 31 | Depreciation A/c | 150 |
| First year | | | | Balance (Revaluation) c/d | 250 |
| | | 400 | | | 400 |
| Jan. 1 | Balance b/d | 250 | Dec. 31 | Depreciation A/c | 180 |
| Dec. 31 | Additions during year | 280 | | Balance (Revaluation) c/d | 350 |
| Second year | | | | | |
| | | 530 | | | 530 |
| Jan. 1 | Balance b/d | 350 | | | |

Alternatively, loose tools are sometimes treated like stock, the commencing balance being debited and the closing balance credited to trading account each year. This is more satisfactory where the revaluation reveals an increase (appreciation instead of depreciation) on account of apprentices, etc., making their own tools in excess of their immediate requirements.

The profit and loss account is shown, debit side only, for the two years, showing the depreciation charge against profits. These debits may be taken direct, as the opposite entry, from the asset accounts themselves, or, temporarily be taken and recorded in a depreciation account.

## Profit and Loss Account

### First year

| | £ | £ | |
|---|---|---|---|
| Depreciation: | | | Gross profit b/d |
| Lease | 500 | | |
| Van | 1000 | | |
| Loose tools | 150 | 1650 | |

## Profit and Loss Account

### Second year

| | £ | £ | |
|---|---|---|---|
| Depreciation: | | | Gross profit b/d |
| Lease | 500 | | |
| Van | 750 | | |
| Loose tools | 180 | 1430 | |

The assets side of the balance sheet for the two years will be shown as follows:

| Balance Sheet as at December 31 | | | |
|---|---|---|---|
| First year | | | |
| Fixed assets | £ | £ | |
| Lease | | 5000 | |
| Less: deprec. | | 500 | 4500 |
| Van | | 4000 | |
| Less: deprec. | | 1000 | 3000 |
| Loose tools | | 400 | |
| Less: deprec. | | 150 | 250 |
| | | | 7750 |

| Balance Sheet as at December 31 | | | |
|---|---|---|---|
| Second year | | | |
| Fixed assets | £ | £ | |
| Lease | | 4500 | |
| Less: deprec. | | 500 | 4000 |
| Van | | 3000 | |
| Less: deprec. | | 750 | 2250 |
| Loose tools | | 250 | |
| Additions | | 280 | |
| | | 530 | |
| Less: deprec. | | 180 | 350 |
| | | | 6600 |

## 16.2 PROVISION FOR DEPRECIATION ACCOUNT

The modern and up-to-date method of dealing with the depreciation of fixed assets, a legal requirement too of the Companies Acts, is to leave the asset at its cost price, debit revenue in the ordinary way with the annual charge, but credit this depreciation charge to a Provision for Depreciation Account instead of the asset account.

The aggregate and cumulative depreciation shown as a credit balance on this account is deducted from the original cost of the asset on the balance sheet, so that members and creditors of the Company can see the extent of the capital expenditure, and the position with regard to renewals and replacements, in particular with regard to wasting assets (those which reduce in value through general usage, wear and tear, or obsolescence).

An example is shown of a machine bought three years ago for £2000. It is to be depreciated by fixed instalments of £200 a year.

Machinery (asset) Account

| | | | £ | | | | |
|---|---|---|---|---|---|---|---|
| Year 1 | Cheque | CB | 2000 | | | | |

Provision for Depreciation Account

| | | | £ | | | | £ |
|---|---|---|---|---|---|---|---|
| Year 1 | Balance c/d | | 200 | Year 1 | P & L Account | | 200 |
| | | | | Year 2 | Balance b/d | | 200 |
| Year 2 | Balance c/d | | 400 | | P & L Account | | 200 |
| | | | | Year 3 | Balance b/d | | 400 |
| Year 3 | Balance c/d | | 600 | | P & L Account | | 200 |
| | | | | Year 4 | Balance b/d | | 600 |

The profit and loss account will be debited with this fixed instalment of £200 each year, and the fixed asset will be shown on the balance sheet for the first three years thus:

```
Year 1
                                   £     £
Machinery at cost               2000
Less:  aggregate deprec.         200  1800

Year 2

Machinery at cost               2000
Less:  aggregate deprec.         400  1600

Year 3

Machinery at cost               2000
Less:  aggregate deprec.         600  1400
```

## 16.3   DISPOSAL OF FIXED ASSETS

Where a fixed asset is sold or taken in part-exchange its original cost must be credited to the asset account as it is now being *taken out of the books.* This original cost must now be divided between the sum realised on disposal (for scrap etc.) and that part representing *depreciation already written off,* and the balance or difference will be treated as *profit or loss on disposal,* to be adjusted on the revenue account at the year end.

**Illustration**
On January 1 a firm's plant and machinery account stood at its original cost of £40,000 with its related provision for depreciation account showing a credit balance of £24,500.

A new machine, was bought for £3000 on June 30, estimated to have a working life of ten years, ignoring scrap value in this instance for depreciation purposes, and adopting the fixed instalment basis as before. The total debit to revenue excluding the depreciation on the new machine, for the current year, was £4500.

On the last day of the trading year a machine bought five years previously for £2000, and depreciated at £250 per annum as part of the gross charge to revenue, was sold for £400.

The plant and machinery account and the provision account will be made up on these lines:

Plant and Machinery Account

| | | £ | | | £ |
|---|---|---|---|---|---|
| Jan. 1 | Original cost b/f | 40,000 | Dec. 31 | Cash proceeds | 400 |
| June 30 | Cheque (new machine) | 3,000 | | Transfer to Prov. for Deprec. A/c | 1,250 |
| | | | | Loss on sale | 350 |
| | | | | Balance c/d | 41,000 |
| | | 43,000 | | | 43,000 |
| Jan. 1 | Balance b/d | 41,000 | | | |

Provision for Depreciation Account

| | | £ | | | £ |
|---|---|---|---|---|---|
| Dec. 31 | Transfer from P & M A/c | 1,250 | Jan. 1 | Balance b/f | 24,500 |
| Dec. 31 | Balance c/d | 27,900 | Dec. 31 | P & L debit £ on old machy 4,500 on new machine 150 | 4,650 |
| | | 29,150 | | | 29,150 |
| | | | Jan. 1 | Balance b/d | 27,900 |

Balance Sheet as at December 31

| | |
|---|---|
| | Fixed assets |
| | Plant & Machinery 41,000 Less: aggregate deprec. 27,900  13,100 |

## 16.4   SCRAP VALUE

Where machinery or motor vehicles are depreciated by the fixed instalment method, the estimated scrap value on disposal of the old asset must be taken into account.

If a new machine, costing £2000, is estimated to have a working life of five years, with a scrap value at the end of that period of £200, a fixed instalment of £360 each year will be written off the asset account, calculated thus:

Original cost of asset          £2000
*Less*: estimated scrap value __200__
                                1800 to be written off
                                        over five years.

When considering the method of depreciation to adopt, the following points should be considered:

(a)  the effective life of the machine or vehicle
(b)  its estimated scrap value
(c)  the frequency of additions (capital)
(d)  likely repairs and maintenance (revenue)
(e)  likelihood of being superseded by more up-to-date models.

In examination questions take particular note of the *dates*, whether depreciation is to be for *one month* or *one year*, and also whether the percentage is a *straight 20 per cent* or *20 per cent per annum.* Another thing, make sure whether the amount to write off is based upon the original cost of the asset, or the *cost plus additions* during the year.

Bear in mind, too, that depreciation is not a cash figure, and in no way affects the cash book. It is an estimated amount of loss or expense of a fixed asset, caused through usage, wear and tear and sometimes obsolescence (going out of date). Most fixed assets, sooner or later, have to be replaced, often by more expensive assets, and it is only at the replacement stage that a large sum of money for further capital finance will be needed.

## 16.5   BAD DEBTS

Occasionally, a credit customer cannot pay what he owes.

Frequent reminders may be ignored, and then, at the end of the financial year, you may decide to threaten him with legal proceedings or put the matter in the hands of a debt-collection agency.

Bad and doubtful debts are reviewed at each year end, and those considered irrecoverable are transferred from the personal accounts in the sales ledger to the Bad Debts Account in the nominal ledger.

The debtors' accounts are closed (although proceedings may still go on) and the debit balance on bad debts account is treated as a loss and expense to the business and written off to profit and loss account.

## 16.6   BAD DEBTS RECOVERED

Any payments received from old debtors (or their trustees) are not credited to the personal account already written off, but to a Bad Debts Recovered Account.

Dividends or compositions (of so much in £) are paid by trustees in bankruptcy or by the liquidator of a company, and the creditor of an old debt of say £20 might consider himself lucky to receive £5 as a first and final settlement.

Small traders either credit their profit and loss accounts with occasional bad debts recovered, or take the credit to reduce the debit balance on bad debts account, and simply show the net debit to profit and loss account.

## 16.7   PROVISION FOR BAD DEBTS

Some debts are *doubtful – not bad,* and a general provision is sometimes made to cover a listed category of this nature, as a proportion of them may prove to be irrecoverable, involving a loss to the business.

The 'provision' takes the form of a percentage of the total trade debts, the listed total of the debtors. Normally the percentage is small, around 2 or 3 per cent, but in certain trades where the credit risk is greater, it could be as high as 10 per cent.

With regard to *doubtful* debts as distinct from those known to be irrecoverable, note that the firm is always hopeful of full recovery. It is not wise to identify all slow payers as 'doubtful' and a specific provision against individual debtors should not be publicised.

Another thing, bear in mind that *actual bad debts* to be written off and a *provision* against the possibility of additional bad debts are two distinct things. The former refers to debit account balances being charged against profits as known and actual losses, whereas the latter is more of a reserve or restriction of profit (a form of insurance) to safeguard the possibility of further loss. The provision is adjustable too; it can be increased or decreased, and in some instances it can be credited back to profit and loss account as no longer required. As with depreciation, no money passes. It is purely a reduction of asset values on paper to show the balance sheet in its true perspective.

## 16.8   CREATING THE PROVISION

A small trader lists the total of his trade debtors at December 31, amounting to £5000. Actual bad debts during the year have already been written off, and we are only concerned with the provision account, and its *creation in the first instance*. The trader consults his accountant and decides that a provision of 4 per cent of the debtors' total would be adequate.

The book entries simply involve a credit to provision account and its corresponding debit to the profit and loss account, thus:

**First Year**

Bad Debts Provision Account

| | | | | Dec. 31 | P & L A/c | | £ 200 |
|---|---|---|---|---|---|---|---|

Profit and Loss Account for year ended Dec. 31

| Bad Debts Prov. A/c | £ 200 | | | |
|---|---|---|---|---|

The *full* amount of the provision (£200) has been brought into the books, and debited to profit and loss account this *first year*.

*Second year and after*
There is already a credit balance of £200 on provision account. Consequently only the *increase or decrease of the existing provision* is taken to profit and loss account.

**Second Year**
The trade debtors total has increased to £6000, and the same rate of 4 per cent is to be maintained.

Bad Debts Provision Account

| | | | | Dec. 31 | Balance b/f from first year | | £ 200 |
|---|---|---|---|---|---|---|---|
| | | | | 31 | P & L A/c increase of provision to £240 (i.e. 4% of £6000) | | 40 |

Profit and Loss Account (second year)

| Bad Debts Prov. A/c | £ 40 | | | |
|---|---|---|---|---|

Note that only the *increase* of the provision is debited against profits in this second year, bringing the *credit balance* on provision account up to £240.

## Third Year

In the third year trade has fallen off through fierce competition, and the debtors balances now only total £4000; the same percentage is to be maintained as before.

In addition, the *actual bad debts* experienced in this third year, amounting to £65, has been written off the debtors' accounts in the sales ledger and transferred to bad debts account.

Bad Debts Provision Account

| Dec. 31 Third year | P & L A/c decrease of provision to £160 (4% of £4000) | | £ 30 | Dec. 31 | Balance b/f from second year | | £ 240 |
|---|---|---|---|---|---|---|---|

Profit and Loss Account (third year)

| | Transferred from Bad Debts Account (see below) | | £ 65 | Bad Debts Prov. A/c decrease written back (see above) | | £ 80 |
|---|---|---|---|---|---|---|

Bad Debts Account

| Dec. 31 31 | AB Smith CD Brown | SL SL | £ 24 41 | Dec. 31 | Transfer to P & L A/c | | £ 65 |
|---|---|---|---|---|---|---|---|

The assets side of the balance sheet is shown in brief detail with regard to the provision accounts over these three years. Note that it is always the *last provision* which is deducted from debtors on the balance sheet.

Assets side of the Balance Sheet

| | Current assets | £ | £ |
|---|---|---|---|
| Year 1 | Trade debtors<br>Less: provision | 5000<br>200 | 4800 |
| Year 2 | Current assets<br><br>Trade debtors<br>Less: provision | <br><br>6000<br>240 | <br><br>5760 |
| Year 3 | Current assets<br><br>Trade debtors<br>Less: provision | <br><br>4000<br>160 | <br><br>3840 |

*Note* that the full amount of the provision is debited to the profit and loss account *only in the first year*.

Once created, there is only an *annual adjustment* (increase or decrease of the provision) to be *debited or credited* to profit and loss account.

On the balance sheet the net trading profit brought forward has been reduced by the amount of the provision increase, and there is a corresponding reduction of net assets as the provision is deducted from debtors. Alternatively, where the provision is reduced, the net profit is increased and net assets also show an increase.

## QUESTIONS

**1.** A small manufacturer with a rapidly expending trade asks for your advice in connection with the depreciation of his fixed assets, listed as follows:

(a) Buildings and premises which cost him £20,000 five years ago.
(b) Machinery and plant shown in the books at cost £12,000 and now with an estimated value of £8000.
(c) A five-ton truck which cost £2500 three years ago.
(d) The lease of a warehouse bought two years ago for £2000 with still eight years to run.
(e) Loose tools valued at £500 a year ago; now estimated to be worth £600.

First you decide to bring each asset account to its real or approximate valuation. Next to consider the method of depreciation most suitable to adopt, and then, third, you decide to show how these assets will appear *one year after the adjustment in asset values have taken place,* showing the up-to-date debits for depreciation to profit and loss account (and the balance sheet figures) at the end of the first trading year after adjustment of values.

**2.** It has been the practice for a company to show its fixed assets at cost in the balance sheet and maintain a depreciation provision account for each asset, deducting the aggregate credit balances from each related asset on the balance sheet.

On January 1, the beginning of the financial year, the books reflected the fixed asset position as follows:

|  | Machinery and Plant | Motor Vechicles |
|---|---|---|
|  | £ | £ |
| Cost plus additions to date | 45,500 | 6,600 |
| Aggregate depreciation to date | 21,250 | 2,150 |

During the year additional purchases of £3200 were made to the machinery, and an old vehicle, bought two years before for £2500, was sold for £1500 (shortly before the end of the trading year).

Write up (a) The plant account allowing for the continuing depreciation figure of 10 per cent on the reducing balance of the asset; (b) the motor vehicles account allowing for the continuing depreciation figure of 20 per cent on the reducing balance of the asset; and (c) the depreciation provision accounts for the two assets.

Show how these assets would appear on the balance sheet of the Company as at December 31, after the year-end adjustments.

**3.** Joan Curtis owes her garage £75 for repairs to her car. Her insurance company refuses to meet the claim. She offers the garage £25 and agrees to pay £5 a month for the next ten months. The garage proprietor agrees.

Miss Curtis pays three instalments and then is made bankrupt. Her trustee in bankruptcy pays the garage a composition of 20p in the £. There is to be no further distribution for unsecured creditors. The balance on the customer's account is written off as a bad debt.

Show the account of Miss Curtis and bad debts account in the books of the garage.

**4.** Edward Cann's provision for bad debts account stands at £150 on January 1.

By the end of the year he has written off two debtors' accounts amounting to £64, transferring their balances to bad debts account.

An amount of £15 has been recovered from a defaulter whose account was written off the previous year.

Trade debtors at December 31, the end of the trading year, stand at £6800. Mr Cann decides to increase his provision to 3 per cent of the total debtors for this year.

Show separate bad debts and provisions for bad debts accounts and also the entries affecting his balance sheet.

5. Jane Draper has a small gown shop but her credit trade is quite substantial. However, she makes an annual provision of 4 per cent of her total debtors to safeguard the likelihood of bad debts.

Her trade debtors at January 1 totalled £9500, and at December 31, the end of her trading year £8750.

The actual bad debts written off during the year amounted to £132, and a payment of £18 had been received from a Mrs Simpson (whose account was written off two years ago) who had now returned from the United States. A first and final dividend of 10p in £ had been received from the trustee in bankruptcy of a Mrs Florence Dalton, whose £40 account had been written off the year before.

From the above information, make up Jane Draper's bad debts and provision for bad debts accounts.

6. Angela Wray has a good little business, but has difficulty in reducing her bank overdraft by more than one hundred pounds or so occasionally. Fortunately, she has a sympathetic bank manager who realises that her premises are worth at least five times the balance sheet value.

This is her recent balance sheet:

| | | £ | | £ | £ |
|---|---|---|---|---|---|
| Capital Account July 1 | | 8,000 | Fixed assets | | |
| Net profit for year | | 3,000 | Premises at cost | 4,600 | |
| | | ——— | Machinery at cost | 2,400 | 7,000 |
| | | 11,000 | | | |
| Less: drawings | | 2,500 | Current assets | | |
| | | ——— | Stock | 1,800 | |
| | | 8,500 | Debtors | 2,500 | |
| | | | Cash | 100 | 4,400 |
| Trade creditors | 1,500 | | | ——— | |
| Bank overdraft | 1,400 | 2,900 | | | |
| | | 11,400 | | | 11,400 |

On the advice of her boy friend Jeremy, Angela decides to rearrange her balance sheet and try to develop her credit trade through more publicity and by enlisting the aid of nationwide suppliers and their showcards.

The following adjustments are made to the balance sheet to present a 'true and fair view' of her financial affairs:

(a) Premises are to be revalued at £20,000.
(b) Machinery and equipment is to be revalued at half its cost price (i.e. £1200) and application is to be made to the bank for a long-term loan or increased overdraft in order to buy modern plant and machinery.
(c) Stock is to be written down to £1500.

(d) A provision for bad debts is to be created at 4 per cent of the debtors' total to safeguard the increased credit trade.

(e) Machinery and equipment will in future be depreciated by 15 per cent on the reducing balance.

You are required to redraft the balance sheet of Miss Wray, giving full effect to these adjustments.

# YEAR-END ADJUSTMENTS

The reason and purpose for the making of certain adjustments at the end of the trading period is to arrive at the correct trading profit and to show, as far as possible, the true financial position on the balance sheet.

We have already dealt with some adjustments. The commonest one is closing stock, brought to the credit of trading account at the year-end and debited to stock (asset) account and shown as part of the property of the business on the balance sheet. In the last chapter, too, there were adjustments in connection with depreciation and bad debts provision.

## 17.1 EXPENSES OWING OR ACCRUED

Typical expenses under this heading are wages and salaries due at the year-end, but not yet paid; and outstanding accounts for electricity, gas and printing, etc. Ordinary trade creditors' accounts are not included in this category, as they have already been listed separately.

## 17.2 WAGES OWING

If money is owing to work-people at the year-end, they become (temporarily) creditors of their employers and the sum due to them must be added to the wages bill for the year. This often happens when the last day of the old year is at the beginning or in the middle of the working week, wages normally being paid on a Thursday or a Friday.

The following accounts are self-explanatory:

Wages Account

| | | £ | | | £ |
|---|---|---|---|---|---|
| Dec. 31 | Cash Book or Wages Book total paid during year | 8500 | Dec. 31 | Transfer to Trading Account | 8750 |
| 31 | Creditors for wages c/d | 250 | | | |
| | | 3750 | | | 8750 |
| | | | Jan. 1 | Balance b/d | 250 |

Trading Account for the year

| | £ | £ | | | |
|---|---|---|---|---|---|
| Wages | 8500 | | | | |
| Add: wages owing | 250 | 8750 | | | |

Balance Sheet as at Dec. 31

| Current liabilities | | |
|---|---|---|
| | £ | |
| Trade creditors | - | |
| Expense creditors | | |
| Wages owing | 250 | |

*Note.* The credit balance shown on wages account at January 1, being the amount due to employees, will be absorbed or cancelled by the first wages payment made in the New Year.

## 17.3 RENT ACCRUED OR OWING

In the rent account shown below, the rent has been paid for the first three quarters of the year, but was not paid for the fourth quarter until January 8 in the New Year. Consequently, the amount owing to the landlord at December 31, the close of the financial year, must be shown as a current liability in the balance sheet. Nevertheless, in so far as working out the profit on the year's trading, the full rent expense for the year is chargeable.

Rent Account (£1000 a year)

| | | | £ | | | | £ |
|---|---|---|---|---|---|---|---|
| Mar. 31 | Cheque | | 250 | Dec. 31 | Profit & Loss Account - full rental for year | | 1000 |
| July 1 | " | | 250 | | | | |
| Oct. 5 | " | | 250 | | | | |
| Dec. 31 | Rent owing c/d | | 250 | | | | |
| | | | 1000 | | | | 1000 |
| | | | | Jan. 1 | Creditor for rent | | 250 |

The full annual rental is £1000, which is charged to profit and loss account. The payment for the final quarter is delayed but nevertheless the amount outstanding must be included as part of the total expense. The payment made on January 8 in the New Year settles the amount outstanding.

Profit and Loss Account

| | £ | £ | | | | |
|---|---|---|---|---|---|---|
| Rent paid | 750 | | | | | |
| <u>Add</u>: rent owing | 250 | 1000 | | | | |

Balance Sheet as at December 31

| | £ | | |
|---|---|---|---|
| <u>Current liabilities</u> | | | |
| Trade creditors | - | | |
| Expense creditors | | | |
| Rent owing | 250 | | |

## 17.4 PAYMENTS IN ADVANCE (OR PRE-PAYMENTS)

These are benefits still to be received – for payments made but not yet used up. Consequently, the charge to profit and loss account must be reduced, and the amount not yet used up brought down as an asset and shown among the current assets on the balance sheet.

## 17.5 INSURANCE PAID IN ADVANCE

In this illustration an annual premium of £60 is paid on April 1 against fire and theft risks. The firm's financial year closes on December 31, which means that *one-quarter of the premium already paid is not used up* at the date of the balance sheet. It is dealt with in this way in the accounts and on the balance sheet:

Insurance Account

| Apr. 1 | Cheque | £ 60 | Dec. 31 | Profit & Loss A/c | £ 45 |
|---|---|---|---|---|---|
| | | | 31 | Amount paid in advance c/d | 15 |
| | | 60 | | | 60 |
| Jan. 1 | Balance b/d (insce pre-paid) | 15 | | | |

Profit and Loss Account

| | £ | | | |
|---|---|---|---|---|
| Insurance | | | | |
| <u>Less</u>: amount | 60 | | | |
| pre-paid | 15 | 45 | | |

Balance Sheet as at December 31

| | Current assets | |
|---|---|---|
| | | £ |
| | Insurance pre-paid | 15 |

The £60 premium is the first insurance payment, covering twelve months to April 1 the following year. In the next year and future years the full annual sum of £60 will be debited against profits, but £15 will always be carried forward as 'paid in advance' as long as this particular policy is operative.

Among other adjustments at the end of the financial year will be those affecting any loan or mortgage interest, and commissions both owing and to be received. Sometimes, too, part of a large advertising campaign may be carried forward, as the payment may have been made near to the end of the financial year, and yet the benefit may well be felt for several months.

The important thing to remember with regard to all adjustments is that there must be a carry-forward on the account affected, which also appears as a current asset or a current liability on the balance sheet.

**Illustration**              Final Accounts and Adjustments

Trial Balance December 31

| | £ | £ |
|---|---|---|
| Capital Jan. 1 | | 8,240 |
| Drawings | 2,000 | |
| Machinery Jan. 1 | 4,000 | |
| Van Jan. 1 | 600 | |
| Stock Jan. 1 | 1,200 | |
| Purchases and sales | 3,608 | 9,895 |
| Returns | 125 | 86 |
| Discounts | 293 | 351 |
| Rent and rates | 940 | |
| Carriage on purchases | 92 | |
| Carriage on sales | 142 | |
| Bad debts | 48 | |
| Trade debtors | 1,580 | |
| Trade creditors | | 1,304 |
| Heating | 154 | |
| General expenses | 78 | |
| Advertising | 134 | |
| Bad debts provision | | 100 |
| Office salaries | 2,350 | |
| Warehouse wages | 2,440 | |
| Bank overdraft | | 364 |
| Cash in hand | 56 | |
| Fittings Jan. 1 | 500 | |
| | 20,340 | 20,340 |

Prepare a trading and profit and loss account for the year ended December 31 and a balance sheet as at December 31, taking the following information into account:

(a) Stock on hand, December 31 £1450.

(b) Warehouse wages owing £40; monthly salaries owing £88.

(c) Rates pre-paid £60. Insurance (included in General Expenses) pre-paid £15.

(d) Bad debts provision to be reduced to 5 per cent of the debtors.

(e) The proprietor had taken £100 of goods from the business for his own use.

(f) Depreciate machinery by 15 per cent; vans by 20 per cent; Fittings by £25.

(g) Charge 50 per cent of the heating expense to trading account.

## Model answer

Trading and Profit and Loss Account
for the year ended December 31

| | £ | £ | | £ | £ |
|---|---|---|---|---|---|
| Stock Jan. 1 | | 1200 | Sales | 9895 | |
| Purchases | 3608 | | | | |
| Add: carriage inwards | 92 | | Less: returns in | 125 | 9770 |
| | 3700 | | | | |
| Less: returns out 86 | | | | | |
| and goods with- | | | | | |
| drawn for own use 100 | 186 | 3514 | | | |
| | | 4714 | | | |
| Less: Stock Dec. 31 | | 1450 | | | |
| | | 3264 | | | |
| Warehouse wages | 2440 | | | | |
| Wages owing | 40 | 2480 | | | |
| Heating (50%) | | 77 | | | |
| Gross profit c/d | | 3949 | | | |
| | | 9770 | | | 9770 |
| Discounts allowed | | 293 | Gross profit b/d | | 3949 |
| Rent and rates | 940 | | Discounts received | | 351 |
| Less: pre-paid | 60 | 880 | Decrease in bad debts | | |
| Carriage on sales | | 142 | provision | | 21 |
| Bad debts | | 48 | Net Loss to | | |
| Heating (50%) | | 77 | Capital Account | | 499 |
| General expenses | 78 | | | | |
| Less: pre-paid insce | 15 | 63 | | | |
| Advertising | | 134 | | | |
| Office salaries | 2350 | | | | |
| Add: salaries owing | 88 | 2438 | | | |
| Depreciation: | | | | | |
| Machinery | 600 | | | | |
| Van | 120 | | | | |
| Fittings | 25 | 745 | | | |
| | | 4820 | | | 4820 |

Balance Sheet as at December 31

| Capital and liabilities | £ | £ | £ | Fixed assets | £ | £ | £ |
|---|---|---|---|---|---|---|---|
| Capital account | | | | Machinery | | 4000 | |
| Balance Jan. 1 | | 8240 | | Less: deprec. | | 600 | 3400 |
| | | | | | | | |
| Less: drawings | 2100 | | | Van | | 600 | |
| and net loss | | | | Less: deprec. | | 120 | 480 |
| on trading | 499 | 2599 | | | | | |
| | | | 5641 | Fittings | | 500 | |
| | | | | Less: deprec. | | 25 | 475 |
| Current liabilities | | | | | | | 4355 |
| | | | | | | | |
| Trade creditors | | 1304 | | Current assets | | | |
| Bank overdraft | | 364 | | | | | |
| Accruals | | | | Stock Dec. 31 | | 1450 | |
| Salaries | 88 | | | Debtors | 1580 | | |
| Wages | 40 | 128 | | Less: provision | 79 | 1501 | |
| | | | 1796 | Prepayments | | 75 | |
| | | | | Cash in hand | | 56 | |
| | | | | | | | 3082 |
| | | | 7437 | | | | 7437 |

*Note* (a) The owner of this business withdrew supplies totalling £100 for his own use. He reduces his purchases available for sale and benefits personally, so the adjustment is:

Debit to Drawings A/c and credit to Purchases A/c

increasing drawings and reducing purchases.

(b) The new provision is £79 (5 per cent of £1580) which is a reduction of £21 on the old provision of £100. The excess of £21 no longer required is now *credited back* to profit and loss account, and the new provision, a credit balance in the books, is deducted from debtors in the balance sheet.

## QUESTIONS

1. Adjust the three nominal accounts mentioned underneath to show the correct debit to trading or profit and loss account at the end of the financial year.

(a) Total wages paid £128,700. The financial year ends on a Tuesday, December 31. Wages owing to workmen (from the previous Thursday) amount to £2800.

(b) The rates account shows a debit of £360 on December 31, but £180 of this amount covers the half-year period to March 31 in the new year.

(c) At the end of the financial year there is a debit of £24 on insurance account. A comprehensive premium to cover theft and fire had been paid on March 1 for twelve months.

2. (a) The rateable value of Deborah Sayle's premises, occupied from April 1, is £240. The current rate in the £ of the local authority for the year ending March 31 is 80p, unchanged from the previous year.

Half-yearly rates have been paid by Miss Sayle on May 8 and October 12 in this particular year. Her own financial accounting period ends on December 31. You are required to make up her rates account to show the net debit to profit and loss account.

From the following figures in your rent account, say which property you own and which property you rent:

(b)

Rent Account

| | | £ | | | £ |
|---|---|---|---|---|---|
| Mar. 31 | Cash - quarter's rent of 32 Main Street | 120.00 | Mar. 30 | Cash - quarter's rent of 35 Main Street | 150.00 |

3. The following details, with regard to electricity consumed, were extracted from the records of John Chapman, a professional man, whose normal trading year ended on December 31.

On January 1, one year before, an amount of £32.30 was owing to the Midlands Electricity Board for the last quarter of the previous year.

During the past year these payments had been made:

| | £ | | £ |
|---|---|---|---|
| January 6 | 32.30 | April 8 | 36.40 |
| July 10 | 18.60 | October 5 | 12.70 |

The account for the last quarter, recently concluded, was £23.90, but this was not received until January 9 in the New Year. Make up the electricity account, showing the full debit to profit and loss account.

4. The actual amounts paid on several nominal accounts are shown on the left of the statement below. These are the debits taken from the nominal ledger to the trial balance at the end of the financial year.

On the right-hand side are the adjustments needed to ensure the correct charge against the year-end profits.

|     |               | £      |                | £   |
|-----|---------------|--------|----------------|-----|
| (a) | Rent          | 840    | Rent owing     | 280 |
| (b) | Rates         | 360    | In advance     | 120 |
| (c) | Wages         | 16,650 | Wages owing    | 440 |
| (d) | Loan interest | 150    | Due            | 150 |
| (e) | Stationery    | 125    | Unpaid account | 15  |
| (f) | Insurance     | 80     | In advance     | 40  |
| (g) | Advertising   | 450    | Carry forward  | 200 |
| (h) | Electricity   | 380    | Unpaid account | 108 |

Show how these adjustments are made on each nominal account and also how the balance sheet will be affected.

5. How would each of the following affect the *gross profit* of a business after the required adjustment has been made? Give your answer in columnar form using three columns for (a) Increase (b) Decrease and (c) No effect.

(a) Closing stock was undervalued by £250.
(b) Machinery account has been debited with £12 repairs.
(c) Carriage outwards £66 had been credited to trading account.
(d) The proprietor had taken £50 of goods for his own use, and no entry had been made in the books.
(e) Sales returns of £15 had been entered on the personal account but not taken off sales account.
(f) The final stock included £85 goods received on December 30, but the invoice had not yet been sent by the supplier.
(g) Warehouse wages of £450 were debited to profit and loss account and the salary of the chief storeman £2500 had been included in office salaries.
(h) Commissions received £150 had been credited to profit and loss account.

6. Andrew Carson's final accounts show a net profit of £2,250 but the following errors and omissions are found later by his auditors. You are asked to make up an amended statement of profit and loss.

(a) Closing stock had been undervalued by £240.
(b) Rates in advance £120 were not taken into account.
(c) No adjustment had been made for wages owing £180.
(d) Bank charges of £10 had been overlooked.
(e) The cost of a second-hand machine had been charged (£300) against profits.
(f) Notification had recently been received of a customer's bankruptcy. The debtor owed £40 and his Trustee intimated that 25p in the £

might be paid. It was considered advisable to reserve against this likely loss.

7. Make up the complete final accounts of Felicity Jones for the year ended June 30 from the following balances, at the same time taking into account the adjustments shown as a footnote.

Trial Balance June 30

|  | £ | £ |
|---|---|---|
| Capital   July 1 |  | 5,800 |
| Drawings for year | 2,620 |  |
| Machinery at cost | 5,250 |  |
| Provision for machinery account |  | 3,000 |
| Fittings | 254 |  |
| Cash | 24 |  |
| Bank overdraft |  | 325 |
| Trade debtors and creditors | 2,375 | 2,284 |
| Provision for bad debts |  | 100 |
| Purchases and sales | 6,800 | 17,222 |
| Returns inwards and outwards | 220 | 180 |
| Discounts allowed and received | 175 | 144 |
| Wages | 5,430 |  |
| Salaries | 3,720 |  |
| Rent and rates | 1,200 |  |
| Carriage outwards | 88 |  |
| Advertising | 450 |  |
| Insurance | 75 |  |
| Miscellaneous expenses | 60 |  |
| Bad debts | 44 |  |
| Commissions received |  | 1,600 |
| Stock   July 1 | 1,870 |  |
|  | 30,655 | 30,655 |

Closing stock at June 30 was £2580.

Depreciation of machinery 10 per cent on reducing balance.

Rates in advance £90   :   insurance in advance £25.

Wages owing at June 30 £105   :   salaries owing £66.

Bad debts provision to be reduced to 4 per cent of the debtors.

Carry forward one-third of the advertising debit.

Miss Jones, in addition to her drawings in cash, had also withdrawn goods for family use, amounting to £125.

8. Prepare the trading and profit and loss account for the month of June, and a balance sheet at June 30, from the following balances extracted from the books of A. Corn, master baker, taking note of the adjustments shown as a footnote.

Trial Balance June 30

|  | £ | £ |
|---|---|---|
| Capital of Mr Corn |  | 5000 |
| Cash in hand at June 30 | 25 |  |
| Balance at bank | 475 |  |
| Trade debtors/creditors | 374 | 284 |
| Purchases/sales | 2300 | 4000 |
| Carriage inwards | 22 |  |
| "       outwards | 32 |  |
| Discounts allowed/received | 20 | 58 |
| Wages | 850 |  |
| Salaries | 430 |  |
| Telephone | 32 |  |
| Drawings | 120 |  |
| Rent and rates | 74 |  |
| Stock   June 1 | 1222 |  |
| Commissions earned |  | 418 |
| Machinery and plant | 3500 |  |
| Fittings and fixtures | 304 |  |
| Returns inwards/outwards | 40 | 60 |
|  | 9820 | 9820 |

*Adjustments*

(a)  Stock at June 30 £1450.
(b)  Depreciate Machinery and Plant by 20 per cent.
(c)  The amount paid in advance for rates was £30.
(d)  Wages owing at month-end £40.
(e)  Telephone account unpaid at June 30 £18.

9.  The following adjustments are to be taken into account in making up the final accounts of The Record Shop for the month of June:

Stock was valued at the month end at £12,666.
The proprietor agreed that he had 'acquired' £72 worth of his record stock for his personal use.
There was a stationary account owing of £18 at June 30, and rates paid in advance amounted to £42.

These are the balances extracted for the month of June:

Trial Balance   June 30

|  | £ | £ |
|---|---|---|
| Capital Account | | 12,800 |
| Sales of recordings | | 15,000 |
| Recording equipment | 5,000 | |
| Office expenses | 2,222 | |
| Office furniture | 844 | |
| Petty cash | 22 | |
| Bank balance | 2,123 | |
| Trade debtors/creditors | 1,828 | 1,335 |
| Supplies bought | 1,914 | |
| Stock of records June 1 | 10,806 | |
| Bad debts | 238 | |
| Stamps and stationery | 87 | |
| Telephone charges | 49 | |
| Wages of technicians | 2,445 | |
| Drawings | 1,000 | |
| Discounts allowed | 375 | |
| Rent and rates | 182 | |
| | 29,135 | 29,135 |

**10.** John Smith is a Stafford wholesaler. His financial position on January 1 was as follows:

| | £ | | £ |
|---|---|---|---|
| Cash in hand | 10.71 | Bank balance | 2464.17 |
| Delivery van | 500.00 | Fittings and fixtures | 370.98 |
| Stock of goods | 4517.81 | | |

Money was owing to him by:

| H. Brown | £750.94 |
|---|---|
| J. Robinson | £270.66 |
| B. Jones | £175.41 |

The outstanding liabilities of John Smith at January 1 consisted of two creditors' accounts:

| S. Johnson | £970.88 |
|---|---|
| L. Green & Co. | £1189.80 |

There was also a long-term loan of £3000 advanced to him by H. Jackson five years ago, and bearing interest at the rate of 6 per cent per annum.

Transactions during the month of January are shown in detail, and your instructions are given underneath.

January
2   Paid back £1000 of loan to H. Jackson
4   Credit sales to H. Brown £349.30

5    Cash sales paid direct to bank £381.71

8    Received cheque from Brown for £730, allowing him discount of £20.94

12   Sold J. Robinson £147 worth of goods

13   Cash sales paid direct to bank £586.59

14   Paid £40 insurance

18   Paid L. Green & Co.'s account in full less discount they allowed of £49.80

19   Bought some goods from S. Johnson £200

23   Cheque received from the trustee in bankruptcy of B. Jones (notified as bankrupt in December) for £87.72 as the first and final dividend

25   Bought from L. Green & Co. £252 worth of stock

29   Cash sales £742.36. Paid into bank the next day

30   Cashed cheque for office cash £150. Various expenses paid in cash, viz. Wages £138.82, Carriage on sales £22.33, and Van expenses £12.91

31   Paid wife's account for new anorak £27.50 and drew £50 in cash for household expenses.

All cheques received were paid into bank the day of receipt.

Your assignment is to open the books by journal entry, and post all transactions to ledger accounts. Enter all transactions for the month of January, and extract a trial balance at January 31. Finally, prepare trading and profit and loss accounts for the month ended January 31 and a balance sheet as at January 31, taking the following adjustments into account:

(a)   the interest accrued on the loan

(b)   rent due to the landlord £25

(c)   insurance paid in advance £20

(d)   reserve 5% on debtors for possible bad debts

(e)   depreciate van by 10 per cent on book value

(f)   stock on hand at January 31 £3335.

# COMPREHENSION AND INTERPRETATION

## 18.1 THE MEANING OF THE BALANCE SHEET

To the ordinary man in the street a balance sheet does not mean very much. He might see a big bank balance and a lot of property and stock, and assume that it is a good business; but if he spots a bank overdraft or some long-term loans he could just as easily form the reverse conclusion. To many others the balance sheet is merely a double list of figures, with totals of corresponding amounts.

But to the accountant and trained businessman a balance sheet has a story to tell. Each group of figures means something, indicating what has happened in the past, and probably what is likely to happen in the future. When these figures are compared with those of earlier years, or against

Balance Sheet of a sole trader (a garage)
as at 31 December

| Capital Account | £ | £ | Fixed assets | £ | £ |
|---|---|---|---|---|---|
| Balance  Jan. 1 | 9,000 | | Goodwill at cost | 2,000 | |
| Add:  profit for year | 3,300 | | Premises at cost | 5,000 | |
| | | | Machinery | 2,600 | |
| | 12,300 | | Van | 850 | |
| Less:  drawings | 3,000 | 9,300 | Fixtures/tools | 250 | 10,700 |
| Fixed liability | | | Current assets | | |
| Mortgage, secured on premises | | 4,000 | Stock  Dec. 31 | 2,400 | |
| | | | Trade debtors | 1,500 | |
| Current liabilities | | | Cash at bank | 680 | |
| | | | Cash in hand | 20 | 4,600 |
| Trade creditors | 1,800 | | | | |
| Expense creditors | 200 | 2,000 | | | |
| | | 15,300 | | | 15,300 |

those of competitors, forecasts can be made of a firm's good health or its retarded development.

The balance sheet is something more than two rows of figures balanced up by the capital account. Let us examine carefully the balance sheet of a sole trader, the proprietor of a small garage, and consider what the story might by *behind the figures.*

## 18.2 CAPITAL OF PROPRIETORSHIP

The 'capital owned' by a sole trader is his personal account in the eyes of the business, £9300 in this instance. A large capital will be represented by correspondingly large assets, a good thing provided that the assets are fully utilised and not grossly over-valued. It will be seen that the garage owner has increased his claim and holding in the business by £300 during the past year, the amount of excess profit over his drawings.

## 18.3 LOAN CAPITAL

There is a mortgage loan due to an outside party, which may have been negotiated at the time the garage was acquired by its present proprietor. There should be terms in writing for repayment of the loan, and concerning interest charges unless it is perhaps a private family loan. The main questions here are (a) is the interest being paid regularly and (b) could a cheaper form of finance be found? The mortgage charge on the security of the premises should be adequate on account of the inflationary value of all forms of property.

## 18.4 TRADE AND EXPENSE CREDITORS

Normally shown separately, trade creditors is the listed detail of suppliers' unpaid accounts at the period close, whereas expense creditors refers to amounts owing for general utility services such as rates and electricity, and perhaps wages and salaries due to employees at the balance sheet date.

## 18.5 FIXED AND CURRENT ASSETS

### (a) Fixed assets
Goodwill (the amount paid to the previous owner or vendor over or in excess of the valuation of the property and stock taken over) is still shown at its original figure, which is probably misleading. It would be better to gradually write off this intangible asset against profits over a few years. Alternatively, goodwill could be offset against the increased value of the premises, which, presumably, would realise a higher price now than their

book value of a few years ago, in particular if the site is well-positioned to attract the attention of car users.

The machinery will include various electrical appliances as aids for car repairs and servicing. Its valuation is not stated, whether it is still shown at cost or whether adequate depreciation has been written off against profits. New and modern replacements may soon be needed, requiring heavy capital expense. What is being done about old and obsolete pieces of equipment? Are they being written down and taken out of the books, and sold as scrap, or are they cluttering up the place in dark and untidy corners?

Capital invested in expensive plant must be made to work. The earning power of the capital falls if machinery is left standing idle, as the heavy depreciation expense is not being recouped out of revenue.

The motor van is probably used as a break-down truck, and, like the machinery, may be in good serviceable condition or in need of extensive repair and possible replacement (at a much increased price) before long.

### (b) Current assets
The main thing about current assets is that there should be a sensible apportionment between stock, debtors and cash, making the working capital a realistic one.

### (c) Stock
Is the stock figure too high? What is its proportion to sales? Too much money tied up in stock means less money to take advantage of good discounts. There is always the likelihood of deterioration and spoilage through carrying excessive stocks.

On the other hand, if the average stock carried is inadequate, business will be lost. A low stock figure at balancing date may be due to the state of the market, lack of funds, the restriction of credit facilities, or to abnormal sales just before the annual stock-taking.

It is a sound policy to value stock at its purchase or cost price, unless a severe drop in the market value warrants a *still lower figure.*

### (d) Trade debtors
This total refers to the money owing to the garage for repair work, servicing and the purchase of oil and petrol on credit. It may be interesting to inquire what credit facilities are available to customers, and ascertain if there is a marked increase of debtors' totals over the year. If the increase is proportionate to the increase in turnover, and also due to general price rises, there is little cause for concern providing the big debtors are still paying their accounts regularly. In some businesses the offer of a small cash discount might get the money in more quickly, but with the competition for petrol and oil, profit margins seldom warrant a discount for settlement of these accounts.

**(e) Cash and bank**

Is there any system of cash control in force? Is the 'cash float' or the petty cash subject to a regular check, and are the cash sales or daily takings paid into the bank day by day? Providing the bank balance averages a few hundred pounds (sufficient for routine expenses and wages) could not part of it be placed temporarily on deposit account? Deposit money earns good interest, and banks no longer insist upon a week's notice for transfer of money back from the firm's deposit to the current account.

## 18.6 BUSINESS PROFITS AND LOSSES

When a trading profit is made, assets are increased or the liabilities are reduced, either in cash or book debts. An increase of assets means an increase of capital.

This is always shown, in the case of a small trader, by the addition of the profit to his capital account.

Conversely, a business loss shows a reduction of net assets with a corresponding decrease of capital account.

When profits are retained in the business, both capital and net assets show corresponding increases. This is another aspect of capital. It is something saved, reserved and put on one side for the benefit of the business, and later perhaps used to purchase new machinery, replace worn-out assets, or to buy larger stocks at higher discounts.

## 18.7 HOW PROFIT IS REPRESENTED BY ADDITIONAL ASSETS

A business was started on January 1 with £2000. Trade purchases and expenses during January amounted to £560. Fixed assets were bought for £1600. Net sales for the month totalled £640, and the stock of goods unsold was valued at £300.

*Ascertainment of profit*

|  | £ |
|---|---|
| Net sales for the month | 640 |
| *Add*: stock at January 31 | 300 |
|  | 940 |
| *Less*: purchases and expenses | 560 |
| Profit for month | 380 |

A balance sheet drawn up on January 31, with the exclusion of trade debtors, creditors and proprietor's drawings, would emphasise the point made about retained profit being represented by net assets:

Balance Sheet as at January 31

| | £ | £ | | £ | £ |
|---|---|---|---|---|---|
| Capital Jan. 1 | 2000 | | Fixed assets | | 1600 |
| Add: profit for month | 380 | 2380 | Current assets<br>  Stock<br>  Bank | 300<br>480 | <br><br>780 |
| | | 2380 | | | 2380 |

The profit made for the month (£380) is represented by a corresponding increase of net assets.

## 18.8 STATISTICS FOR MANAGEMENT

The relationship between gross profit and turnover is important. In many instances a fixed percentage is added to the cost of the goods to arrive at the selling price. This is known as the 'mark-up' percentage. It varies with the different trades, being low in the grocery and provision trade, and high in the automobile and furniture trade. Car factors and furniture retailers have to allow for the heavy expense of large showrooms and salesmen's commissions.

### Cost of sales

A simple form of trading account is now shown to illustrate some bases of comparison, to do with gross profit percentages, cost of sales and rate of stock turnover.

Trading Account
for the month of September

| | £ | | £ |
|---|---|---|---|
| Stock 1 September<br>Purchases less returns | 1,600<br>9,400 | Sales less returns | 12,000 |
| | 11,000 | (net turnover to cash<br>and credit customers) | |
| Less: Stock 30 Sep. | 2,000 | | |
| COST OF SALES<br>Gross profit for month | 9,000<br>3,000 | | |
| | 12,000 | | 12,000 |

The cost of sales (or cost of the goods sold) is worked out on the debit of trading account, and will, of course, be increased by other expenses such as wages and carriage inwards. Note that the cost of sales is not the same as goods bought or purchases, as the stock at the end of the trading period *includes recent purchases.*

## 18.9  GROSS PROFIT PERCENTAGES

Trading results of different periods may be compared by expressing gross profits as percentages of relative turnovers. In the example shown the percentage is worked out thus:

$$\frac{\text{Gross profit}}{\text{Sales}} \times 100, \text{ i.e. } \frac{3,000}{12,000} \times 100 = 25 \text{ per cent}$$

Investigations should be made where there is a wide variation of the gross profit percentage.

## 18.10  RATE OF STOCK TURNOVER

Profits should increase if the rate of stock turnover can be increased.

The number of times the stock can be turned over in the course of a month or a year has a direct bearing upon the gross profit.

The *rate of stock turnover* is found by dividing the *cost of sales* by the *average stock.*

The average stock on the trading account illustrated is:

$$\text{£}1600 + 2000 = \frac{3600}{2} = 1800.$$

The rate of stock turnover will then be:

$$\frac{\text{Cost of sales}}{\text{Average stock}} = \frac{9000}{1800} = 5 \text{ times in a month.}$$

Compare these two businesses:

|  | Average stock | Stock turn | Mark up % on cost |
|---|---|---|---|
| Business A | £1000 | 6 times a year | 40 |
| Business B | £1000 | 3 times a year | 35 |

The second business is not only increasing its turnover by selling at a lower cost. It is also making £400 a year more gross profit, as shown by these workings:

*Business* A

Stock turnover £1000 × 6 = 6000 × 40% = £2400 gross profit

*Business* B

Stock turnover £1000 × 8 = 8000 × 35% = £2800 gross profit

### 18.11  CLAIMS FOR LOSS OF STOCK

When stock is destroyed, perhaps by fire or flood, the claim made on the insurance company must be based on whatever figures are available. If the financial books have been destroyed the previous years' figures will be used as a guide, together with certified statements from suppliers or manufacturers. A trading account is then made up from the date of the last balance sheet to the date of the destruction of the stock.

### Example

Robert Armstrong's stock of goods was destroyed by fire on March 31, except for a salvaged amount valued at £500. Normally his accounts were prepared to December 31. The following figures were obtained from available records:

|                                       | £      |
|---------------------------------------|--------|
| Stock at January 1                    | 2,400  |
| Purchases (January 1 to March 31)     | 8,200  |
| Carriage on purchases                 | 150    |
| Warehousing wages                     | 6,500  |
| Sales (January 1 to March 31)         | 18,000 |

It was ascertained from the trading accounts of the previous five years that Armstrong's average percentage of gross profit to turnover was 30 per cent.

Trading Account for the three months ended March 31

| | £ | £ | | £ |
|---|---|---|---|---|
| Stock Jan. 1 | | 2,400 | Sales for three months | |
| Purchases | 8200 | | to March 31 | 18,000 |
| Carriage inwards | 150 | 8,350 | Final stock figure | |
| Wages | | 6,500 | (difference on account) | 4,650 |
| Gross profit (estimated | | | | |
| at 30% of £18,000) | | 5,400 | | |
| | | 22,650 | | 22,650 |

| Estimated stock at March 31 | £4650 |
|---|---|
| *Less*: value salvaged | 500 |
| Insurance claim | £4150 |

## 18.12 IMPORTANT RATIOS

In addition to the commonest form of ratio already described (gross profit to turnover) the following ratios are put to important use in the world of finance:

### (a) Working capital or current assets to current liabilities

This concerns the liquidity of the business and its ability to pay its routine trading operations and take full advantage of discounts obtainable. A ratio of 2:1 is ideal under normal circumstances, dropping to 1:1 at the month-end when the main suppliers' accounts are paid.

*Example.* $\dfrac{\text{Current assets}}{\text{Current liabilities}} \quad \dfrac{£10{,}000}{£5{,}000} = \text{ratio of 2:1}$

A low ratio means lack of working capital, and a high ratio might indicate that there is too much capital locked up in stock, debtors and cash.

### (b) Quick assets or acid test

Quick assets refer to cash, bank, debtors and investments that can quickly be realised, such as immediate withdrawals from building societies. The ratio of these assets to current liabilities gives a clear indication of the firm's ability to meet its urgent obligations.

*Example.* $\dfrac{\text{Quick assets}}{\text{Current liabilities}} \quad \dfrac{£6000}{£5000} = 6{:}5$

This would normally be regarded as quite a good ratio.

### (c) Average credit or debtors to sales

The ratio is multiplied by 12 (months) to give the average number of months' credit allowed.

*Example.* $\dfrac{\text{Debtors}}{\text{Sales}} \quad \dfrac{£2{,}500}{£15{,}000} \times 12 = 2 \text{ months' credit.}$

The average credit allowed by suppliers can be calculated in the same way (creditors to purchases).

**(d) Net earnings or net profit to capital employed**

Capital employed is the total real assets (which would exclude a grossly inflated goodwill still a debit balance in the books). It also sometimes is interpreted as excluding debtors, as the firm is temporarily deprived of the use of the money owing by credit customers.

*Example.* $\dfrac{\text{Net trading profit}}{\text{Capital employed}} \quad \dfrac{£3,500}{£17,500} \times 100 = 20 \text{ per cent.}$

## QUESTIONS

1. The trading account details for the past two years of Frank Sorrel's business are shown below:

|  | Year 1 £ | Year 2 £ |
|---|---|---|
| Net purchases | 6,700 | 8,000 |
| Net sales | 10,000 | 12,300 |
| Commencing stock at cost price | 1,200 | 1,400 |
| Closing stock at cost price | 1,400 | 1,600 |

Make up a trading account with comparative colums on each side to show the cost of the goods sold (cost of sales), and give the gross profit percentage on turnover for each year.

Calculate the rate of stock turnover and compare the results of the two years.

2. Study the following balance sheet of Richard Telford and then answer the questions printed underneath:

Balance Sheet as at December 31

| | £ | £ | | £ | £ |
|---|---|---|---|---|---|
| Capital Jan. 1 | 26,500 | | Fixed assets | | |
| Net profit | 4,900 | | Machinery at cost | 20,000 | |
| | ——— | | Less: depreciation | 5,000 | 15,000 |
| | 31,400 | | | | ——— |
| Less: drawings | 4,000 | 27,400 | Investments | | |
| | ——— | | 9% Treasury Stock | | |
| Current liabilities | | | (current value £7500) | | 10,000 |
| Trade creditors | 1,360 | | | | |
| Crs. for wages | 240 | 1,600 | Current assets | | |
| | ——— | | Stock | 2,000 | |
| | | | Debtors | 1,500 | |
| | | | Bank/cash | 500 | 4,000 |
| | | ——— | | | ——— |
| | | 29,000 | | | 29,000 |
| | | ════ | | | ════ |

You are required to calculate:

(a) the working capital and the capital employed of this business
(b) the ratio of current assets to current liabilities
(c) the net earnings or net profit to capital employed as a percentage.

Also state what funds might be available for replacement of machinery in the near future, and the alternative forms of finance which might be sought.

3. How would each of the listed items below affect the gross profit of a business *after* the needed amendment or adjustment had been made?

Answer in columnar form, ticking appropriate columns headed 'Increase', 'Decrease' or 'No effect'.

(a) Jessica Hill had been invoiced £5 in error, the goods having been purchased by her sister Monica.
(b) Closing stock was deflated by £100 (its valuation should be £100 more).
(c) Carriage outwards £180 was, in the first instance, debited to trading account.
(d) The bought day book was overcast by £100 but this did not affect the arithmetical accuracy of the trial balance as a compensating error appeared on one of the big creditors' accounts.
(e) Sales returns of £25 had been entered in the returns book but not posted to the credit of the customer's account.
(f) Goods delivered by a wholesaler for £50 on the last day of the financial year had been taken into stock, but the invoice was not received until early in the New Year.

4. Amanda Stewart made up her own year-end accounts, but the Inland Revenue would not accept them, so she asked her accountant cousin to check them over and redraft them in a more acceptable form. Her cousin discovered a number of errors, listed below.

You are invited to study the items listed (a) to (f) and say to what extent, *after amendment,* they will affect the net trading profit, originally worked out at £4250.

(a) Closing stock has been over-valued by £150.
(b) A deposit of £400 for a second-hand car has been debited to Miss Stewart's profit and loss account.
(c) Bank charges of £15 on her last bank statement have not yet been entered in her cash book.
(d) No adjustment has been made for rates in advance £40 and for salaries owing at the year-end £60.
(e) A private golf club subscription of £30 has been charged to sundry expenses, and one of her home electricity bills (for £45) has been charged against the business.
(f) Miss Stewart had also taken goods for her own use and consumption (approximately 4120) during the year.

5. Comparative balance sheets are shown of Janetta Ross for the past two years:

Balance Sheets as at December 31

|  | Year 1 £ | Year 2 £ |  | Year 1 £ | Year 2 £ |
|---|---|---|---|---|---|
| Capital Account | 10,000 | 10,950 | Fixed assets |  |  |
| Net profit | 4,950 | 5,470 | Machinery | 8,000 | 7,200 |
|  |  |  | Fittings | 800 | 720 |
|  | 14,950 | 16,420 |  |  |  |
| Drawings | 4,000 | 5,000 | Current assets |  |  |
|  |  |  | Stock | 1,800 | 2,400 |
|  | 10,950 | 11,420 | Debtors | 2,200 | 2,600 |
|  |  |  | Bank | 750 | 400 |
| Trade creditors | 2,600 | 1,900 |  |  |  |
|  | 13,550 | 13,320 |  | 13,550 | 13,320 |

Your assignment is to consider the figures on the above balance sheets and comment generally upon the financial structure of this business. Is trade improving? What is the position with regard to credit accounts, both debtors and creditors? What about the liquid cash position? Would it not be wise for Miss Ross to reserve part of her drawings and start some kind of investment fund (gilt-edged securities or building society shares) with a view to replacing or modernising some of the machinery and equipment in use, which, of course, may be shown at an inflated value.

Calculate for both years:

(a) the working capital
(b) the percentage of current liabilities to current assets
(c) the percentage of sales to debtors on the basis of
        Year 1 sales £25,000  :  Year 2 sales £30,000.
(d) the net earnings of capital owned on a percentage basis.

6. A trader's stock is destroyed by fire on July 1, except for a small salvaged amount valued at £250.
His stock on January 1 (six months before) was £1800.

The purchases and sales figures for these six months were £6200 and £8800 respectively.

During the past two years he has worked on an average gross profit percentage to turnover of 25 per cent.

Calculate his insurance claim for the stock destroyed.

7. Janina Jones started in business with £2000 (her sole asset) on January 1. Rather unwisely she kept no proper records of her business transactions, and relied on her memory a good deal, in particular with regard to her credit customers. Her boy friend Charles, six months afterwards, listed her assets and liabilities as follows:

|  | £ |  | £ |
|---|---|---|---|
| Equipment/fittings | 1500 | Stock on hand | 1280 |
| Trade debtors | 1420 | Creditors | 880 |
| Cash and bank balances combined |  |  | 900 |

During these six months of trading Miss Jones had paid an additional £1000 into the business bank account, and Charles estimated that she had withdrawn £3400 for her private use. From this information you are required to calculate the approximate profit for the trading period.

# INCOMPLETE RECORDS AND SINGLE ENTRY

If accounting records are incomplete it makes good book-keeping difficult. Double entry, the complete system, cannot be used to advantage.

Final accounts made up from single-entry records often require a fair degree of approximation.

The single-entry system, or rather lack of system, used to be prevalent among many small traders, whose main business was 'cash over the counter'. The records also kept by small clubs and local societies were often incomplete, based largely on a rough form of cash book and perhaps a bank account. The Receipts and Payments Account described in the next chapter is an incomplete record; further information, analysis of payments and distinction between capital and revenue expenditure is necessary before presenting to members a more informative statement.

On the commercial side, neglecting to keep proper books could lead to tax evasion, although this may not be deliberate. The retailer used to rely a good deal on his memory, and it was only when the tax inspector began to over-assess him for income tax that he realised it was in his own interest to start keeping permanent and authentic records.

## 19.1 WHERE CASH RECORDS ARE AVAILABLE

Generally, some sort of cash book is kept, and also a bank account now by the majority of small traders. Some rough record will also be kept of credit customers, and statements from suppliers, when paid, will either be stuck on a hook or thrust away in a drawer. Often though, in very small businesses, there are no records of the present value of business assets, no cumulative record of purchases and sales, and no nominal or expense recorded totals at all.

When an accountant is called in to sort things out and perhaps put the trader on a more business-like basis, he will generally follow this procedure, with a fair amount of approximation where figures are missing and answers to his questions extremely vague.

(a) First he will reconcile the bank columns of the cash book with the bank statement, and then analyse all cash book items, preparing a Cash Summary for the year.

(b) The various nominal accounts can be opened and posted up from the cash book summary, completing that part of the double entry.

(c) Total accounts for debtors and creditors will be made up where credit is in operation. These total accounts have already been explained in Chapter 15. From these total accounts the credit purchases and credit sales for the trading period will be obtained and posted up to their respective accounts in the nominal ledger.

(d) An opening balance sheet (sometimes called a Statement of Affairs) is made out, probably with much approximation in so far as asset values are concerned. The commencing capital (say of one year back) is obtained in this way, being simply the difference between total estimated assets and total estimated liabilities at that particular date. Many discreet questions must be asked of the proprietor, such as:

'Where did you get the money for your new car?'
'How did you manage to find £5000 deposit on your new house?'

The answers to some of these questions may explain a huge cash discrepancy which will in due course be debited to drawings.

(e) When the double entry has been completed, a trial balance is taken out, year-end adjustments are made, and the first full set of accounts made up in the ordinary way.

### Single-entry illustration

John Brown's accountant summarised his client's cash book for the year ended December 31 thus:

| | £ | | £ |
|---|---|---|---|
| Balance b/f | 1,300 | Payments to suppliers | 3,300 |
| | | Wages | 4,200 |
| Cash takings for year | 8,500 | Drawings of J. Brown | 1,900 |
| | | Cash purchases | 270 |
| Money received from | | New counter | 150 |
| credit customers | 940 | Insurance | 30 |
| | | Rates | 280 |
| | | General expenses | 48 |
| | | Balance c/d | 562 |
| | 10,740 | | 10,740 |
| Balance b/d | 562 | | |

John Brown's statement of affairs at January 1, the beginning of the year, is shown here:

| | £ | | £ |
|---|---|---|---|
| Capital | 16,350 | Premises at cost | 13,000 |
| | | Fittings/equipment | 1,350 |
| Trade creditors | 620 | Stock Jan. 1 | 440 |
| | | Trade debtors | 880 |
| | | Cash and bank (combined) | 1,300 |
| | 16,970 | | 16,970 |

The position at the end of the trading year, December 31, with regard to John Brown's assets and liabilities was as follows:

Stock Dec. 31 £420 : Debtors £1170 : Creditors £830

A new refrigerator was bought for the shop costing £180 on December 20, the invoice to be settled in the New Year. £8 had been paid in advance for insurance and £70 for rates. Fixed assets at January 1, a year ago, were to be depreciated at 10 per cent. Wages owing at the year-end amounted to £55.

*Answer*    There is little difficulty in this type of question as long as credit purchases and credit sales are worked out on these lines:

Total Debtors

| | | £ | | | £ |
|---|---|---|---|---|---|
| Jan. 1 | Balance b/f | 880 | Dec. 31 | Cash paid by customers | 940 |
| Dec. 31 | CREDIT SALES | 1230 | 31 | Balance c/d | 1170 |
| | | 2110 | | | 2110 |
| Dec. 31 | Balance b/d | 1170 | | | |

Total Creditors

| | | £ | | | £ |
|---|---|---|---|---|---|
| Dec. 31 | Cash paid to suppliers | 3300 | Jan. 1 | Balance b/f | 620 |
| | Balance c/d | 830 | 31 | CREDIT PURCHASES | 3510 |
| | | 4130 | | | 4130 |
| | | | Dec. 31 | Balance b/d | 830 |

Trading and Profit and Loss Account
for the year ended December 31

| | £ | £ | | £ |
|---|---|---|---|---|
| Stock   Jan. 1 | | 440 | Credit sales | 1,230 |
| Credit purchases | | 3,510 | Cash sales | 8,500 |
| Cash purchases | | 270 | Stock   Dec. 31 | 420 |
| Wages | 4200 | | | |
| "   owing | 55 | 4,255 | | |
| Gross profit c/d | | 1,675 | | |
| | | 10,150 | | 10,150 |
| Insurance | 30 | | Gross profit b/d | 1,675 |
| Less: in advance | 8 | 22 | | |
| Rates | 280 | | | |
| Less: in advance | 70 | 210 | | |
| General expenses | | 48 | | |
| Deprec. equipment | | 135 | | |
| Net trading profit | | 1,260 | | |
| | | 1,675 | | 1,675 |

Balance Sheet of John Brown
as at December 31

| | £ | £ | | £ | £ |
|---|---|---|---|---|---|
| Capital Account | | | Premises at cost | | 13,000 |
| Balance Jan. 1 | 16,350 | | Fittings, etc. | 1,350 | |
| Add: Net profit | 1,260 | | Less: deprec. | 135 | |
| | 17,610 | | | 1,215 | |
| Less: drawings | 1,900 | 15,710 | Additions | 330 | 1,545 |
| Current liabilities | | | Current assets | | |
| Trade creditors | 1,010 | | Stock Dec. 31 | 420 | |
| Wages owing | 55 | 1,065 | Debtors | 1,170 | |
| | | | Prepayments | 78 | |
| | | | Cash/bank | 562 | 2,230 |
| | | 16,775 | | | 16,775 |

## 19.2  WHERE FEW RECORDS ARE AVAILABLE

In instances where there is a complete absence of financial record, perhaps little else other than a bunch of invoices and some jottings in an exercise book used as a rough cash book, the question of profit and the financial state of the business really does become a matter of approximation. This applies to many assessments for tax on small retailers. All the accountant can do, when called in for the first time, is to rely upon his client's memory to a large degree, and gradually establish his figures by a simple reasoning process.

Again, many questions are asked of the proprietor, and the physical evidence of the assets and stock on the premises examined. All available bills and vouchers for capital and revenue purchases are scrutinised, and checks perhaps made with the main suppliers and creditors.

The known or ascertained assets and liabilities are listed in two separate distinct groups, for both the beginning and the close of the trading period, and the proprietor's capital established on each of these two dates by using the simple equation $A = C + L$, where $A$ = assets, $C$ = capital and $L$ = liabilities.

Normally there is a big cash discrepancy, the major part of it being put down to the proprietor's drawings. The estimated drawings figure can be checked roughly from the average gross profit for the type of business and taking into account the apparent living standard of the proprietor and his family.

Finally, any additional new finance or capital assets introduced into the business during the trading period will be noted, and the first official trading profit ascertained by arithmetic in this way:

|  |  |  | £ |
|---|---|---|---|
| CAPITAL at end of trading period | | | |
| | say December 31 $(A - L)$ | | 7,500 |
| Add back: money and goods withdrawn | | | |
| | (i.e. estimated Drawings) | | 3,300 |
| | | | 10,800 |
| Deduct: | CAPITAL at start one year | £ | |
| | ago, January 1 $(A - L)$ | 4,000 | |
| | and additional capital paid in | 1,000 | 5,000 |
| | Net trading profit for year | | £5,800 |

**Illustration**

Joshua Smith has neglected the financial records of his business, but when he realises that the Inland Revenue has over-assessed him for income tax he calls in an accountant friend to work out his trading profit for the year ended December 31.

The book and paper records are almost non-existent, but Smith has a bank account used mainly for the business, and after a good deal of questioning and checking with external creditors, the following statement of affairs is drawn up to show the position one year ago, January 1, the beginning of the trading year under review:

Statement of Affairs January 1

| | £ | | £ |
|---|---|---|---|
| Capital Jan. 1 | 2500 | Van (at valuation) | 1500 |
| Creditors (statements) | 300 | Fittings (invoiced) | 240 |
| | | Stock (invoices) | 320 |
| | | Debtors (rough lists) | 560 |
| | | Bank account | 180 |
| | 2800 | | 2800 |

*Note*   The amount of £2500 for 'Capital' is simply the difference between the listed assets and liabilities on this date.

The following information is obtained, with a fair degree of accuracy on a physical check up to date, of the business assets and liabilities as at December 31, the end of the trading year:

| | £ | | £ |
|---|---|---|---|
| Bank balance | 220 | Trade creditors | 310 |
| Stock | 430 | Trade debtors | 660 |

Fittings were still valued at their original figure.

A new van had been bought on December 30 for £2300 and the old van taken in part-exchange at £1550. The difference had been paid by cheque.

After much checking and questioning the proprietor finally agreed to the approximate figure for his drawings being £2750.

From the above information a Statement of Profit is drawn up in this

Statement of Profit for the year ended December 31

| | £ |
|---|---|
| Capital of proprietor at Dec. 31 ($\underline{A}$ - $\underline{L}$) | 3540 |
| (£220 + 660 + 430 + 240 + 2300 less £310) | |
| Add back:  drawings for year | 2750 |
| | 6290 |
| Less:  Capital on January 1, a year ago | 2500 |
| Net trading profit for year | 3790 |

PROOF        Statement of Affairs as at December 31

| Capital | £ | £ | | £ |
|---|---|---|---|---|
| Balance Jan. 1 | 2500 | | Van at cost | 2300 |
| Profit for year | 3790 | | Fittings | 240 |
| | | | Stock | 430 |
| | 6290 | | Debtors | 660 |
| Less:  drawings | 2750 | 3540 | Bank | 220 |
| Trade creditors | | 310 | | |
| | | 3850 | | 3850 |

## QUESTIONS

1. From the following information prepare a statement showing the trading profit of a retailer and draw up his balance sheet as at June 30, the close of his trading year.

|  | July 1 £ | June 30 £ |
|---|---|---|
| Cash in hand | 5 | 8 |
| Bank account | 225 | 310 |
| Fittings and equipment | 322 | 1410 |
| Credit customers | 256 | 372 |
| Owing to suppliers | 194 | 236 |
| Rent owing | – | 80 |
| Stock | 850 | 940 |
| Van | – | 1500 |

During the year ended June 30 the retailer paid the proceeds of a small insurance policy (£750) into the business. His personal drawings were ascertained to be £3400. When making up his final accounts allow for a bad debt of £30 (shown as a debit balance in the total of £372 above), and depreciate the final balance of Fittings and equipment by 10 per cent.

2. William Fry's cash book for the year ended December 31 is summarised as follows (cash and bank combined):

|  | £ |  | £ |
|---|---|---|---|
| Balance b/f | 150 | Cash paid to credit | |
| Cash takings | 4860 | suppliers | 1210 |
| Cash received from | | Cash purchases | 372 |
| credit customers | 1826 | General expenses | 424 |
| | | Wages | 2636 |
| | | New counter | 85 |
| | | Drawings | 1960 |
| | | Balance c/d | 149 |
| | 6836 | | 6836 |
| Balance b/d | 149 | | |

The following information was extracted from the available records (and excellent memory) of Mr Fry:

|  | Jan. 1 £ | Dec. 31 £ |
|---|---|---|
| Stock on hand | 630 | 705 |
| Fittings and equipment | 315 | 400 |
| Debtors' accounts | 460 | 540 |
| Creditors' accounts | 380 | 430 |
| Loan from wife | 500 | – |

Mr Fry had paid off the loan from his wife during the year out of his private resources.

You are required to prepare a trading and profit and loss account for the year ended December 31 and a balance sheet as at December 31, allowing for 15 per cent depreciation of Fittings and equipment on the final balance of the account and adjusting for £12 insurance prepaid (debited in General expenses).

3. A summary of Sarah Vane's cash transactions for the year ended December 31 is given below; cash and bank balances are combined.

| | £ | | £ |
|---|---|---|---|
| Cash/bank Jan. 1 | 640 | Paid to suppliers | 1250 |
| Cash takings | 2520 | Fittings bought | 280 |
| Rent and rates | 400 | Part-time assistant | 1650 |
| General expenses | 155 | Loan from R. Stone | 1000 |
| | | Receipts from credit customers | 2400 |
| | | Withdrawals of cash for private use | 1300 |

On December 31 Miss Vane owed £92 to her suppliers, and her own credit customers owed her £145. A printing account of £16 still had to be paid, and £32 was owing to the part-time assistant. Insurance paid in advance (included in General expenses) amounted to £18.

Make up the final accounts for Miss Vane as at December 31, taking the stock on hand to be £120.

4. This is John Branston's balance sheet on June 30:

| | | £ | | | £ |
|---|---|---|---|---|---|
| Capital    June 30 | | 10,000 | Fixed assets | | |
| | | | Premises | 8,000 | |
| Current liabilities | | | Machinery | 1,400 | |
| | | | Motor van | 1,860 | 11,260 |
| Trade creditors | 3,200 | | | | |
| Bank overdraft | 450 | | Current assets | | |
| Corporation rates | 150 | 3,800 | Stock June 30 | 1,040 | |
| | | | Debtors | 1,370 | |
| | | | Cash | 130 | 2,540 |
| | | 13,800 | | | 13,800 |

His transactions for the month of July are summarised, in totals, below:

| | | £ |
|---|---|---|
| (a) | Cash sales (cost £320) | 450 |
| (b) | Cash purchases | 140 |
| (c) | Goods bought on credit | 2400 |
| (d) | Goods sold to customers (cost £2200) | 3360 |
| (e) | Payments from customers (banked) | 2820 |
| (f) | Cheque payments to suppliers | 1850 |
| (g) | Cheque paid for Rates (see BS) | 150 |

(h)  Discount allowed to debtors                                              96
(i)  Discount received from creditors                                         72
(j)  Returns from customers (cost £110)                                      180
(k)  Returns to suppliers                                                    145
(l)  Bought new van for £2650 on instalment terms and
     paid deposit of                                                        1650
(m) Received cheque for sale of old van                                     1810
(n)  Personal drawings in cash                                               200
(o)  Sundry office expenses                                                   20
(p)  Paid surplus cash into bank

Your assignment is to draft relevant ledger accounts, in brief detail, from the original entries on the balance sheet and the transactions listed for the month of July, extract a complete new list of totals and balances, and make up an up-to-date balance sheet for John Branston as at July 31. At the same time, express your views upon the financial state of the business.

5. Rosemary Anne opened a small shop on May 1, arranging to settle her suppliers' accounts by cheque, otherwise all business was to be strictly 'cash'. At the end of each week excess cash over £5 is to be paid into the bank.

Rosemary Anne was much too busy to bother keeping proper book-keeping records, but at the end of three months she had to call on her brother David to help sort out the financial tangle enmeshing her. She managed to produce the following information:

|  |  | £ |
|---|---|---|
| Bank lodgments: | Paid in on opening bank account May 1 | 500 |
|  | Total weekly bankings | 2820 |
|  |  |  |
| Cheques drawn: | Fittings/equipment | 250 |
|  | Suppliers' accounts | 2736 |
|  | General expenses | 25 |
|  | Landlord (rent) | 200 |
|  | Wrapping material, etc. | 18 |
|  | Electricity | 23 |
|  | Part-time assistance | 210 |

The bank had deducted £5 for charges, and there was an overdraft of £147 on July 31.

Rosemary Anne had made notes on her till records of £250 expenses paid out of cash, including £100 for business purchases. Her stock of goods on July 31 was estimated at £508. She then owed her main supplier £238, and £17 was due to the Electricity Board. Insurance paid in advance (included in General expenses) was £10.

David first of all made up a summary from cash book details, and then prepared total accounts for both suppliers and the expense creditors. He managed to establish his sister's drawings at £225 for the three months.

Complete the final accounts of the business from this information, allowing for 20 per cent depreciation of the Fittings and equipment.

# CHAPTER 20

# NON-TRADING CONCERNS AND CLUB ACCOUNTS

## 20.1 NON-TRADING ORGANISATIONS

Clubs, societies and most associations are formed for the use and benefit of members, not for the purpose of trading. The main income of these organisations is derived from subscriptions and donations, and where there is a surplus of income over expenditure it is used for the benefit of the club or the well-being of its members.

Annual accounts, often audited by a member, are presented at the annual general meeting each year. These accounts show in summary form the total income of the club or society and the manner in which it has been spent.

In the case of small societies where cash (or the bank balance) is the only asset, and small expenses are paid by an appointed treasurer, it will probably only be necessary to produce a receipts and payments account.

## 20.2 RECEIPTS AND PAYMENTS ACCOUNT

This is simply a classified summary of all cash transactions for the period, normally one year. *Every* receipt of subscription or donation or casual profit is included, whether referring to the period under review or not. Likewise, *every* payment made during the same period is included in the summary, whether paid in arrear or in advance. No distinction is made between capital and revenue.

The receipts and payments account is a cash book summary. It starts with the commencing cash and bank balance (or bank overdraft). Money received is debited. Money paid is credited. It finishes with the closing cash and bank balances, brought down in the ordinary way just like a cash book.

In all examination questions, think of the receipts and payments account as a *cash book*. Write the words 'cash book' after its new heading and then there will be no confusion.

On the debit side is listed all money receipts such as subscriptions, donations, gate money, and money surpluses from dances, whist drives and raffles, etc.

On the credit side, apart from the general expenses such as wages, stationery, maintenance, lighting and heating, will also appear all asset purchases bought (nets, furniture, etc.).

## 20.3 INCOME AND EXPENDITURE ACCOUNT

A receipts and payments account tells less than half the story. The club may have acquired certain assets. There may be money due from members at the end of the season, and sometimes there are stocks of refreshments, in tins or bottles, to be carried over from one period or season to the next.

An income and expenditure account is then made up, often based upon the receipts and payments account (or cash book), but including various adjustments to show the *actual* income and expenditure for the period.

This means that capital payments (for assets, etc.) will be excluded in establishing the club's net revenue, whether a surplus or a deficit for the period.

It is also usual to present a balance sheet with this type of account.

The long-sounding term 'income and expenditure' simply disguises the profit and loss account with which we are familiar. Treat this new account exactly as you would treat the profit and loss account of a trading business. Write the words 'profit and loss account' in pencil under the new heading until you are used to it.

The main points to consider before studying the illustration which follows are:

(a) In examination questions it is often customary to combine cash and bank for simplicity.

(b) The term 'income' takes the place of 'cash sales or daily takings' of a trading firm. The income from subscriptions, donations and sundry receipts for the *year under review* is taken to the credit of income and expenditure account, in the main posted from the debit of the cash book.

(c) All the expenses of running and managing the club will be debited to income and expenditure account. But remember to *exclude all capital and fixed asset payments*. All permanent assets acquired for the use of the club will be debited to individual asset accounts.

(d) Adjustments are made to show only the *real* income and the *real* expenditure for the period.

(e) Stocks are dealt with in the ordinary way, and sometimes a small trading account is made up where there is a bar, the surplus or deficit on bar trading being carried down to the lower income and expenditure account. Stocks of stationery are adjusted on stationery purchases, and stocks of refreshments carried over adjusted on refreshment purchases.

(f) The commencing capital of the club, sometimes called the Accumulated Fund, often needs to be worked out in this type of examination question. It will be found by listing all the assets and property belonging to the club, including commencing cash and bank balances and subscriptions owing by members (debtors) at the start, less any liabilities at the start (which might include subscriptions paid in advance by other members).

## 20.4 ILLUSTRATION

The Ashfield Tennis Club was formed on April 1 with a membership of 100. Subscriptions of £5 each were to be paid by the end of June. The elected chairman of the club made a gift of part of his own large garden, which was well turfed and valued at £1000.

The treasurer prepared the following summary in the form of a receipts and payments account for the three months ended June 30:

| | £ | | £ |
|---|---|---|---|
| Subscriptions received | 465 | Wages of groundsman | 450 |
| Sundry receipts: | | New nets | 320 |
| | | Cost and erection of | |
| Teas | 84 | temporary clubhouse | 1200 |
| Dances/socials | 248 | General expenses: | |
| | | | |
| Temporary loans from | | Teas | 35 |
| senior members free | | Dances/socials | 170 |
| of interest | 1500 | Printing/stationery | 24 |
| | | Heating/lighting | 32 |
| | | | |
| | | Balance c/d | 66 |
| | —— | | —— |
| | 2297 | | 2297 |
| | ══ | | ══ |
| Balance b/d (cash in | | | |
| hand) | 66 | | |

One of the accountant members of the club proposed that this cash summary should be extended to an income and expenditure account to give a more realistic view of the revenue position, and a balance sheet also prepared as at June 30. His proposal was adopted, and it was also decided to take the following adjustments into account when making up a new set of accounts:

(a) Of the figure £465 subscriptions received, £15 had been paid in advance (for the next season), and ten members had not yet paid their subscriptions for the current season.
(b) Wages owing to the groundsman at June 30 amounted to £35.
(c) Creditors for electricity £10; and for printing £8.
(d) Stocks of refreshment, mainly bottled, valued at cost £22.
(e) The nets were to be revalued at £250 as at June 30.

**Redrafted Accounts**

Income and Expenditure Account
for the three months ended June 30

| | £ | £ | | £ | £ |
|---|---|---|---|---|---|
| Wages paid | 450 | | Subscriptions | | |
| owing | 35 | 485 | account: | | |
| Printing/stationery | 24 | | Actual receipts | 465 | |
| Account owing | 8 | 32 | Arrears due | 50 | |
| Heating/lighting | 32 | | | 515 | |
| Account owing | 10 | 42 | Less: paid in | | |
| | | | advance | 15 | 500 |
| Deprec. of nets | | 70 | Receipts from | | |
| Surplus (excess | | | teas, dances | | |
| income over | | | and socials | 332 | |
| expenditure) | | 20 | Less: expenses | 205 | |
| | | | | 127 | |
| | | | Stock on hand | | |
| | | | June 30 | 22 | 149 |
| | | 649 | | | 649 |

Note that subscriptions must show the actual revenue for the period, the amount paid plus the amount due from members. In this instance the figure is £500, but in time some members will become defaulters and be struck off the membership list. The correct figure to be taken to the income and expenditure account may be more easily understood by making up a Subscriptions Account in this manner:

Subscriptions Account

| June 30 | | £ | June 30 | | £ |
|---|---|---|---|---|---|
| 30 | Subs. paid in advance by members c/d | 15 | 30 | Actual receipts as per cash book | 465 |
| 30 | INCOME & EXPENDITURE ACCOUNT | 500 | 30 | Subs. still owing by members c/d | 50 |
| | | 515 | | | 515 |
| July 1 | Debtors for subs. | 50 | July 1 | Creditors for subs. | 15 |

Note that the subscriptions for the following year or period will be adjusted on the above account. Meanwhile, these debit and credit balances will be taken to the balance sheet shown below:

Balance Sheet of the Ashfield Tennis Club
as at June 30

| Accumulated Fund | | £ | £ | Fixed assets | | £ | £ | £ |
|---|---|---|---|---|---|---|---|---|
| Balance April 1 | 1000 | | | Land | | | 1000 | |
| Add: surplus (income over expenditure) | 20 | | 1020 | Clubhouse | | | 1200 | |
| | | | | Equipment | | 320 | | |
| Loan accounts | | | 1500 | Less: deprec. | | 70 | 250 | 2450 |
| Current liabilities | | | | Current assets | | | | |
| Subs. in advance | | 15 | | Stock refreshments | | | 22 | |
| Creditors for electric | | 10 | | Debtors for subs. | | | 50 | |
| " " printing | | 8 | | Cash/bank | | | 66 | 138 |
| " " wages | | 35 | 68 | | | | | |
| | | | 2588 | | | | | 2588 |

## QUESTIONS

1. Prepare suitable accounts for your tennis club from the information below, given to you by your treasurer. The season has just ended at October 31.

|  | £ |
|---|---|
| Balance of Accumulated Fund (November 1 one year ago) and which included cash and bank balances totalling £130 | 4250 |
| Clubhouse, asset balance at cost | 4000 |
| Nets and equipment as per last balance sheet | 550 |
| Equipment bought during year | 150 |
| General expenses of club | 180 |
| Wages of part-time staff | 880 |
| Rent paid up to July 31 (ground rental) | 120 |
| Arrears of rent at October 31 | 40 |
| Profit on dances and socials | 135 |
| Subscriptions received during year | 1290 |
| (£20 arrears for previous year and £30 paid recently in advance of season just ended) | |
| Cash and bank balances combined at October 31 the end of present season | 245 |

In making up the income and expenditure account, please allow for the following:

(a) Depreciation of nets and equipment £100.
(b) £60 owing for groundsman's wages.
(c) £45 still owing by members for current subscriptions.

2. Your assignment is to convert the receipts and payments account, shown below, into an income and expenditure account, and to draw up a balance sheet as at December 31, taking into account the supplementary information listed overleaf.

Receipts and Payments Account - year ended December 31

| Jan. | | £ | Dec. | | £ |
|---|---|---|---|---|---|
| 1 | Bank balance | 450 | 31 | Payments for bar supplies | 5150 |
| Dec. | | | | Printing/postages | 130 |
| 31 | Subs. received for: £ | | | Rent and rates | 1280 |
| | current year 1520 | | | General expenses | 420 |
| | previous year 110 | | | New furniture | 360 |
| | next year 60 | 1690 | | Staff wages | 1800 |
| | | | | Honorarium for | |
| | Bar sales | 7250 | | Secretary | 150 |
| | Hire of rooms | 220 | | Balance c/d | 440 |
| | Sundry receipts | 120 | | | |
| | | 9730 | | | 9730 |
| Dec. | | | | | |
| 31 | Balance b/d | 440 | | | |

**Additional Information**

|  | January | December |
|---|---|---|
|  | £ | £ |
| Bar stocks | 340 | 400 |
| Creditors for supplies | 510 | 390 |
| Wages owing | 60 | 40 |
| Rent due | 180 | 180 |
| Rates paid in advance | 120 | 140 |
| Subscriptions owing | 130 | 150 |
| Fixed assets (valued at cost less depreciation): |  |  |
| Furniture | 880 | 1240 |
| Equipment | 200 | 200 |

At a recent meeting it was decided to reduce the Furniture Account to show a final balance of £1100, and to depreciate Equipment Account by 20 per cent.

**3.** Rosanna Peel has a typing agency. She rents a small office for £360 a year and starts business on July 1.

A summary of her cash transactions for the first month is given, cash and bank combined.

|  | £ |  | £ |
|---|---|---|---|
| Balance July 1 | 500 | Office furniture | 150 |
|  |  | Typewriter | 80 |
| General and casual receipts | 215 | Postages | 10 |
|  |  | Sundry expenses | 35 |
|  |  | Advertising | 24 |
| Payments on contract invoices | 180 | Rent (two months in advance) | 90 |
|  |  | Drawings | 200 |

Invoices sent out to credit customers for contract work during July totalled £240. At the end of the month the stationery on hand (purchases were under sundry expenses) was valued at £16. In addition, one stationery account for £25 was unpaid.

Make up Miss Peel's profit and loss account for the month of July, and a balance sheet as at July 31.

**4.** A year ago the balance sheet of Sara Long showed her financial affairs as follows:

|  | £ |  | £ |
|---|---|---|---|
| Capital Account | 2200 | Fittings and equipment | 1200 |
|  |  | Stock | 500 |
| Trade creditors | 650 | Trade debtors | 800 |
|  |  | Bank | 350 |
|  | 2850 |  | 2850 |

An analysis of her cash book for the year gave this information, in total:

| Jan. | | £ | Dec. | | £ |
|---|---|---|---|---|---|
| 1 | Balance | 350 | 31 | Cash purchases | 44 |
| Dec. | | | | Office fittings | 75 |
| 31 | Cash takings | 1430 | | General expenses | 42 |
| | Payments from | | | Payments to | |
| |    credit customers | 5675 | |    suppliers | 2236 |
| | | | | Salaries | 2800 |
| | | | | Drawings | 1500 |

Miss Long valued her closing stock at £650. At the year-end her credit customers owed her £920, and she owed £780 to her suppliers.

Prepare a complete set of final accounts for Miss Long, depreciating fittings and equipment by £175.

**5.** The following details of the Sundowners' Social Club have been extracted in summary form from the cash book for the year ended December 31:

| Jan. | | £ | Dec. | | £ |
|---|---|---|---|---|---|
| 1 | Balance at bank | 350 | 31 | Bar supplies, etc. | 6,250 |
| Dec. | | | | Refreshments | 870 |
| 31 | Bar takings | 8,800 | | Wages | 4,200 |
| | Profits from | | | General expenses | 186 |
| |   raffles and | | | Furniture | 310 |
| |   socials | 626 | | Printing/postages | 65 |
| | Misc. receipts | 230 | | Repairs | 105 |
| | | | | Crockery | 23 |
| | Subscriptions: | | | Books/magazines | 272 |
| | Current year | 3,600 | | Entertainers' fees | 450 |
| | Arrears of subs. | 120 | | Concert expenses | 660 |
| | In advance | 80 | | Secretary's | |
| | | | |   honorarium | 100 |
| | | | | Balance c/d | 315 |
| | | 13,806 | | | 13,806 |
| Jan. | | | | | |
| 1 | Balance b/d | 315 | | | |

Other information obtainable from the club's records:

| | January 1<br>Beginning of year | December 31<br>End of year |
|---|---|---|
| | £ | £ |
| Freehold premises at cost | 10,000 | 10,000 |
| Furniture and fixtures | 2,500 | 2,810 |
| Bar stock | 520 | 575 |
| Stock of refreshments | 105 | 138 |
| Equipment and crockery | 225 | 248 |
| Wages owing | 68 | 44 |
| Electricity account unpaid | – | 36 |

You are required to prepare a separate bar trading account, a general income and expenditure account, and a balance sheet as at December 31. The wages bill should be divided equally between the bar and the general account; the cost of the books and magazines written off completely, and the furniture account depreciated by 10 per cent on the balance at January 1.

# INTRODUCTION TO
# PARTNERSHIP ACCOUNTS

A common definition of partnership is 'the relationship which exists between two or more persons carrying on business with a view to profit'.

The ordinary books of account, the cash book, day books, purchase and sales ledgers are posted up exactly in the same manner as those of a sole trader, and the net trading profit ascertained in the same way as before. It is only from this stage that there is a change in procedure.

The net trading profit (or loss) must be split up between the partners in the proportions they have agreed to divide profits and losses. The division or allocation of profit (or loss) is shown in the Appropriation Account, an extension of the profit and loss account.

## 21.1  SEPARATE CAPITAL ACCOUNTS

Each partner has a separate capital account, which normally is shown at the original fixed amount plus additional capital introduced.

## 21.2  INTEREST ON CAPITAL

Where capitals vary appreciably it is sometimes decided to allow each partner interest on his capital, thus providing some measure of compensation to those partners who might invest their surplus funds in investments outside the firm.

## 21.3  CURRENT ACCOUNTS

These take the place of the Drawings Account of the sole trader. The share of profit due to each partner is credited to his current account together with any interest on capital. Sums withdrawn on account of profits are debited. Current accounts are made up, in vertical form, and shown on the firm's balance sheet, quite separate from individual capital accounts.

## 21.4  PARTNERSHIP SALARY

Sometimes a junior partner spends much more of his time and effort on the firm's business than some of his co-partners, and is paid a small salary as a form of compensation. This salary is debited to Partnership Salaries Account, appears as a debit on the trial balance and is charged to the appropriation account. If unpaid at the balance sheet date it must be credited to the partner's current account and shown as a liability still due to him.

## 21.5  INTEREST ON DRAWINGS

In order to curb heavy withdrawals in anticipation of profits interest is sometimes charged on drawings. This interest is debited to the partner's current account and credited (as a gain to the firm) to the appropriation account. The interest is calculated from the date of the withdrawal to the end of the trading period. *For example*, say interest on drawings is to be charged at 5 per cent per annum, and one partner draws £960 on each of the following dates: March 31; June 30; September 30, and December 31. This partner, at December 31, the end of the trading year, would be charged £36, £24, and £12 for the withdrawals on the first three dates (nothing for the last day of the year). This total of £72 Interest on Drawings would be *credited* to the firm's appropriation account, and debited, together with his drawings of £3840, to his current account.

## 21.6  PARTNERSHIP AGREEMENT

All rules and conditions within the firm are laid down by the partners themselves. Normally, a formal written agreement is drawn up by a solicitor, but intention could be implied by past custom. In the event of dispute and the absence of any agreement, written or implied, partnerships are governed by the Partnership Act 1890.

## 21.7  THE APPROPRIATION ACCOUNT AND BALANCE SHEET

*A* and *B* are in partnership, sharing profits and losses two-thirds and one-third respectively.

On January 1 *A*'s capital was £5000, and *B*'s was £2000.

According to the partnership deed each partner is entitled to 5 per cent interest on capital, and *B* is also to be credited with £1500 a year salary for the additional work he does on behalf of the firm. The partners private withdrawals during the year were *A* £3500 and *B* £2500. The net trading profit for the year was £7850.

From the above information show the profit and loss appropriation account, the partners' capital and current accounts and a balance sheet as at December 31.

Profit and Loss Appropriation Account

| | £ | | £ |
|---|---|---|---|
| Interest on Capital: | | Net trading profit b/d | 7850 |
| A | 250 | | |
| B | 100 | | |
| Salary of B | 1500 | | |
| Shares of profit: | | | |
| A: two-thirds | 4000 | | |
| B: one-third | 2000 | | |
| | 7850 | | 7850 |

Capital Accounts (remaining at fixed amounts)

| | | A | B | | | A | B |
|---|---|---|---|---|---|---|---|
| | | £ | £ | Jan. 1 | Balances | £ 5000 | £ 2000 |

Current Accounts

| | | A | B | | | A | B |
|---|---|---|---|---|---|---|---|
| | | £ | £ | | | £ | £ |
| Dec. 31 | Drawings | 3500 | 2500 | Dec. 31 | Interest on Capital | 250 | 100 |
| | Balances c/d | 750 | 1100 | | Salary | | 1500 |
| | | | | | Shares of net trading profit | 4000 | 2000 |
| | | 4250 | 3600 | | | 4250 | 3600 |
| | | | | Jan. 1 | Balances b/d | 750 | 1100 |

Balance Sheet of A and B as at December 31

| | £ | £ | |
|---|---|---|---|
| Capital Accounts | | | |
| A | 5000 | | |
| B | 2000 | 7000 | |
| Current Account   A | | | S U N D R Y |
| Share of profit | 4000 | | |
| Add: Int. on Capital | 250 | | |
| | 4250 | | A S S E T S |
| Less: Drawings | 3500 | 750 | |
| Current Account   B | | | |
| Share of profit | 2000 | | |
| Add: Int. on Capital | 100 | | |
|      and salary | 1500 | | |
| | 3600 | | |
| Less: Drawings | 2500 | 1100 | |

*Note* that the partners' current accounts on the balance sheet correspond vertically to the horizontal format in the private ledger.

## 21.8  GOODWILL

A new business has no goodwill. It still has to be earned and developed. As a business grows and expands so does its reputation and connection. That is its 'goodwill'.

When the proprietor of a good business decides to retire he will expect to receive considerably more money for the sale of his business than just the value of his stock, fittings and equipment. The goodwill of a business is seldom measurable until the business is sold or a new partner is taken into the old firm. In the latter case the existing partners put their own valuation on the goodwill figure.

The value of goodwill on the sale of a sole trader's business is the difference between the price received by the vendor (seller) and the value of net assets acquired (total assets less creditors) by the purchaser and new owner.

## 21.9  ADMISSION OF NEW PARTNER

The old partners transfer a share of their established business to the new partner on his admission to the firm. It is only reasonable that they should expect to be compensated in some way for the surrender of a portion of their profits.

In addition to his capital the new partner may be asked to pay a premium for entrance to the firm. This premium would be shared by the old partners in the ratios in which they previously shared profits and losses, and may either be paid to them direct, by way of private transaction, or be paid into the bank account of the firm and withdrawn afterwards. It is simply a matter of private arrangement.

If the new partner (perhaps the managing clerk of the old firm) has difficulty in providing a premium in addition to his own capital, the old partners may elect to create a Goodwill Account in the books, debiting the amount decided upon as the *goodwill figure to a new asset account*, and *crediting their old capital accounts in the same proportions as they previously shared profits and losses.*

By raising the values of their capital accounts the old partners increase their holding upon the assets of the new firm, benefiting themselves on retirement, and, in the meantime, interest on capital will be increased on the larger credit balances.

**Illustration**
X and Y share profits and losses in the proportions two-thirds and one-third. This is their balance sheet on December 31.

| Capital Accounts | £ | Fixed assets | £ 5000 |
|---|---|---|---|
| X | 4500 | Current assets | |
| | | Stock/debtors | 2500 |
| Y | 2000 | Bank | 500 |
| Trade creditors | 1500 | | |
| | 8000 | | 8000 |

X and Y (the old firm) decide to admit Z as a partner on January 1 on the following terms:

(a) Z is to receive one-quarter of the profit and X and Y are to have the same proportions as before.
(b) A goodwill account is to be brought into the books at £6000 to compensate the old partners for their past efforts in building up the firm's connection.
(c) Z is to bring in £3000 as capital.

Show and complete all ledger accounts affected by these new financial arrangements, and make up a balance sheet for the new firm X, Y and Z as at January 1. See page 182.

**Division of partnership profits**
On the admission of a new partner it will be necessary to adjust the profit-sharing ratios for all partners.

**Example**
X and Y are in partnership sharing profits and losses two-thirds and one-third respectively.

They admit Z as a partner to take a fourth share on the same basis as Y in the old firm.

The proportions are worked out thus:

Z will take $\frac{1}{4}$ of profits leaving $\frac{3}{4}$ for other two.
X will take $\frac{2}{3}$ of $\frac{3}{4} = \frac{1}{2}$ share of profits.
Y will take $\frac{1}{3}$ of $\frac{3}{4} = \frac{1}{4}$ share of profits.

## Cash Book

| | £ | | £ |
|---|---|---|---|
| Balance | 500 | Balance c/d | 3500 |
| Z's Capital | 3000 | | |
| | 3500 | | 3500 |
| Balance b/d | 3500 | | |

## Goodwill Account

| | £ | | £ |
|---|---|---|---|
| Capital Accounts: | | Balance c/d | 6000 |
| X | 4000 | | |
| Y | 2000 | | |
| | 6000 | | 6000 |
| Balance b/d | 6000 | | |

## Capital Accounts (new firm)

| | X £ | Y £ | Z £ | | X £ | Y £ | Z £ |
|---|---|---|---|---|---|---|---|
| Jan. 1 Balances c/d | 3500 | 4000 | 3000 | Dec. 31 Balances b/f | 4500 | 2000 | 3000 |
| | | | | Cash | | | |
| | | | | Goodwill: | | | |
| | | | | X: two-thirds | 4000 | | |
| | | | | Y: one-third | | 2000 | |
| | 8500 | 4000 | 3000 | | 8500 | 4000 | 3000 |
| | | | | Jan. 1 Balances b/d | 8500 | 4000 | 3000 |

## Balance Sheet of the new firm X, Y and Z as at January 1

| Capital Accounts | £ | £ | | £ | £ |
|---|---|---|---|---|---|
| X | 8500 | | Goodwill | 6000 | 11,000 |
| Y | 4000 | | Fixed assets | 5000 | |
| Z | 3000 | 15,500 | Current assets: | | |
| Trade creditors | | 1,500 | Stock/debtors | 2500 | 6,000 |
| | | | Bank | 3500 | |
| | | 17,000 | | | 17,000 |

## 21.10   AMALGAMATION OF SOLE TRADERS

Two sole traders may decide to amalgamate their businesses and become partners.

This is a simple examination question, providing the capital account of each sole trader is adjusted according to the revaluation of his own assets and liabilities *before the amalgamation takes place.*

Make up separate balance sheets for each sole trader at the new values agreed upon, and then lump together the assets and liabilities on the combined final balance sheet showing separate capital accounts for each partner.

### Illustration
Grey & Green decide to amalgamate their businesses on January 1. Their own final balance sheets on December 31 were as follows:

Grey's Balance Sheet as at December 31

|  | £ |  | £ |
|---|---|---|---|
| Capital | 8,000 | Machinery | 6,000 |
|  |  | Furniture | 350 |
| Creditors | 2,450 | Stock | 1,850 |
|  |  | Debtors | 2,500 |
| Bank overdraft | 250 |  |  |
|  | 10,700 |  | 10,700 |

Green's Balance Sheet as at December 31

|  | £ |  | £ |
|---|---|---|---|
| Capital | 7,500 | Machinery | 4,000 |
|  |  | Van | 1,400 |
| Creditors | 800 | Fittings | 230 |
|  |  | Stock | 970 |
|  |  | Debtors | 1,200 |
|  |  | Bank | 500 |
|  | 8,300 |  | 8,300 |

It is agreed that the following adjustments shall be made before amalgamation.

Machinery is to be depreciated by 20 per cent in both instances.

The van is to be revalued at £1000.

A provision of 5 per cent is to be made for bad debts.

Grey is to pay off his bank overdraft by cashing a small private insurance policy.

**Answer**

The two balance sheets will be redrafted, quite separately, as follows:

Grey's Balance Sheet redrafted

| | £ | | | £ |
|---|---|---|---|---|
| Capital | 6925 | Machinery | | 4800 |
| | | Furniture | | 350 |
| Creditors | 2450 | Stock | | 1850 |
| | | Debtors | 2500 | |
| | | Less: Prov. 125 | | 2375 |
| | 9375 | | | 9375 |

Green's Balance Sheet redrafted

| | £ | | | £ |
|---|---|---|---|---|
| Capital | 6240 | Machinery | | 3200 |
| | | Van | | 1000 |
| Creditors | 800 | Fittings | | 230 |
| | | Stock | | 970 |
| | | Debtors | 1200 | |
| | | Less: Prov. 60 | | 1140 |
| | | Bank | | 500 |
| | 7040 | | | 7040 |

Balance Sheet of Grey and Green as at January 1

| | £ | £ | | | £ |
|---|---|---|---|---|---|
| Capitals | | | Machinery | | 8,000 |
| | | | Van | | 1,000 |
| Grey | 6925 | | Furniture/fixtures | | 580 |
| Green | 6240 | 13,165 | | | |
| | | | Stock | 2820 | |
| Creditors | | 3,250 | Debtors 3700 | | |
| | | | Less: Prov. 185 | 3515 | |
| | | | Bank | 500 | 6,835 |
| | | 16,415 | | | 16,415 |

*Note* It is laid down by Section 24 of the Partnership Act, 1890, that *in the absence of either written or implied evidence, partners will share profits and losses equally*, irrespective of the balances of their capital accounts.

## QUESTIONS

1. Draw up the profit and loss appropriation account and show the capital and current accounts of Abbott & Bullock from these details extracted from the books of the firm on December 31, the end of their trading year.

|  | Capitals | Current Accounts | Drawings |
|---|---|---|---|
|  | £ | £ | £ |
| Abbott | 8000 | 880 credit | 4800 |
| Bullock | 6000 | 80 debit | 5200 |

Bullock is to be credited with a salary of £1040 per annum for the extra work he does for the firm, and each partner is to be credited with 5 per cent interest on capital. The net trading profit for the year was £11,100.

2. Hobbs & Duckworth are partners with capitals of £5000 and £3000 respectively. They share proportions of profit according to their capital ratios.

On January 1 they admit Leyland and give him a quarter-share in the firm. Leyland brings in £2000 as capital and pays a premium of £1000 for entry, this amount being withdrawn immediately by the old partners. A goodwill account of £4000 is raised on Leyland's admission.

Give the journal entries recording these transactions and state the new profit-sharing ratios of the firm as from January 1, assuming the old partners adopt the same basis as before.

3. You are required to determine _B_'s share of profit and show his current account from the following information:

Cash Book

| Jan. |  |  | £ | June |  |  | £ |
|---|---|---|---|---|---|---|---|
| 1 | Capital | | | 30 | Salary _B_ | | 600 |
|  | Accounts: | | | Dec. | | | |
|  | _A_ | | 16,000 | 31 | Drawings: | | |
|  | | | | | _A_ | | 4,000 |
|  | _B_ | | 8,000 | | | | |
|  | | | | | _B_ | | 3,200 |

_A_ and _B_ share profits and losses three-fifths and two-fifths respectively. Allow for 5 per cent interest per annum on capital and 6 per cent on drawings.

_B_'s withdrawals were £800 at the end of each quarter – March 31, June 30, September 30 and December 31. _A_ had made two withdrawals of £2000 each on June 30 and December 31.

_B_ is entitled to a salary of £1200 a year.

The net trading profit for the year ended December 31 was £10,268 before charging interest and salary.

**4.** Louth and Tennyson are sole traders who decide to amalgamate their businesses on July 1.

On June 30 their financial positions were as follows:

(a) Louth – premises £10,000, fittings £450, stock £1000, bank overdraft £350, cash in hand £30, trade debtors £1240, and trade creditors £860.
(b) Tennyson – machinery and equipment £8600, stock £2200, bank balance £680, trade debtors £1730, trade creditors £1340, and cash on hand £70.

The new partners decided that they would occupy Louth's premises, to be revalued at £15,000. Tennyson previously had rented his premises.

Fittings, machinery and equipment are to be depreciated by 10 per cent and stock also reduced by 20 per cent.

Both partners withdrew their own cash balances, and Louth paid off his bank overdraft privately. The new firm commenced business with Tennyson's bank balance, and he paid into the partnership account a sum of money to give him a similar holding in the firm as his partner.

Show the opening journal entries and the balance sheet of Louth Tennyson & Co. as at July 1.

**5.** The trial balance of Witham & Welland at December 31 shows the net trading profit *before* making up the appropriation account:

|  | | £ | £ |
|---|---|---:|---:|
| Capital accounts: | Witham | | 8,000 |
| | Welland | | 6,000 |
| Current accounts: | Witham | 120 | |
| | Welland | | 220 |
| Drawings: | Witham | 3,600 | |
| | Welland | 4,200 | |
| Net trading profit for year | | | 8,390 |
| Partnership salaries account | | 500 | |
| Rates in advance | | 350 | |
| Insurance in advance | | 80 | |
| Expense creditors | | | 150 |
| Trade debtors | | 2,300 | |
| Trade creditors | | | 2,920 |
| Premises at cost | | 9,000 | |
| Fittings/equipment less depreciation | | 1,850 | |
| Van less depreciation | | 1,250 | |
| Stock December 31 | | 2,000 | |
| Cash and bank | | 430 | |
| | | 25,680 | 25,680 |

Welland has withdrawn only half of the salary to which he is entitled (£1000 a year). Make the adjustment, allow each partner 8 per cent interest on capital and draw up the balance sheet of the firm as at December 31.

**6.** The following balances are extracted from the books of Ellen and Emily White, relating to the year ended on June 30 and *after* the net trading profit of £5,500 has been ascertained.

|  | £ | £ |
|---|---:|---:|
| Ellen White: Capital account |  | 4,000 |
| Current account |  | 220 |
| Emily White: Capital account |  | 3,000 |
| Current account | 130 |  |
| Net trading profit for the year |  | 5,500 |
| Fittings and fixtures | 550 |  |
| Stock at June 30 | 2,250 |  |
| Trade debtors | 2,500 |  |
| Trade creditors |  | 2,710 |
| Provision for bad debts |  | 100 |
| Freehold premises at cost | 5,000 |  |
| Cash in hand | 40 |  |
| Cash at bank | 710 |  |
| Drawings accounts: Ellen White | 2,500 |  |
| Emily White | 1,850 |  |
|  | 15,530 | 15,530 |

You are required to make up the appropriation account of the firm, and a balance sheet as at June 30, taking into account these additional adjustments:

(a) interest to be allowed on capitals at 6 per cent annum.
(b) £500 to be transferred to a General Reserve Account.
(c) the provision for bad debts to be increased to £150.

7. The following balances have been extracted from the books of John and Henry Brown at December 31, at the end of their first trading year:

| | £ | | £ |
|---|---:|---|---:|
| Bank overdraft | 500 | Machinery repairs | 250 |
| Cash in hand | 50 | Plant and machinery | 4,300 |
| Commission paid | 80 | Commission earned | 420 |
| Carriage on purchases | 70 | Carriage on sales | 110 |
| Fittings and fixtures | 400 | Rates paid | 160 |
| Cash sales | 350 | Cash purchases | 230 |
| Sundry debtors | 4,000 | Sundry creditors | 2,800 |
| Discounts received | 30 | Discounts allowed | 40 |
| General expenses | 370 | Bills receivable | 750 |
| Insurance | 90 | Salaries | 3,150 |
| Rent paid | 300 | Provision for bad debts | 200 |
| Credit purchases | 8,000 | Credit sales | 14,000 |
| Embezzlement loss | 550 | | |

The position with regard to the capital and drawings accounts of the two brothers was as follows:

| Capital Accounts January 1 | Drawings Accounts December 31 |
|---|---|
| John Brown £5000 | John Brown £1800 |
| Henry Brown £3000 | Henry Brown £1600 |

The firm's premises were rented at a nominal figure from a relative, and at the balance sheet date there was a quarter's rent in arrear. These other adjustments are to be taken into account when you prepare a trading and profit and loss account for the first year of the partnership, and a balance sheet as at December 31:

(a) The stock at December 31 was valued at £1200. This included £50 of goods delivered but not yet invoiced.
(b) Only nine months' rent has been paid, and insurance paid in advance amounts to £30.
(c) General expenses includes £100 additions to office furniture, and £10 annual subscription to John Brown's golf club.
(d) Interest on capital at 5 per cent is to be allowed to each partner.
(e) Plant and machinery is to be depreciated by 10 per cent per annum, and the provision for bad debts reduced to 3 per cent of the debtors.

8. The balance sheet of Leslie Frost on July 1 was as follows:

| Liabilities | £ | Assets | £ |
|---|---|---|---|
| Capital | 6500 | Machinery | 5000 |
| Bank overdraft | 250 | Motor van | 800 |
| Creditors | 750 | Stock | 1200 |
| | | Debtors | 500 |
| | 7500 | | 7500 |

He takes Paul Snow into partnership with him on the following terms: Snow is to pay £2000 into the business bank account and bring in office furniture and equipment worth £500. He will receive a one-third share of the business profit of the new firm, when ascertainable. Both partners agree not to withdraw any money from the business for six months.

On December 31 the balances in the books, after ascertaining a net trading profit of £3000, were:

| | £ | | £ |
|---|---|---|---|
| Bank | 1345 | Stock as valued | 2625 |
| Trade debtors | 930 | Motor van | 750 |
| Trade creditors | 980 | Machinery | 6900 |
| Furniture and | | Wages owing | 60 |
| equipment | 450 | Insurance paid | |
| | | in advance | 40 |

You are required to make up the partnership appropriation account for the six months, and a balance sheet of the firm as at December 31, allowing interest on capitals at 6 per cent per annum.

# MANUFACTURING

# ACCOUNTS AND

# PRODUCTION COSTS

## 22.1  MANUFACTURING ACCOUNT : WORKS COST : COST OF SALES

The manufacturing account shows details of the cost of manufacture or production; consequently this type of account is a characteristic of firms (usually large public companies) making their own products.

The main expense and bulk costs of most manufactured articles occur long before the retail stage, determining to a large degree the ultimate selling price to the public.

The manufacturer must obtain his raw material at ever-increasing world commodity prices, and provide an efficient labour force and the machinery of production months ahead of his estimated demand for his product.

The manufacturing account precedes the normal trading account we already know, and comprises, almost entirely, all debit items in connection with the cost and expense of production, often split into two main groups, the Prime Cost of Production, and the Factory or Works Cost of Production.

The closing stock of raw materials is deducted from the commencing stock, plus purchases of raw materials, and an adjustment made for work in progress (sometimes called 'partly finished goods') and then the total expense on this account (which is the Cost of Production) is brought down as a debit to trading account, to take the place of the ordinary trade purchases of our acquaintance; but remember, some finished goods may also be bought from outside suppliers.

Stocks need to be segregated carefully in this type of question. Note that there are stocks of raw material and partly finished goods (work in progress) in the manufacturing account, and stock of finished goods in the trading account, both at the *beginning and at the close* of the accounting period. *All closing stocks* must be brought into the balance sheet.

## Manufacturing Account Illustration

Manufacturing, Trading and Profit and Loss Account
for the month of October

| | £ | | £ |
|---|---|---|---|
| Stock of raw materials | | Cost of production carried | |
| Oct. 1 | 2,000 | down | 52,400 |
| Purchases of raw material | 15,000 | | |
| Carriage on raw material | 250 | | |
| | 17,250 | | |
| Less: Stock of raw | | | |
| material Oct. 31 | 1,250 | | |
| Materials consumed | 16,000 | | |
| | £ | | |
| Factory (direct) | | | |
| wages | 24,225 | | |
| Factory (direct) | | | |
| expenses | 6,375  30,600 | | |
| Prime cost | 46,600 | | |
| Indirect wages | 2,500 | | |
| Indirect expenses | 1,000 | | |
| Deprec. of plant | 2,000  5,500 | | |
| Work in progress | | | |
| Oct. 1 | 3,800 | | |
| Less: Work in | | | |
| progress Oct. 31 | 3,500  300 | | |
| Factory/Works Cost | 52,400 | | 52,400 |
| Cost of production b/d | 52,400 | Market value of goods | |
| | | produced c/d | 60,900 |
| Estimated gross profit on | | | |
| manufacture to show | | | |
| market price of produc- | | | |
| tion c/d | 8,500 | | |
| | 60,900 | | 60,900 |
| Stock of Finished Goods | | Sales less returns | 98,000 |
| Oct. 1 | 4,750 | | |
| Purchases FG | 2,350 | | |
| Market value of manufactured | | | |
| goods b/d | 60,900 | | |
| Warehousing expenses | 1,725 | | |
| | 69,725 | | |
| Less: Stock FG Oct. 31 | 5,525 | | |
| Cost of Sales | 64,200 | | |
| Gross Profit c/d | 33,800 | | |
| | 98,000 | | 98,000 |
| Salaries | 6,700 | Gross profit b/d | 33,800 |
| Carriage outwards | 820 | Gross profit on | |
| Office expenses | 2,380 | manufacture b/d | 8,500 |
| Advertising | 3,600 | Discounts received | 700 |
| Discounts allowed | 600 | | |
| Net profit for month | **28,900** | | |
| | £43,000 | | £43,000 |

Sometimes the examiner introduces a figure for the market value of goods manufactured into the question, in this instance £60,900, in order to disclose an estimated 'profit on manufacture'. It is reasonable to assume that the real value of the manufactured goods at the end of the production line is substantially higher than that shown by the revenue and costing records of the firm, mainly due to the time element and the ever-increasing costs of labour and raw material.

In instances of this nature the 'profit on manufacture' is brought down from the debit of manufacturing account to the *credit of profit and loss account* where it joins the gross profit on trading. The ultimate net trading profit is the same, but the adjustment ensures a fairer view of the gross profit percentage and enables management to compare their own production costs with the prices of finished goods on the open market.

## 22.2 PRIME AND FACTORY COSTS

Prime cost varies with the turnover. The basic cost of production comprises materials used in manufacture, and the direct wages and expenses identified as being integral parts of the production scheme or project under way.

A manufacturer's prime cost includes the cost of his raw materials consumed, carriage on those materials and any other direct expenses which can be allocated to that particular batch of his production, plus the total wages to all workmen paid in that production process.

To arrive at the factory or works cost, certain factory 'overheads' must be added to the prime cost. These are referred to as indirect expenses and comprise miscellaneous expenses such as fuel, power, heating and lighting, wages of foremen, cleaners and greasers, and the depreciation of the machinery and equipment in use. The total Factory or Works Cost of Production is thus ascertained, to be brought down to the debit of trading account, subject to any adjustment through the introduction of the market value of the manufactured goods, mentioned above.

## 22.3 FIXED AND VARIABLE OVERHEADS

Profit and loss account expenses are also termed 'overheads'. They may be 'fixed' or 'variable'. Examples of fixed expenses are rent, rates, lighting and heating of the office, insurance and office salaries. An increase in turnover would not have any appreciable effect on these expenses. They remain fairly static until the landlord decides to increase the rent, or the local valuation office increases the rating assessment by another 20p in the pound. Electricity and fuel bills continue to increase, but we regard these as normal, due to inflation and not the result of a bigger trade turnover.

On the other hand, discounts allowed and delivery and van expenses would show a marked increase following a big improvement in the credit sales turnover, and bad debts reserve might have to be raised on the higher debtors' total. Commissions paid to travellers and salesmen would certainly be higher, and the debit for advertising might well be much larger than the previous year, but remember here there is often a delayed action with a big publicity campaign. The large boost of sales at the beginning of the new year could be the result of money spent on publicity at the back end of the old trading year. These are examples of variable expenses affected by, or having some bearing on, the turnover.

## QUESTIONS

1. Prepare a manufacturing and trading account for the month ended December 31 from the following information:

|  |  | December 1 £ | December 31 £ |
|---|---|---|---|
| Stocks { | Raw materials | 45,000 | 42,500 |
|  | Work in progress | 6,750 | 9,330 |
|  | Finished goods | 32,400 | 35,640 |

| | £ | | £ |
|---|---|---|---|
| Purchases (raw materials) | 82,220 | Gross sales | 225,000 |
| Carriage ” ” | 1,500 | Returns inwards | 3,000 |
| Salaries of Works Manager | | Fuel and power | 8,720 |
| and maintenance staff | 6,700 | Production wages | 44,500 |
| Factory expenses and overheads | 5,850 | Deprec. of plant | 4,500 |
| Machinery repairs | 1,260 | | |

Show clearly the cost of raw materials consumed, the cost of production and the cost of sales.

2. From the balances below prepare accounts to disclose:

(a) the cost of production  (b) cost of materials used
(c) cost of goods sold      (d) gross profit on manufacture
(e) gross profit on sales    (f) net trading profit for month

|  | | January 1<br>£ | January 31<br>£ |
|---|---|---|---|
| Stocks | Raw material | 6400 | 7200 |
| | Finished goods | 5800 | 6500 |
| | Work in progress | 1500 | 1200 |

|  | £ |  |  |
|---|---|---|---|
| Purchases of raw material | 22,200 | Office salaries | 3,500 |
| Manufacturing wages | 15,500 | Sales | 85,000 |
| Warehousing wages | 1,600 | Carriage outwards | 330 |
| Carriage on raw material | 620 | Rent received | 250 |
| Office/showroom rates | 660 | Warehouse expenses | 380 |
| Depreciation of factory | | Sales returns | 550 |
| plant and machinery | 800 | Selling expenses | 2,400 |
| Discounts received | 690 | Discounts allowed | 720 |
| Heating/lighting of factory | 1,750 | General expenses | 1,200 |
| Heating/lighting of office | | Advertising | 780 |
| and showroom | 480 | Insurances (general) | 200 |
| Factory rates and insurance | 1,450 | | |

*Note* Manufactured goods are to be transferred to the Sales Department at the current market value of £56,000.

3. A few years ago Aunt Emily left her niece Doris Brown a fairly substantial legacy. Miss Brown could have left the money in gilt-edged securities and lived quite comfortably on the investment income. Instead, she decided to purchase a small machine shop and ladies' outfitters, and use the trade name 'Roxana' for her products.

The trial balance below was taken out for the month of June (see p. 194).

The stocks on hand at June 30 were:

| Raw materials | £450 |
|---|---|
| Finished goods | £800 |

Work in progress was valued at £380; expenses accrued were workshop wages £110 and warehouse wages £80. Further depreciation for machinery to be 10 per cent on cost, and bad debt provision to remain as it stands.

You are required to prepare a complete manufacturing, trading and profit and loss account for the month ended June 30, and a balance sheet as on that date.

|  | £ | £ |
|---|---|---|
| Capital Account   Miss Brown | | |
|   Original investment | | 8,000 |
| Drawings and current account | | |
|   Credit balance June 1 | | 50 |
|   Cash withdrawn during month | 500 | |
| Freehold premises at cost | 6,000 | |
| Machinery/equipment at cost | | |
|   plus additions to date | 3,400 | |
| Aggregate deprec. on machinery | | |
|   etc. | | 1,200 |
| Motor van at cost | 2,200 | |
| Aggregate deprec. on van | | 600 |
| Stock June 1   Raw materials | 840 | |
|              Finished goods | 1,500 | |
| Purchases   Raw materials | 3,750 | |
| Wages:  Workshop | 5,320 | |
|         Warehouse | 2,400 | |
| General warehousing expenses | 620 | |
| Net sales | | 18,400 |
| Trade debtors and creditors | 1,830 | 1,440 |
| Discounts | 120 | 180 |
| Advertising | 270 | |
| Rates and insurance: | | |
|   Apportioned to machine shop | 280 | |
|   and warehouse/office | 140 | |
| Provision for doubtful debts | | 100 |
| Office salaries | 800 | |
| General expenses | 120 | |
| Work in progress June 1 | 550 | |
| Cash in hand | 80 | |
| Bank overdraft | | 750 |
| | 30,720 | 30,720 |

# INTRODUCTION TO COMPANY ACCOUNTS

## 23.1 PUBLIC AND PRIVATE COMPANIES

Most limited companies are associations of people formed in accordance with procedures laid down by the Companies Acts of 1948, 1967 and 1976.

These associations have a common capital subscribed by members, and their purpose in almost every instance is to engage in some form of commercial or industrial enterprise with a view to making a trading profit.

A limited company is a legal entity, incorporated by registration with the Registrar of Joint-Stock Companies, and subject to certain checks and conditions imposed by the Registrar to safeguard the interests of both members and creditors.

The main advantage of a limited company is the limitation of the personal liability of its members. If a member (shareholder) has paid up the full amount due on his allotted shares, or if he has had shares transferred to him which are fully paid, then he has no further liability for the debts and obligations of the company of which he is a member.

The limited company, through its large capital and additional cash resources, has unlimited scope for expansion and development, and its continuity is assured, i.e. it is not affected by the death or personal interests and inclinations of individual members.

On the other hand, the real owners of the business (the shareholders) take no active part in the company's affairs beyond voting at meetings and re-electing directors to manage the company.

The two main types of limited companies are: (a) Private companies and (b) Public companies

| Private Companies | Public Companies |
|---|---|
| Minimum limit of two members and maximum of fifty, excluding past and present exployees. | Minimum of seven members and no maximum |
| Need only have one director. | Must have at least two directors. |
| Shares not issued for public subscription, and cannot be sold without consent of members. | Public subscription for shares the big feature. Shares may also be freely transferred and sold and are often quoted on the Stock Exchange. |
| Much less publicity and no general quotations on Stock Exchange. | |

## 23.2 TYPES OF SHARE CAPITAL

*Nominal, Authorised or Registered Capital* – the amount the company is authorised to raise, as laid down in the Memorandum of Association. Note that the full amount need not necessarily be issued.

*Issued or Subscribed Capital* – the nominal amount of share capital issued and subscribed by the public.

*Called-up Capital* – the amount required from members on application, allotment and call accounts.

*Paid-up Capital* – the amount actually received from members, which may not be the same as that 'called up' as there may be some 'calls in arrear' (money due not yet paid).

*Uncalled Capital* – the difference between the company's Called-up Capital and the nominal value of the Issued Capital.

*Example*    K.C. Ltd has an authorised capital of £100,000 consisting of 100,000 shares of the nominal value of £1 each. Half of the authorised capital was issued and taken up. The position at June 30 was that 75p on the issued shares had been called up, and all calls due had been paid except for one member with a holding of 200 shares who had not yet paid his last call of 25p.

In this instance the balance sheet of K.C. Ltd will depict the following on the Capital and Liabilities side:

K.C. Ltd   as at June 30

| Share Capital | | |
|---|---|---|
| Authorised Capital | | £ |
| 100,000 shares of £1 each | | 100,000 |
| Issued Capital | £ | |
| 50,000 shares of £1 each | | |
| 75p per share called up | 37,500 | |
| Less: Calls in arrear | 50 | 37,450 |

*Note* in the example above:

| | |
|---|---|
| The authorised capital is | £100,000 |
| Issued capital is | £50,000 |
| Called-up capital is | £37,500 |
| Paid-up capital is | £37,450 |
| Uncalled capital is | £12,500 |

## 23.3  CLASSES OF SHARES

There are three main classes of shares – Preference, Ordinary and Deferred, but again these might be varied on the following lines:

*Preference Shares* have the right to receive dividends of a fixed percentage before other classes participate, and they may also be preferential for repayment of capital in the event of winding up.

*Cumulative Preference Shares* are entitled to any arrears of dividend being made up before the claims from other groups.

*Participating Preference Shares* carry the entitlement to share in further profits after payment of their fixed dividend, usually after a certain maximum dividend has been paid to Ordinary. Shareholders.

*Redeemable Preference Shares* are sometimes issued subject to certain conditions by the company for redemption at a later date.

*Ordinary Shares* form the bulk of a company's shares as a general rule. These shares carry no special rights or preferences like the Preference Shares, either for dividend or in the event of winding up. Although much more speculative than preference shares, they may earn considerable dividends in boom years. Sometimes they are split into two classes:

*Preferred Ordinary* carrying a fixed rate of dividend *after* preference claims have been met, and *Deferred Ordinary* with no fixed dividend but the entitlement to take the surplus profits after all other claims have been met.

*Deferred or Founders' Shares* are sometimes issued as fully paid to the original promoters and directors for their services in formation, but they only rank for dividend after all other classes have received their quotas.

## 23.4 NEW TERMS

*Stock* is bulk capital which can be divided into fractional amounts. Shares must be fully paid before conversion into stock.

*Share Certificates* are issued under the company's seal certifying that the person named is the owner of a number of shares of a certain class.

*Debentures* are loans. A debenture holder is a creditor of the company. Debentures carry a fixed rate of interest, similar to preference shares, but no voting rights are attached as debenture holders are not members of the company. Mortgage debentures are secured on some property of the company (premises or machinery), whereas naked debentures are loans or bonds made under the seal of the company. Debentures may be redeemable or irredeemable, and debenture interest is a charge and must be paid whether the company either makes a profit or incurs a loss.

*Preliminary or Formation Expenses* are incurred when a new company is floated, and will include legal fees and stamp duty, accountants' fees for investigations and reports, underwriting commission on the share issue, and the cost of printing the Memorandum and Articles of Association. This expense may be considerable, and sometimes remains as a debit balance for a year or two before being 'written off' against profits. The balance is carried forward as a fictitious asset, below the current assets on the balance sheet, until written off.

## 23.5 SHARE ISSUES

The trading records and the account books of a limited company are similar to those of a privately owned one-man business or a partnership, but one main distinction is in the way a company raises its capital, in particular the public limited company, through public subscription. The interests of both the shareholders and the creditors must be protected by law, and consequently the final accounts of limited companies are subject to strict control by the Companies Acts.

### Share issue of a Public Company

Examination questions on share issues generally involve payment of the nominal value of the shares by instalments. The procedure with regard to the financial side is thus:

|  | Debit | Credit |
|---|---|---|
| 1. When the application money for the shares is received from the public | Bank | Application and Allotment Account |
| 2. Where issue is over-subscribed, certain application money is returned to unsuccessful applicants with Letters of Regret | Applic./ Allot. A/c | Bank |
| 3. Allotment to successful applicants confirmed by letter, with request for sum now due on allotment. It is at this stage where the entries on Share Capital Account first appear. | Applic./ Allot. A/c | Share Capital A/c |
| 4. The allotment money comes in | Bank | Applic./Allot. A/c |
| 5. Directors ask for first (and perhaps final) call | Call A/c | Share Capital A/c |
| 6. Call money comes in | Bank | Call A/c |
| 7. Where call money remains unpaid after a reasonable period and reminders of the member's commitment remain unheeded. | Calls in Arrear | Call A/c |

*Note* (a) It is usual to combine Application and Allotment Accounts
(b) It is only *after the application stage* that the Share Capital Account comes into existence, being built up by credit entries at each subsequent stage *before the money is received on allotment and on call* from the members of the company.

**Illustration**

DRS Ltd offer to the public 100,000 Ordinary Shares of £1, payable by instalments as follows:

> 20p on application
> 30p on allotment
> 50p first and final call

Applications are received for 150,000 shares. £4000 is returned to unsuccessful applicants asking for less than 100 shares, and the allotment money is adjusted with regard to those successful applicants whose own applications have been reduced. The balance of the allotment money and the full amount of the first and final call were received without complication. These are the book entries:

Cash Book

| | £ | | £ |
|---|---|---|---|
| Applic./Allot. A/c | 30,000 | Refund of Applic. money | 4,000 |
| " " | 24,000 | Balance c/d | 100,000 |
| First & Final Call | 50,000 | | |
| | 104,000 | | 104,000 |
| Balance b/d | 100,000 | | |

Application and Allotment Account

| | £ | | £ |
|---|---|---|---|
| Share Capital A/c | 50,000 | Cash Book | 30,000 |
| Refund of money CB | 4,000 | " " | 24,000 |

Ordinary Share Capital Account

| | £ | | £ |
|---|---|---|---|
| Balance c/d | 100,000 | Applic./Allot. A/c | 50,000 |
| | | First/Final Call | 50,000 |
| | | Balance b/d | 100,000 |

First and Final Call

| | £ | | £ |
|---|---|---|---|
| Share Capital A/c | 50,000 | Cash Book | 50,000 |

Balance Sheet of DRS
after share issue

| Authorised and Issued | | | |
|---|---|---|---|
| Share Capital | | | |
| | £ | | £ |
| 100,000 Ordinary Shares of £1 fully paid | 100,000 | Bank or assets acquired | 100,000 |

## 23.6 CALLS IN ARREAR

Calls in arrear are unpaid calls and debit balances on defaulting share-holders' accounts, members who have applied for shares but are unable to meet the instalments due. At the beginning of this chapter the call arrears were shown, in total, as a deduction, on the balance sheet, from the Issued Share Capital.

To explain the accounting entries let us assume that John Smith, a company member in the last illustration, had applied for 500 shares, and paid his application and allotment money, but was unable to meet the final call of 50p.

The accounts affected are the cash book and the Final Call Account, now amended as follows:

Cash Book

| | £ | | £ |
|---|---|---|---|
| Applic./Allot. A/c | 30,000 | Money refunded | 4,000 |
| "       " | 24,000 | Balance c/d | 99,750 |
| First/Final Call | 49,750 | | |
| | 103,750 | | 103,750 |
| Balance c/d | 99,750 | | |

First and Final Call

| | £ | | £ |
|---|---|---|---|
| Share Capital | 50,000 | Cash Book | 49,750 |
| | | Transfer to Calls in Arrear | 250 |

Calls in Arrear Account

| | £ | | |
|---|---|---|---|
| Transfer from First and Final Call | 250 | | |

John Smith has a contractual obligation to pay the balance of the sum due on the shares allotted to him, but his debt is not shown in the trade debtor's total. The debit balance will be transferred to Calls in Arrear Account, to be deducted from the Issued Share Capital on the balance sheet in this manner:

Balance Sheet of DRS as at .......

| Authorised and Issued | | | |
|---|---|---|---|
| Share Capital | | | |
| | £ | | £ |
| 100,000 Ordinary Shares at £1 each | 100,000 | Bank or assets acquired | 99,750 |
| Less:   Calls in arrear | 250 | | |
| | 99,750 | | |

After giving John Smith reasonable notice to pay the sum of £250, the Company will stipulate that his shares will be forfeited by a certain date and sold, probably to another member.

## 23.7  SHARES ISSUED AT A PREMIUM

A successful company may decide to issue further shares at a premium, i.e. above par value. The premium is normally paid with the allotment money, the book entries being:

> debit cash and credit allotment account when allotment money (plus premium) is received.

The premium is then transferred to a Share Premium Account and remains a credit balance in the books, a *capital reserve* not available for transfer back to the revenue account and paid away in dividend, which might be the case with regard to a general reserve. On the balance sheet a capital reserve is positioned under its own heading between the Issued Share Capital and the Revenue Reserves, thus:

| Authorised and Issued | | |
|---|---:|---|
| Share Capital | £ | |
| 200,000 Ordinary Shares of £1 fully paid | 200,000 | B A N K   A N D |
| Capital Reserve Share premium account | 10,000 | |
| | | N E T   A S S E T S |
| Revenue Reserves General reserve account | 20,000 | |
| P & L undistributed profit | 5,000 | |

## 23.8  SHARES ISSUED AT A DISCOUNT

A Company that has been incorporated for at least one year may apply for Court permission to issue shares at a discount.

The amount of discount will be credited to Application and Allotment Account, the debit being taken to Share Discount Account. This debit will be shown on the balance sheet as a *fictitious asset*, under its own heading at the bottom of the assets, until either written off against profits or offset against a capital reserve such as premium on shares.

## 23.9  PRESENTATION OF FINAL ACCOUNTS

The net trading profit of a limited company is carried down to the credit of an appropriation account where it joins any balance of undistributed profit from the previous year.

Appropriations of profit, transfers to reserve, dividends paid and dividends recommended by directors are debited to this account and the balance is carried forward to the balance sheet, to be shown under the heading of revenue reserves and undistributed profits.

Profit and Loss Appropriation Account

| | £ | | £ |
|---|---|---|---|
| Transfer to General Reserve | 5,000 | Balance b/f from last year | 2,500 |
| Preference dividend for half-year paid | 8,000 | Net trading profit b/d | 33,000 |
| Preference dividend now due | 8,000 | | |
| Ordinary dividend proposed | 10,000 | | |
| Balance, undistributed profit carried forward | 4,500 | | |
| | 35,500 | | 35,500 |

Interest on debentures and directors' fees should not be debited to the appropriation account as they are specific charges and expenses of the company and not appropriations of profit.

The members at their annual general meeting have still to approve and adopt the recommendations of their directors in so far as allocations to reserves and the declaration of dividends.

The liabilities side of the balance sheet now takes the following form:

| Authorised Capital | | | |
|---|---|---|---|
| | | £ | |
| 200,000 10% Preference Shares of £1 | | 200,000 | |
| 100,000 Ordinary Shares of 50p each | | 50,000 | |
| **Issued Capital** | | | |
| 160,000 10% Pref. Shares of £1 fully paid | | 160,000 | |
| 100,000 Ordinary Shares of 50p fully paid | | 50,000 | |
| Capital Reserve | | | SUNDRY |
| Share premium account | | 5,000 | |
| Revenue Reserves | | | ASSETS |
| | £ | £ | |
| General reserve | 20,000 | | |
| Addition | 5,000 | 25,000 | |
| P & L balance b/f | | 4,500 | 29,500 |
| Current Liabilities | | | |
| Trade creditors | | 8,400 | |
| Expense creditors | | 620 | |
| Dividends proposed: | | | |
| Preference | | 8,000 | |
| Ordinary | | 10,000 | 27,020 |

A dividend is an entitlement to a portion or allocation of profit, normally expressed as a percentage. It must be recommended for payment by the directors and approved by members at their annual general meeting.

Interim dividends are sometimes paid by well-established companies, and generally preference shareholders are paid half-yearly. Income tax is deducted *at the source* by the company (ignored in these small examples). *Both the dividends paid and those recommended are debited to the appropriation account,* transferred from the Dividend Account in this manner:

Share Dividend Account - 10% Preference

| | | | £ | | | £ |
|---|---|---|---|---|---|---|
| June 30 | Bank | CB | 8,000 | Dec. 31 | Appropr. A/c (interim paid) | 8,000 |
| Dec. 31 | Balance c/d | | 8,000 | 31 | Appropr. A/c (final declared) | 8,000 |
| | | | 16,000 | | | 16,000 |
| | | | | Jan. 1 | Balance c/d | 8,000 |

Note that this credit balance (£8000) appears under the heading of current liabilities in the balance sheet. When paid to members, early in the New Year, bank is credited and the above account debited and closed.

A similar account would be made out for the ordinary shareholders. Remember though, that shareholders will receive only net warrants, after deduction of the standard rate of income tax.

## 23.10 CAPITAL AND REVENUE RESERVES

There is a marked distinction between these two classes of reserve. A capital reserve comes into existence through a gain or capital profit such as a premium or bonus on the sale of shares over and above their par value. Since it cannot be paid away in dividend, it becomes a permanent form of reserve, until it can perhaps be offset against a capital loss.

A general reserve, on the other hand, indicates that money is being withheld from dividend distribution to strengthen the financial position of the business. The working capital of the business is increased or improved, with greater finance available to buy further supplies or to obtain good discounts. Sometimes a sum of money is invested outside the business equivalent to the amount debited to the appropriation account. It is then called a Reserve Fund and a corresponding account for the investment appears on the assets side of the balance sheet.

## 23.11 THE ANNUAL RETURN

Directors are responsible to lay the annual accounts before members at least once during each calendar year, and to send to the Registrar of Joint-Stock Companies an *annual return* giving particulars of directors and members, and also a copy of the last balance sheet and profit and loss account.

## 23.12 STYLE OF PRESENTATION

Financial statements should 'tell their story' in clear, unmistakable language so that members of companies and other interested parties can interpret the meaning and full significance of the figures in front of them.

Prominent headings and groupings of items are main features of company accounts, and correct presentation of the final accounts, from the examiner's standpoint, is often as important as their accuracy.

Most limited companies present their annual accounts in a vertical narrative style. The information given by statements shown in this way enables the trained accountant and manager to see not only the results of trading and the financial position at a certain date, but also *how* the results have been achieved and *what* assets are actually represented by the share capital of the company.

The Companies Acts insist that a clear distinction is made between charges and appropriations of profit. Full disclosure must be made of 'directors' remuneration showing the distinction between fees and salaries, amounts withdrawn from or transferred to reserves, interest on loans, overdrafts and debentures, taxation owing or reserved, dividends paid and proposed, profits and losses of a non-recurrent nature, and income from quoted and unquoted investments'; this part of the profit and loss account disclosing this information being referred to as 'the published section', illustrated thus:

Published Profit and Loss Account of a Company
for the year ended December 31

| | £ | £ | £ | Previous year's figures |
|---|---|---|---|---|
| Net trading profit from General P & L Account | | | 107,000 | |
| Directors' fees | 15,000 | | | |
| Directors' other emoluments | 2,400 | 17,400 | | |
| Audit fees | | 2,000 | | |
| Debenture interest | | 4,000 | | |
| Depreciation of plant | | 22,000 | | |
| Deprec. of vans and equipment | | 1,600 | 47,000 | |
| Net profit for year | | | 60,000 | |
| Less: Corporation Tax | | | 28,000 | |
| Profit after tax | | | 32,000 | |
| Transfer to General Reserve | | 2,000 | | |
| Proposed dividend Ordy Shares | | 25,000 | 27,000 | |
| Retained profit for current year | | | 5,000 | |
| Add: P & L credit balance from last year | | | 2,250 | |
| Undistributed profit taken to balance sheet | | | 7,250 | |

*Note* the grouping of essential information and the distinction between charges and appropriations of profit on the 'published section' of the profit and loss account.

The vertical narrative style of both the revenue account and the balance sheet, now shown, lends itself to comparison and ease of explanation with its footnotes and figures of the previous year, shown in anticipation of members' questions. Note that the balance sheet now shown, discloses at a glance the working capital, net assets and the equity of the company.

Balance Sheet as at December 31

| Fixed assets | Cost | Aggregate deprec. | Book value | | Comparative figures of last year |
|---|---|---|---|---|---|
| | £ | £ | £ | £ | |
| Buildings | 75,000 | - | 75,000 | | |
| Machinery | 220,000 | 88,000 | 132,000 | | |
| Vans, etc. | 16,000 | 6,400 | 9,600 | 216,600 | |

Investments (quoted)
10,000 12% Pref. Shares in RST Ltd     10,000
   (market value £8500)

| Current Assets | £ | £ |
|---|---|---|
| Stock | 9,500 | |
| Trade debtors | 15,300 | |
| Prepayments | 450 | |
| Bank deposits | 38,000 | |
| Current account | 2,400 | 65,650 |

| Less Current Liabilities | | |
|---|---|---|
| Trade creditors | 6,650 | |
| Expense creditors | 350 | |
| Corporation Tax | 28,000 | |
| Proposed dividend | 25,000 | 60,000 |
| Working capital | | 5,650 |

Net Assets     232,250

Less 10% Debentures (secured on
  buildings)     40,000

    192,250

The assets of the Company are represented by:

Authorised Share Capital     £
200,000 Ordinary Shares of £1     200,000

Issued Share Capital
150,000 Ord. Shares of £1 fully paid     150,000

Capital Reserve
Share premium account     15,000

| Revenue Reserves | £ | £ |
|---|---|---|
| General reserve | 18,000 | |
| Addition this year | 2,000 | 20,000 |
| P & L credit balance | | 7,250    27,250 |

    192,250

# QUESTIONS

1. Distinguish between:

(a) Authorised, Issued and Paid-up Capital.
(b) Ordinary and Preference Shares.
(c) Debentures and a long-term Bank Loan.
(d) Money payable by company members on application, allotment and call.

2. Record the following information in ledger accounts and prepare a balance sheet as at December 31.

(a) Company DRS Ltd was formed with an authorised share capital of £250,000 composed of 500,000 Ordinary Shares of 50p.
(b) 200,000 shares were issued to the public at a premium of 20p per share. The whole issue was fully subscribed and allotted.
(c) New premises were purchased for £50,000 and formation expenses amounted to £5500.

3. A public limited company issued 100,000 Preference Shares of £1 each at a premium of 10p and £30,000 12 per cent Debentures at a discount of 5 per cent.
Applications were received for 120,000 shares and the money surplus to requirements was returned.
The share issue was placed on this basis:
25p on application, 35p on allotment (which included the premium) and 50p a month after allotment.
All amounts on application and allotment were duly received and banked, but one member who had applied for 200 shares could not pay his final call. He was warned that unless he settled the amount due within fourteen days his shares would be forfeited. He promised to make immediate arrangements with his bank.
The debentures were subscribed in full and the money banked. You are required to:

(a) Give the cash book and ledger entries with regard to both issues.
(b) Show the balance sheet entries at this stage.

4. The WHT Company Ltd was registered with an authorised capital of £100,000 consisting of 100,000 Ordinary Shares of £1 each.

The full amount of capital was issued at a premium of 20 per cent and all monies received from members.
Six months after commencing business the following balances were extracted from the books, *subsequent* to ascertaining the net trading profit for the six months, and making certain allocations and distributions from that profit.

| | Book<br>balances |
|---|---|
| | £ |
| Plant and machinery (cost £57,500, depreciation to date £3500) | 54,000 |
| Van (cost £3000, depreciation £300) | 2,700 |
| Freehold premises at cost | 60,000 |
| Investments 8% Treasury Stock (market value £2880) | 3,200 |
| Stock October 31 | 6,500 |
| Trade debtors | 8,200 |
| Provision for bad debts | 205 |
| Trade creditors | 5,600 |
| Expense creditors | 380 |
| Share premium account | 20,000 |
| General reserve | 2,000 |
| Reserve for taxation | 4,000 |
| Ordinary dividend proposed | 5,000 |
| Credit balance of P & L appropriation account (undistributed profit) | 3,165 |
| Bank balance October 31 | 3,500 |
| Formation expenses not yet written off | 2,250 |

You are required to draft the balance sheet as at October 31 to show the working capital and the equity or net worth of the Company.

5. The RAS Company Ltd has an authorised share capital of £100,000 divided into 50,000 10% Preference Shares of £1 each and 50,000 Ordinary Shares of £1 each, all issued and fully paid. The preference shares had been issued at a premium of 10 per cent.

For the year ended June 30 the directors recommended payment of the second part of the preference dividend, but made no recommendation for the ordinary shareholders. At the year-end the balance of the debenture interest was still to be paid. The directors also recommended the transfer to General Reserve the sum of £2000, and the profit and loss 'published part' of the appropriation account is to include annual depreciation charges of 10 per cent on cost for Machinery and plant, and 25 per cent on cost for Motor vehicles.

Draft the published section of the profit and loss account and make up the balance sheet of the company in compliance with the Companies Acts from the information above and the balances extracted from the books at June 30, shown below:

Buildings (cost £80,000): Machinery and plant (cost £50,000, book balance now £35,000 before this year's depreciation): Motor vehicles (cost £6000, book balance £4500 before deprec.): Stock June 30 £15,700: Bank balance £5200: Cash in hand £120: Trade debtors £18,300: Creditors for rates £420: Trade creditors £6600: Directors' fees £15,000: Audit fees £1800: Net trading profit for current year £34,000: P & L credit balance from last year £3300: General Reserve Account Balance brought forward £10,000: Debit for Preference Dividend for half-year £2500: 12 per cent Debentures £20,000: Debit for payment of half-year's interest to debenture holders £1200: Capital reserve (Preference Premium Account £5000).

Aspects of taxation may be ignored.

6. RHJ Ltd was registered as a private company three years ago with an authorised capital of £100,000 consisting of 10,000 Preference Shares of £1 each and 90,000 Ordinary Shares of £1 each. The preference shares were issued to the original directors and promoters, and so far only 40,000 of the ordinary shares have been issued, confined, in the main, to one particular family group, the relatives of the founder of this old-established retail business, now formed into a limited company. There are three full-time working directors of the company, who share all office and administration work, and are paid on a monthly salary basis, plus nominal directors' fees of £250 each half-year.

The following balances were extracted from the books of the company for the year ended December 31.

| | £ | £ |
|---|---|---|
| Premises at cost | 36,000 | |
| Machinery (cost £25,000) | 19,500 | |
| Fixtures and fittings at cost | 1,000 | |
| Delivery van (bought 6 months ago) | 2,000 | |
| Purchases and Sales | 65,000 | 113,500 |
| Returns inwards/outwards | 240 | 360 |
| Warehouse wages | 9,205 | |
| Directors' fees and salaries | 13,430 | |
| Stock   January 1 | 5,500 | |
| Petty cash | 50 | |
| Bank balance | 11,700 | |
| Treasury Stock (£4000 nominal bought two weeks before end of trading year at 85) | 3,400 | |
| Trade debtors/creditors | 8,850 | 6,250 |
| Provision for bad debts | | 400 |
| Accountancy charges | 500 | |
| General expenses (including rates) | 1,025 | |
| Insurance | 480 | |
| Warehouse heating/lighting | 920 | |
| Office heating/lighting | 410 | |
| Debenture interest to June 30 | 300 | |
| 12% Debentures | | 5,000 |
| Preference dividend paid at June 30 | 500 | |
| Interim dividend (5% on Ordinary Share Capital) paid June 30 | 2,000 | |
| Undistributed profit brought forward from previous year | | 6,500 |
| 10% Preference Share Capital | | 10,000 |
| Ordinary Share Capital (fully issued with no calls in arrear) | | 40,000 |
| | 182,010 | 182,010 |

You are required to prepare the trading and profit and loss appropriation account of the Company for the year ended December 31, and a balance sheet as at December 31, giving effect, as far as possible, to the requirements of the Companies Acts, and taking into account the adjustments listed below:

(a) The stock valuation at December 31 was £6200.
(b) Insurance paid in advance at the year end was £120; wages owing to own workpeople £200.
(c) Depreciate machinery by 10 per cent on cost, and depreciate the new van by 20 per cent per annum.
(d) The provision for bad debts is to be adjusted to 4 per cent of the total debtors' balances.
(e) Transfer £10,000 to Taxation Reserve; otherwise ignore other taxation aspects.
(f) Provide for debenture interest now due.
(g) The directors recommend payment of the dividend on the Preference Shares for the second half of the year.
(h) If profits are available, allow for a further 10 per cent dividend on the Ordinary Shares, making a total dividend of 15 per cent for the year.

# APPENDIX

# APPENDIX

## A.1 BASIC DOCUMENTS OF ACCOUNTING

**(a)**

```
                    ORDER

No. 1234                  A. Bray & Co.
                          8 Main Street
Messrs P. Jay Ltd         Kingford
The Square
Heriton                   2 May ..

Please supply:
```

| Catalogue number | | |
|---|---|---|
| 56/A6 | 5 doz. | men's socks navy & grey 50p each |
| 88/B4 | 3 doz. | assorted ties 80p each |
| | | Signed: T. Brown Manager |

The initiation of a commercial transaction normally starts with the ORDER. This may be verbal (perhaps by telephone), or it may be typed or written, often on an official order form, as illustrated here.

**(b)**

```
        ADVICE/DESPATCH NOTE

              P. Jay Ltd
              The Square
              Heriton        6 May ..

Messrs A. Bray & Co.
8 Main Str, Kingford


Dear Sirs,

     We have today despatched to you,
by our own van, the following goods,
in accordance with your Order No. 1234
of 2 May ..

     56/A6 5 doz. men's socks (navy
               and grey)
     88/B4 3 doz. assorted ties

     Credit of £2.50 will be allowed
on the return of the packing case.

               Signed:  S. Smith
                        Director
```

The firm receiving the order first checks on the availability of supplies, and then confirms by ADVICE or DESPATCH NOTE that the goods are on the way.

A DELIVERY NOTE (similar to the Advice Note) is normally sent with the goods to enable the receipts storeman to check the contents of the package on its arrival. The delivery note is signed and handed back to the carrier as proof of delivery.

(c)                    Invoice

```
No. 6346
                 The Square
                 Heriton        6 May ..

Messrs A. Bray & Co.
8 Main Str, Kingford

     B O U G H T   O F   P. Jay Ltd
     (V.A.T. regd  no.  915 2868 34)
```

| Ref. | | £ |
|---|---|---|
| 56/A6 | 5 doz. men's socks navy & grey @ 50p | 30.00 |
| 88/B4 | 3 doz. assorted ties @ 80p | 28.80 |
| | | 58.80 |
| | V.A.T. at 10% | 5.88 |
| | | 64.68 |
| | Package (returnable) | 2.50 |
| E. & O.E. | | 67.18 |

The goods have been ordered, delivered, checked and now put to stock, on shelves or in drawers.

The initiation of the financing part of a credit transaction starts with the supplier's INVOICE, now illustrated, sent to A. Bray & Co., the firm ordering the goods as part of their general merchandise on retail sale to the public.

(d)            Credit Note

```
No. 348                   The Square
                          Heriton

                          15 May ..
```

| CREDITED BY P. Jay Ltd | |
|---|---|
| By return of one packing case... recd 14 May | £2.50 |

The CREDIT NOTE, often printed or written in red, acknowledges a claim for an allowance or reduction of the goods charged by the supplier.

In this instance the claim is for the return of the container, but in many cases it refers to the claim of the buyer for unsuitable or damaged goods.

(e)  Statement

| | P. Jay Ltd |
| | The Square |
| | Heriton |

Note that the packing case or container is first charged on the invoice (in case it is not returned) and then credited and deducted on the monthly STATEMENT.

31 May ..

Messrs A. Bray & Co.
8 Main Street
Kingford

| | | | £ | £ |
|---|---|---|---|---|
| May 6 | To goods Inv. no. 6346 | | 67.18 | |
| 15 | Less C/N for returned case | | 2.50 | 64.68 |
| 3½% one month | | | | 64.68 |

Assuming no payment during the month of May has been made by the customer and debtor, A. Bray & Co., their account will appear in the sales ledger of P. Jay Ltd thus:

Dr.                          A. Bray & Co.                          Cr.

| May 6 | SDB | | £ 67.18 | May 15 31 | SRB Balance c/d | | £ 2.50 64.68 |
|---|---|---|---|---|---|---|---|
| | | | 67.18 | | | | 67.18 |
| June 1 | Balance b/d | | 64.68 | | | | |

Note that the full amount of the sale (the price of the goods plus V.A.T.) is posted to the account of the customer, but P. Jay Ltd will still be responsible to account to H.M. Customs and Excise for the V.A.T. tax added to the invoice in this transaction.

## A.2  V.A.T. INPUT AND OUTPUT PROCEDURE

It is always the consumer (or purchaser) who bears the full brunt of the government charge known as 'Value Added Tax', best explained by illustration:

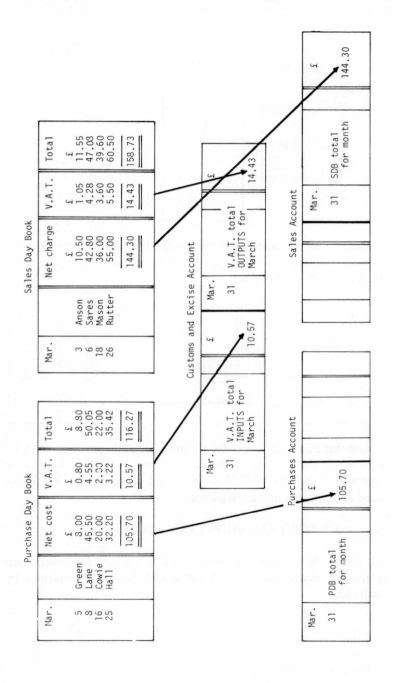

**Purchase Day Book**

| Mar. | | Net cost | V.A.T. | Total |
|---|---|---|---|---|
| | | £ | £ | £ |
| 5 | Green | 3.00 | 0.80 | 8.80 |
| 8 | Lane | 45.50 | 4.55 | 50.05 |
| 16 | Cowie | 20.00 | 2.30 | 22.00 |
| 25 | Hall | 32.20 | 3.22 | 35.42 |
| | | 105.70 | 10.57 | 116.27 |

**Sales Day Book**

| Mar. | | Net charge | V.A.T. | Total |
|---|---|---|---|---|
| | | £ | £ | £ |
| 3 | Anson | 10.50 | 1.05 | 11.55 |
| 6 | Sares | 42.80 | 4.28 | 47.03 |
| 18 | Mason | 36.00 | 3.60 | 39.60 |
| 26 | Rutter | 55.00 | 5.50 | 60.50 |
| | | 144.30 | 14.43 | 158.73 |

**Customs and Excise Account**

| Mar. | | £ | Mar. | | £ |
|---|---|---|---|---|---|
| 31 | V.A.T. total INPUTS for March | 10.57 | 31 | V.A.T. total OUTPUTS for March | 14.43 |

**Purchases Account**

| Mar. | | £ |
|---|---|---|
| 31 | PDB total for month | 105.70 |

**Sales Account**

| | | £ |
|---|---|---|
| Mar. | | |
| 31 | SDB total for month | 144.30 |

*Note*  (a) V.A.T. has been charged at 10 per cent.

(b) The amount due to Customs and Excise Account (£3.86 owing to the government) will be settled by cheque, crediting the cash book and debiting the above account at the end of the agreed period for settlement.

(c) The combined amounts shown in the total column of each day book are taken to the personal accounts, so that the tax is always borne by the customer.

## A.3  BIN CARDS AND STOCK RECORDS

Records of stores received and issued must be kept by all organisations where goods are bought either for resale or for further processing into finished goods.

The size and nature of the storehouse and the extent of stores control will vary according to the size and nature of the business, whether a huge manufacturing concern or a small garage and workshop.

In the engineering industry the heavy bulk stores and liquids in special containers will be stored at ground level, while the lighter and easier-to-handle stores and components will be placed on accessible racks and shelving, whereas the smaller and more easily misplaced stores would be kept in bins for greater security.

Each rack or bin will be numbered clearly and a Bin Card will be attached, although the detailed record of receipts and issues may be kept in the Cost Office.

This is a simple form of Bin Card:

BIN (or stock) CARD

| No. of bin | 28 | Location | outer end of<br>left bay | Max. Qty | 400 |
| --- | --- | --- | --- | --- | --- |
| | | | | Min. Qty | 100 |

Description of store    Bracket, angle iron 5 cm

Code number    RJ 44

| | RECEIPTS | | | ISSUES | | | BALANCE IN STOCK |
| --- | --- | --- | --- | --- | --- | --- | --- |
| Date<br>Feb. | GRB | Qty | Date<br>Feb. | SR | Qty | | |
| 1 | | | 1 | | | | 250 |
| | | | 5 | 328 | 30 | | 220 |
| | | | 8 | 406 | 24 | | 196 |
| | | | 15 | 454 | 48 | | 148 |
| 20 | 224 | 200 | | | | | 348 |
| | | | 25 | 517 | 16 | | 332 |

GRB = Goods Received Book    SR = Stores Requisition

## A.4   WAGES AND LABOUR RECORDS

The working hours of employees are carefully recorded and vouched by time-recording clocks in most industrial organisations, although a small percentage still adopt the metal disc or tally method. Where the latter system is in force, each workman has his individual number impressed upon the tally, which he removes from a board and drops into a box on arrival and departure from work. The time-keeper supervises the arrival and departure of the main work force, and makes up his Time Book and his own records from the tallies deposited in the box and those still left on the board.

These time records are needed for the calculation of wages, based upon three main methods of payment:

(a) *Time basis* at so much an hour, with a higher rate of overtime.

(b) *Piece work* or payment by results, dependent upon the number of articles produced within a given time.

(c) *Bonus systems* which provide incentives to greater effort and higher pay rates for speedier output, the employer benefiting through reduced overhead expense.

Time recording is not only essential for time rates, but is important too for piece rates and bonus systems as oncost is often adopted as a percentage of the time taken.

In addition to the recording at the 'gate', the workman also makes up his own daily or weekly *time sheet* or *job card,* which provides a check on his clock record. The Wages Abstract is made up from the time sheet and job cards, and the cost clerks use it to work out the labour costs and charges to be debited to the various jobs and processes at all stages of production in the works.

A specimen time sheet of one workman is shown, followed by the relevant entry in the Wages Book (or Pay Sheet) with approximations for P.A.Y.E. and National Insurance.

# T I M E   S H E E T

No. 220                                Week ending  20 May ..

Name  A. R. Lee                        Dept    Assembly

| DAY | JOB NO. | HOURS | OVERTIME |
|---|---|---|---|
| THURSDAY | 168 | 7 | |
| FRIDAY | " | 7 | 1 |
| SATURDAY | 216 | 4 | |
| SUNDAY | | | |
| MONDAY | 186 | 7 | 2 |
| TUESDAY | " | 7 | 1 |
| WEDNESDAY | " | 7 | |

| Foreman's signature | Total normal hours          39 | Overtime hours  4 | Total hours   43 |
|---|---|---|---|
| W. W. Day | Normal rate at £1.80 | | O/T rate at 1½ |
| | Gross wage + overtime | £ 70.20 10.80 —— £81.00 | Checked  J. R. S. |

WAGES BOOK

(or PAY SHEET)

week ending   May 20 ..

| Clock No. | Name | EARNINGS | | | TAX DETAILS from PAYE | | | | DEDUCTIONS | | | | Net pay | Employer's NIC |
|---|---|---|---|---|---|---|---|---|---|---|---|---|---|---|
| | | Basic | O/T | Gross pay | Aggreg. to date | Tax due | Tax paid | Refunds | Tax | NIC | Hosp. fund | Total deductions | | |
| | | £ | £ | £ | £ | £ | £ | £ | £ | £ | £ | £ | £ | £ |
| 220 | Lee AR | 70.20 | 10.80 | 81.00 | 515.00 | 78.00 | 63.00 | – | 15.00 | 1.75 | 0.25 | 17.00 | 64.00 | 3.50 |

The total of the 'Net pay' column will be the total drawn from the bank for the pay packets each week. Alternatively, the bank will be asked to pay the net wages in this column direct to the workmen's bank accounts by credit transfer.

The firm's accountant can check, from the Wages Book, the total basic wages and overtime of each workman, the amount due to the Inland Revenue for tax deducted, and the up-to-date position with regard to National Insurance contributions.

## PAY PACKETS

**Computation of number and denomination of notes and coin**
*Example.* Assume that the net pay, after all deductions, for a total work
force of six employees is listed as follows:

|  |  | £ |
|---|---|---|
| Workman No. | 122 | 55.20 |
| " | 123 | 66.28 |
| " | 125 | 72.75 |
| " | 128 | 76.84 |
| " | 129 | 82.35 |
| " | 130 | 68.47 |
|  |  | 421.89 |

The secret of the computation is to work downwards from the higher
denominational note of £5 (or £10 or £20), through the 'silver' and on
to the lowest copper coin, thus:

| | £5 | £1 | 50p | 10p | 5p | 2p | 1p |
|---|---|---|---|---|---|---|---|
| 55.20 | 11 | - | - | 2 | - | - | - |
| 66.28 | 13 | 1 | - | 2 | 1 | 1 | 1 |
| 72.75 | 14 | 2 | 1 | 2 | 1 | - | - |
| 76.84 | 15 | 1 | 1 | 3 | - | 2 | - |
| 82.35 | 16 | 2 | - | 3 | 1 | - | - |
| 68.47 | 13 | 3 | - | 4 | 1 | 1 | - |
| | 82 | 9 | 2 | 16 | 4 | 4 | 1 |

| £410 + 9 | £1 + £1.60 + 20p | 8p + 1p |
|---|---|---|

£419 + £2.80 + 0.09

Total £421.89

## A.5   AN EXTENSION OF THE SLIP SYSTEM

The banks made use of the system long before the trading and merchanting firms found that it could be adapted suitably for their purposes.

The principle involved in the slip system is that each original document (invoice, cash receipt, credit note, etc.) is used in posting both the permanent form of original record (day book or cash book) and also the ledger account. The object of the slip system is to avoid repetitive work and the delay of copying from a copy. Where machine accounting is in use, both or all the original documents are prepared at the same time.

The slip system is of great advantage where accounts need to be posted at speed, the exact position of a person's account being available on request. This, in particular, applies to banking, where it is the practice for the counter clerks to pass back to the ledger clerks (in the office area in the background) the paying-in slips together with the receipts to be credited to a customer's account, and also cheques cashed across the counter.

Some firms have dispensed with the orthodox form of sales day book by taking a short cut in this manner: instead of entering details from their copy invoices in the day book, they staple the invoice copies in book form, and post each debtor's account direct from this record. At the same time a cumulative total is made of the daily sales, to be posted to Sales Account at the end of the month. The sales returns are dealt with in the same way, in reverse.

After all, the sales day book is simply a list of copy invoices assembled in date order, the dates and amounts being copied and posted again to the customers' personal accounts, with the cumulative total of the day book being posted at the end of the month to the credit of Sales Account.

The Sales (Debtors') Ledger could also be dispensed with by taking three copies of the original invoice sent to the customer. One copy would be filed alphabetically in a separate personal folder for each customer; another copy would be used as a build-up for his monthly statement, and the third copy would replace the old day book copy and provide the totals for the credit of Sales Account and also for Sales Control. The customer's statement would be made up and ready for dispatch at the end of the month, and the totals of all debtors' statements listed to provide a check on Sales Control; an effective self-balancing system is essential where short-cut accounting methods are in use.

As the customers pay their accounts their statements, with copy invoices attached, would be stamped 'Paid' and filed away in an 'Accounts Paid' cabinet.

A similar procedure could be followed on the purchase side. The Bought Day Book and the Creditors' Ledger could be by-passed, and after machine operators had extracted the information needed for the Purchases Account and Purchase Control, the suppliers' invoices would be filed away in folders, in batches for ease in checking. At the end of the month there would be an immediate check on the creditors' statements, which, when paid, would be filed away in a 'Suppliers' Accounts Paid' cabinet.

Adaptations of the slip system are likely to involve much paper work, special copy paper or the use of multi-coloured forms and varied rulings. Attachments are fitted to typewriter carriages, successive forms of stationery fed into the typewriter, and several copies made at one operation. The despatch, delivery and accounts copies are all made up at the same time as the original invoice is typed.

Book-keeping and ledger posting machines have a separate mechanism fitted for adding and subtracting, and a balance may be struck at any stage by depressing the typewriter key. These machines can post at one operation:

(a) the debit to the customer's account;
(b) the details for his monthly statement;
(c) a cumulative total of individual debits for posting to the Sales Account.

## A.6   EXAMINATION GUIDANCE AND TECHNIQUE

A few hints are given here about the best way to approach accounting examinations; further help on how to study effectively and pass examinations will be found in Richard Freeman's *Mastering Study Skills*, also in this series.

### (a) Effective study

As long as examinations remain competitive (dependent upon a number of places or on a percentage of passes) a fair proportion of marginal candidates will pass and a fair proportion will fail, simply because of their study methods and examination technique.

Make sure that you will not be marginal.

The pass percentage in most elementary examinations is between 35 and 45 and the candidate who has worked through his course with a fair degree of concentration should be able to keep well above the border line.

### (b) The time factor

Most candidates taking accounting and book-keeping examinations could double their marks if double the time were allowed. Since time is an all-important feature, as much practical work as you can include in your scheme of work is the keynote to this problem. In your preparation time yourself against the clock, and repeat papers you have answered before in two-thirds or half the time you have taken previously.

If you can choose your own place in the examination hall, make sure of good lighting, but avoid too much sun. Appropriate an additional desk or chair if possible, as you will need plenty of elbow-room for working on double foolscap paper.

Put your watch in front of you, ten minutes fast!

### (c) The examination paper

In some accounting examinations the choice of questions is severely limited. Sometimes every question must be answered.

Examiners, however, must set a fair representative paper with not more than one question of the same type (e.g. you would not have two questions on bank reconciliation or on petty cash, but you might have one on each).

Many candidates fail simply through not interpreting the questions properly. This is lack of comprehension, failure to understand written English and follow the instructions laid down. You must aim at pleasing the examiner. After all, *he* is marking *your* paper. Get the proper sense of the question, and answer it *his* way and not your own. Do not reframe the question to suit yourself.

### (d) Easier questions first

After glancing quickly through the whole paper, go through it again slowly and carefully, weighing up each question, and making sure you understand exactly what the examiner wants to know.

There is no need to answer the questions in numerical order. Select the easiest question you can answer and do it first. It will give you greater confidence before attempting the more difficult ones. Get all the smaller and lower mark questions out of the way to begin with, even if you can only answer part of these questions. At least you will earn a few marks by doing this, instead of perhaps forfeiting them in the rush work at the end, particularly if you are stuck on a big final account which has already taken up far too much of your time.

If there is a compulsory question which you do not like the look of, leave it for a while until you have regained your 'second wind' and then you will tackle it with greater confidence. If it is a real bogey, something you know little about, spend your last twenty to thirty minutes on it making some attempt to master it, and leave all your workings for the examiner to see; the latter may reap those marginal marks, after all!

When you realise that you have done something foolish such as deducting the wrong amounts for returns in your trading account, do not scratch out and start altering figures. Simply add a footnote, drawing the examiner's attention to the error, and *amend only your final figures.* You will not lose any marks if this is neatly done.

### (e) In brief

Always use a ruler. Never draw lines freehand. Never scratch out. Just rule through.

Bring down balances on all accounts where there are balances. Never leave in suspension.

Make additions and calculations in pencil first, and then ink-in after rechecking; but never attempt to do a whole question in pencil as you cannot afford the time.

Never cramp headings on final accounts or above ledger accounts. Leave a good space between a number of ledger accounts shown vertically on a page, at least one inch.

In questions requiring written answers, tabulate where possible.

Use a fresh sheet of paper for each question so that you can come back to any unfinished work.

### (f) Complete the paper

Your chances of success will be immeasurably brighter if you aim at a target of *moderately good marks on the paper as a whole,* rather than attempting maximum marks on two or three questions. Assuming that all questions carry equal marks, it is better to earn half marks on five questions instead of two-thirds of the marks on only three completed questions.

Do all you can on one question before starting the next one, but *do not spend any time looking for mistakes in balancing.* Finish the paper first and then, if there is still time, start checking for errors.

More marks will be gained through speed and neatness than those lost through inaccuracy. Outside the examination hall, accuracy, of course, is essential, but then there is no set time limit for the localisation of errors.

Proper headings neatly spaced, allocation of the assets and liabilities to their correct groupings, a clear distinction between the capital of proprietorship and the outside debts of the business, and an orderly well-balanced presentation of any type of final account are all important features likely to catch the examiner's eye.

# ANSWERS TO
# PROBLEM QUESTIONS

Chapter

| | | |
|---|---|---|
| 2 | 4 | Capital £650 |
| | 5 | BS £1080 |
| | | |
| 3 | 3 | Cash £920, Cap £1940, BS £2140 |
| | 4 | (a) £13,500, (b) £10,850 and £3470, (c) £820 |
| | 5 | Cash £1130, Cap £13,950 |
| | | |
| 4 | 1 | Balances Jan. 31 £435, Feb. 28 £535, Mar. 31 £555 |
| | 3 | Cash £435, TB £905 |
| | 4 | Profit £135, Cap £435, BS £435 |
| | 5 | Cash £375, BS £1005 |
| | 6 | Cash £373, TB £713, Profit £133, BS £373 |
| | | |
| 5 | 2 | Cash £443.80 |
| | 3 | TB £1247.50 |
| | 4 | Cash £548.00 |
| | 5 | TB £1499.60 |
| | 6 | Cap £710, TB £2650 |
| | 7 | TB £3400 |
| | | |
| 6 | 2 | £4800, 33⅓ per cent, 50 per cent |
| | 3 | (a) £1620, (b) £12,800 |
| | 5 | (a) GP £358.50, NP £317.80 |
| | | (b) GP £267.50, NP £219.00 |
| | | |
| 7 | 1 | Cash £545, Cap £4975, Stock £1800, Debtors £1900, Creditors £2850, WC reduced by £105 |
| | 2 | BS totals (a) £787.80, (b) £869.00 |
| | 3 | COS £13,860, GP £7780, NP £5388, Cap 13,388, BS £13,768 |
| | 5 | Cash £317, TB £824, GP £68, NP £30, BS £495 |
| | | |
| 8 | 1 | Cash £92.30, bank £500.40 |
| | 2 | (a) Cash £54.00, bank £513.50 |
| | | (b) Cash £8.50, bank £638.20 |
| | | (c) Cash £51.40, bank £612.80 |

Chapter

| | | |
|---|---|---|
| 8 | 4 | Cash £37.60, bank £562.20 |
| | 5 | Discounts £3.95 and £6.33, cash £55.80, bank £418.08 |
| | 6 | Discounts £33 and £16, cash £76, bank £331 |
| 9 | 1 | Cash book bank balance £194.45 |
| | 2 | Bank statement £421.28 |
| 10 | 1 | Balance £9.88, refund £30.12 |
| | 2 | Balance £13.57, refund £36.43 |
| | 3 | Bank £886, PC £26, TB £2423 |
| 11 | 1 | PDB £156, SDB £200 |
| | 2 | Debit £119.79 |
| | 3 | Cash £44, bank £382, debtors £391, creditors £243, V.A.T. account £20 debit, £30 credit, TB £3912 |
| | 4 | Cash £52, bank £696, debtors £618, creditors £1014, TB £4422 |
| | 5 | Purchases £6315, sales £10,778 |
| | 6 | Bank £518.20, cash contra £177.90, discounts £4 and £13.40 |
| | 7 | TB £4840 |
| 12 | 5 | GP (a) £667, (b) £514, NP £435, Cap £3455, BS £4003 |
| 13 | 2 | £59.00 debit |
| | 3 | £102.25 credit |
| | 5 | Garrett £139.00 debit, Gilbert £144.00 credit |
| 14 | 1 | £52.00 debit |
| | 2 | BS £5230 |
| | 3 | Bank £890.20, TB £3319.40 |
| | 4 | BS £2679.60, Capital £2144.10 |
| | 5 | TB £2700 |
| 15 | 1 | Bank £423.60, SL £208.90, BL £192.00 |
| | 2 | Sales control £1460.40, purchases control £877.30 |
| | 3 | Credit purchases £3370, credit sales £5940 |
| | 4 | GP £2123 |
| | 5 | Sales control £6566 debit |
| 16 | 2 | Aggregate deprec. plant £26,120, vehicles £3150 |
| | 3 | Bad debts £28 |
| | 4 | Provision increase £54, bad debts £49 |
| | 5 | Provision increase £30, bad debts £110 |
| | 6 | Cap £22,300, FA £21,200, CA £4000, BS £25,200 |
| 17 | 2 | P & L debit £144, in advance £48 |
| | 3 | Net debit £91.60 |
| | 6 | Amended profit £2690 |
| | 7 | GP £5682, NP £1593, Cap £4648, BS £7428 |

Chapter

| 17 | 8 | GP £1036, NP £236, BS £5458 |
| 9 | GP £12,573, NP £9,444, BS £22,525 |
| 10 | TB £9579.64, NP £195.90, BS £7476.28 |

18   1   Stockturn (a) 5 times (b) 5.2 times
GP (a) 35 per cent (b) 37.5 per cent
2   (a) £2400 and £29,000, (b) 5:2, (c) 16.9 per cent
4   Amended profit £4660
5   (a) £2150 and £3500, (b) 54.8 per cent and 35.2 per cent, (c) 8.8 per cent and 8.7 per cent, (d) 49.5 per cent and 50 per cent
6   Insurance claim £1150
7   Profit £4620, Cap £4220

19   1   NP £5239, Cap £4053, BS £4369
2   NP £2101, Cap £1316, BS £1746
3   NP £1608, Cap £948, BS 2088
4   NP £1126, Cap £10,926, BS £15,459
5   Cash takings £3300, NP £46, BS £723

20   1   Surplus £60, Acc. Fund £4760, BS £4890
2   Surplus £390, Acc. Fund £1760, BS £2430
3   NP £347, Cap £647, BS £672
4   NP £1948, Cap £2648, BS £3428
5   Loss on bar £320, net deficiency £76, Acc. Fund £13,676, BS £13,836

21   1   Current accounts: Abbott £660, Bullock £240
2   Goodwill to capital accounts:
H £2500, D £1500
Profit-sharing ratios 15:9:8
3   B's share of profit £3200, current account £928
4   BS £35,370, capitals each £16,585, T paid in £6015
5   BS £17,260, current accounts, Witham £55, Welland £135, both credit
6   BS £10,900, current accounts Ellen £225, Emily £465
7   BS £10,280, current accounts JB £360, HB £470
8   BS £13,040, current accounts LF £2015, PS £985

22   1   (a) £86,220, (b) £155,170, (c) £70,070
2   (a) £41,820, (b) £22,020, (c) £57,280, (d) £14,180 (e) £27,170, (f) £32,020
3   Cost of production £10,360, GP £4240, NP £2970, BS £12,900

23   2   Capital reserve £20,000, bank £64,500
3   Capital reserve £10,000, bank £139,900
4   WC £3015, equity £122,915, BS £125,165
5   P & L credit balance £4600, WC £28,600, net assets £141,600, equity £121,600, BS £121,600
6   GP £38,995, net profit on trading £20,016, undistributed profit £9516, BS £85,766

# INDEX